Education, Manpower, and Development in South and Southeast Asia

Muhammad Shamsul Huq

The Praeger Special Studies program—utilizing the most modern and efficient book production techniques and a selective worldwide distribution network—makes available to the academic, government, and business communities significant, timely research in U.S. and international economic, social, and political development.

Education, Manpower, and Development in South and Southeast Asia

PRAEGER SPECIAL STUDIES IN INTERNATIONAL ECONOMICS AND DEVELOPMENT

Praeger Publishers   New York   Washington   London

Library of Congress Cataloging in Publication Data

Shamsul Huq, Muhammad.
    Education, manpower, and development in South and
Southeast Asia.

    (Praeger special studies in international economics
and development)
    Includes bibliographical references.
    1. Education—Economic aspects—South Asia.
2. Human capital—South Asia.   3. Education—South
Asia.   I. Title.
LC67.S66S48   370'.954   74-19336
ISBN 0-275-09120-1

PRAEGER PUBLISHERS
111 Fourth Avenue, New York, N.Y. 10003, U.S.A.
5, Cromwell Place, London SW7 2JL, England

Published in the United States of America in 1975
by Praeger Publishers, Inc.

Dedicated
with the deepest appreciation
to
my fellow workers in the field of
education and development

This study was planned in the winter of 1970 as a follow-up of my earlier work, Education and Development Strategy in South and Southeast Asia.* By that time the development movement in the Third World had reached a new critical phase, with a turbulence building up behind the success story of growth in several nations.

The inadequacy of the gross national product (or income) as an indicator of development is tragically demonstrated in the case of Pakistan, the Fourth Five-Year Plan (1970-75) of which underlines the rising discontent among the people and the sharpening of the conflict between economic growth and social justice, since the previous plans resulted in increasing unemployment, mounting prices, declining real wages, and increasing inequalities in income. The economic disparity between the two regions of the country greatly accentuated all of these ills in the eastern region, which had the larger population. Physically separated from the west by over a thousand miles, it was gradually driven to a point of complete alienation by the concentration of the wealth and power in a small minority in the western region, which had predominated ever since the creation of the state.

The first warning of the coming storm was the near-revolution of early 1969, which caused the collapse of the then dictatorship as an anticlimax to its much publicized celebration of the decade of development. At first this warning seemed to have an effect, as if the ruling coterie could see the writing on the wall. The first nationwide elections were ordered and held, and the elected national assembly was called to meet and prepare a constitution to restore democracy. Then suddenly the armed might of the vested interests struck the people of the eastern region, perpetrating one of the greatest human tragedies in history; it was under these cataclysmic conditions that my country, Bangladesh, was born, with many deep and searing wounds.

The message this study attempts to convey to the developing world and also to the international development community, thus, naturally bears an imprint of the traumatic experiences of my people. The most important factor sustaining me in my present work has been my hope that our sister nations in the developing world may be spared similar agonies and be enabled to choose a growth path based on a clear recognition that it is man who is both the end and agent of development. Growth theories that leave the vast mass of people in a state of unemployment or underemployment, that fail to provide education and

---

*Honolulu: East-West Center Press, 1965.

productive skill, and that tolerate malnutrition and ill health, stand thoroughly condemned by the experiences of the past twenty years.

As one closely associated with educational planning and development during the last two decades, I was gradually and inexorably led to the conclusion that the continuing crisis in education was a part of the larger crisis in development. Reform efforts in education cannot play a worthwhile role except within a broader growth model aimed at the development and utilization of human capital. I have therefore adopted a frame of study in which educational problems are viewed as linked to those in other sectors of development, and I have followed a global and intersectoral approach in my effort to study the major problems facing education in the developing countries, with the focus on South and Southeast Asia.

Chapter 1 in this study attempts to identify and analyze the major challenges in the field of education as well as the social and economic factors to which they are related in a web of interdependent and interlocking action.

Chapter 2 provides a global perspective of the problems that developing countries have in common. For example, the growth pattern shows grotesque distortions resulting from a growth strategy that stresses the development of a small, capital-intensive modern sector. This has led to increasing deterioration in the general level of living and the sharpening of the people's demand for social justice, thus generating socially and politically explosive situations.

Chapter 3 examines the implications of the multidimensional concept of development, along with the various approaches to a study of the dynamics of development, indicating that growth is not static, but rather that it is a continuous and dynamic process involving a series of adjustments from one short-run equilibrium to another and that there can be many variations in technique of growth.

The role of education in development is examined as part of the broader concept of development, and quality of life is examined as the central component of development. The widening disparity between the industrial and the developing countries and the related question of how much growth and what style of life the latter should seek are examined in this connection. The inescapable conclusion is that the most pervasive goal to motivate both development and education must be the development and utilization of human capital, in which the developing world is rich.

Chapter 4 is devoted to an examination of some of the major studies of the concept of human capital and its formation through investment in education, as carried out in the United States, the USSR, and Japan. Attention is given to the limitations and implications of the findings of these studies. An important issue raised is the need for an educational system designed to fit the economic and social needs of a nation; how this "fit" can be achieved remains a major challenge for the developing countries.

Chapter 5 describes several approaches to the development of various theoretical plan-models to meet this challenge and points out their advantages and disadvantages. The need for empirical research to collect information to feed these models is indicated, in order that the results from the application of these models to a developing country may be satisfactory.

Chapter 6 shifts the focus to development in South and Southeast Asia and examines the developing economic and social situation in light of the provisions of the national development plans. The experiences of several countries in this region in meeting their major problems are highlighted, with special emphasis on experiments in labor-intensive techniques and development of the rural sector, both of which offer enormous possibilities for the utilization of human capital.

Chapter 7 examines the educational structures in the region with special reference to their production mechanisms and other systemic features determining their internal and external efficiency, in light of the changes considered necessary to enable education to perform effectively as an instrument of development.

Chapter 8 summarizes the conclusions derived from the preceding chapters and presents them in the form of a conceptual framework of planning strategy, including some suggested changes in the international aid program that would aim it more effectively toward the goals of development.

As observed in Chapter 2, one of the ironic and frustrating paradoxes of the last two decades has been that at the end of the last decade the developing countries could boast a much faster rate of growth in their armed forces than in their economies and social services. The external aid received for investment in military hardware and establishment far exceeded the aid for economic and social development. Should the amount of aid used during the past two decades to arm the developing countries to fight among themselves, now be channeled to equip them to fight the hunger, ignorance, and disease that continue to afflict their people, the present decade might see the dawn of a new day, a day of sunshine and peace for all the world.

Finally, I should like to stress that the present study is purely an academic exercise in probing into the state of development and education, actuated by my professional interest and also by my sense of a deepening crisis in both development and education. The views expressed here are entirely my own, except where they have been specifically attributed to other sources. As in all cases of aggregation, the comments and conclusions may not be wholly applicable to actual situations in all of the nations under study. Even where they are so applicable, they are not intended in any way to belittle the heroic efforts all of these nations are making. This study is essentially a plea for shifting the focus of growth to the people through a planned symbiosis in educational and economic development. Its purpose will have been amply fulfilled if it succeeds, even in some measure, in getting this plea across to all who are concerned with development and education.

ACKNOWLEDGMENTS

At the outset I should like to acknowledge most gratefully that a fellowship grant from the Woodrow Wilson International Center for Scholars in Washington, D.C., enabled me to undertake the present study. At the Center, which is located in the historic Smithsonian Institution building and enriched by the presence of scholars drawn from diverse nations and disciplines, I found the academic atmosphere intellectually as stimulating as the excellent facilities for research available there were conducive to my work.

One of the most attractive features of the Center was its friendly staff. It would have been impossible for me to complete my study within the specified time without the willing and valued assistance of the directing, administrative, library, and secretarial staff of the Center. Space does not allow me to mention these good friends individually, as I would have wished, but I am deeply grateful to all of them.

My wife and I owe a special debt of gratitude to the then director of the Center, Benjamin H. Read, and his gracious wife for their unfailing kindness, the solicitude they showed for our welfare, and the help they extended to us during the hour of our need, which was well beyond the call of their duty.

The materials received from the governments of the countries included in my study and from various international agencies, such as the United States Agency for International Development, UNESCO, and the World Bank, were of immense help. I am grateful to them. In this connection I would especially mention the assistance received from Director General Rene Maheu of UNESCO, Director Duncan Ballantine of the World Bank, and Dr. Myron Vent of the U.S. Agency for International Development.

I am also thankful to my fellow scholars at the Center, who helped me with their valuable comments at various stages during the progress of my study. My special thanks are due to Dr. Lincoln Gordon and Dr. Chester Cooper for their kind assistance in seeking a publisher for this study.

I must also mention gratefully the help and support that came from my wife. Not only did she take great pains in making for our younger son and me "a home away from home," but she also proved to be a tower of strength during a most trying period, as we passed our days in great anguish, waiting for the liberation of our country.

My sincere thanks are also due to my colleagues at the Foundation for Research on Educational Planning and Development in Bangladesh, and especially to Mr. Yousuf Hasan, who helped me in various ways while I was revising parts of the manuscript.

I am also thankful to many other kind friends not mentioned here by name for the assistance they rendered in connection with this study.

CONTENTS

152 - 205

LIST OF TABLES

1

THE CRISIS IN EDUCATION AND DEVELOPMENT

The developing countries are currently experiencing an unprecedented crisis engulfing all sectors of development, necessitating a searching appraisal spanning all aspects of planning strategy. They have reached this stage through a rather slow, but traumatic, discovery that the growth achieved by them has caused more pains than gains; that their plan-models have raised more problems than they have solved; and that the late 1970s and early 1980s will be a period of crucial test for the developing countries with formidable problems looming large on the horizon of their development or in the task ahead of them.

The resurgence of the nations of the Third World made an unprecedented demand on their educational systems to meet new national goals of economic and social development. This demand for education could not be entirely explained by the high esteem in which it was traditionally held in these countries, nor by the higher status accorded to educated people during the colonial period, but was largely the logical outcome of a process of conscious shift in values that had started with the struggle for freedom.

The emotional fervor in the aspirations of the people, which had served as the driving force in this struggle, also had an important intellectual content. Political liberation was seen as an essential first step in giving them access to science and technology and thus to a new era of progress and prosperity. Education appeared to be the path to follow to reach this destination, enabling the emergent countries to use the advances in science and technology to achieve a fuller and better life for their people, as had the rich industrialized countries.

THE UNFULFILLED DEMAND FOR EDUCATION

Thus in the minds of the people and their leaders a new and far-reaching importance was added to the traditional values of education.

This implied a vastly changed and expanded role for education, which was not adequately indicated, and far less measured, by the targets, programs, and projects in the national plans, which as a matter of fact reflected the present resource-constraint more than the national aims and needs in education.

In order to identify the major implications of the popular notion of the role of education, which has many ramifications bound up with deep-seated social and psychological factors, this role is conceptualized through a simple theoretical formulation, which is that of an idealized demand for education. As far as it can be inferred from the available literature on the subject,[1] this demand would draw on a synthesis of old and new values and require the supply of education to be comparable in quantity, quality, and instrumental role to that of the education systems in the more developed parts of the world. "Social demand" is used in this study to distinguish this idealized demand, on the one hand, from the "plan-demand" which is based on the economic and social targets in the national plans, and from the "private demand," representing the demand for education of individuals according to their own perception of their needs. Private demand is naturally influenced by economic and social status, by the existing elitist structure of the society, and by market conditions. "Market demand" ordinarily concerns the finished products of the educational system depending on the structure of the labor market and influences educational inputs and outputs only indi-rectly over a period of time. Its immediate effect can be seen in the prevailing surpluses and shortages in various occupations.

These terminological distinctions are important in the context of the situation in the developing countries, which is profoundly influ-enced by the manner in which these interacting demands operate on national development.

In the first place, the "social demand" represents the potential demand for trained manpower to meet the objectives of maximum econ-omic and social development and utilization of human resources. Based on the enrollment norms at the various levels in the industrial countries, an approximate profile of the quantitative dimension of the "social demand" for education, compared to that of the existing status of edu-cation in the developing countries, is shown in Table 1.1.

The disequilibrium between this social demand and the supply of education is a source of serious tension, which is of course accentu-ated by the backlog of illiteracy involving two-thirds of the adult popu-lation. Tension is also generated by the conflicting aims of the private and "plan-demand." The attempted adjustment between these two de-mands has taken various forms, such as growth in the number of public and private schools, measures to regulate such schools, overcrowded classrooms within the educational system, competitive and restricted admissions, double-shift schools, redesigned curricula, and new courses to meet the demands for new skills. Such makeshift, fragmen-tary measures have been mere palliatives intended to ease the tension,

TABLE 1.1

"Social Demand" for Education in Developing Countries and
and Actual Enrollment at Various Levels, 1966/67[a]

	First Level	Second Level	Third Level
Social demand[b]	324	128	25
Number enrolled	175	33	4

[a]Excluding mainland China, North Korea, and North Vietnam.

[b]On the basis of enrollment in industrial countries.

Source: UNESCO Statistical Year Book, 1969, and World Bank
Education Sector Working Paper, September 1971.

and they did not eliminate the causes of it. These causes lay in the
traditional concepts of education as well as in the structure of society
in the developing countries, including the traditional elitist social
hierarchy; the employment structure; the continuing influence exerted
by the employment structure on the market demand for formal education;
and the rising demand for increasing access to educational, economic,
and social opportunities. The production function peculiar to educational
dynamics acts on the increasing supply in one stage of education to
cause increasing demand in other stages.[2]

The resulting stress varies according to the intensity of the pressure of the social demand, which is, however, capable of endangering
national stability and progress, depending on the degree of the public
consciousness of the social demand for education and the system's
response to it. This danger can be overlooked by the planner only at
grave peril, as demonstrated by events in a number of countries.

Many of the other challenges and problems in the educational
sector seem to stem from this unfulfilled demand associated with the
new role of education. It should perhaps be stressed here that quantitative expansion of education, though important, is only one of the
several components of the task implied in this role. A closer look at
the national policies and plans will show that the task for education in
the developing countries is one that is without any parallel in enormity
and complexity and extends beyond the sector of education into society
as a whole. In this task, education is viewed as an instrument of
change with a dual function, to change the society and also to change
itself. It is to change the society by breaking through its crust of outmoded traditions, salvaging its inner values and revitalizing its life
impulse with selected values from the modern world; it is to change
itself in structure, becoming abundant, efficient, and productive and
a part of the mainstream of the world's growing knowledge.

Such a role for education is vividly conceptualized in the national development plans and policies in Southeast Asia. The report of the Education Commission and the First Five-Year Plan (1973-78) of Bangladesh both visualize a key role for education in the reconstruction of the society, reflecting the basic principles of socialism, democracy, nationalism, and secularism as embodied in the country's constitution.[3]

India's plans and policies also stress the paramount role of education as an instrument of social change to achieve national objectives. The third five-year plan of India stated,

> Education is the most important single factor in achieving rapid development and technological progress and in creating a social order founded on values of freedom, social justice and equal opportunity. [4]
>
> India with thousands of years of history, bears even now the powerful impress of her distinctive features. . . . They are in fact a set of moral and ethical values which have governed Indian life for ages past, even though people may not have lived up to them. These values are a part of India's thinking, even as, more and more, that thinking is directed to the impact of the scientific and technological civilization of the modern world.[5]

The Government of India Resolution on the Report of the Education Commission in 1964 contained the following description of the role of education:

> Education has always been accorded an honoured place in Indian society. The great leaders of the Indian freedom movement realized the fundamental role of education and throughout the nation's struggle for independence, stressed its unique significance for national development. . . . The Government of India is convinced that a radical reconstruction of education . . . is essential for economic and cultural development of the country, for national integration and for realizing the ideal of a socialistic pattern of society. This will involve a transformation of the system to relate it more closely to the life of the people; a continuous effort to expand educational opportunity; a sustained and intensive effort to raise the quality of education at all stages; an emphasis on the development of science and technology; and the cultivation of moral and social values. [6]

According to Indonesia's first five-year plan,

> Education must be closely linked with the need as well as possibilities of economic and social development so that

it can equip pupils for their life, and fulfill community
needs. . . . Education must undergo some reforms in order
to make schools an integral, suitable and useful part of
the life of the community. [7]

Malaysia's second plan stated,

Besides having a strong manpower orientation, education
and training programmes will contribute significantly
towards promoting national unity. They will play a vital
role in increasing productivity and income of all Malay-
sians, as well as in greater urbanization of the Malays
and other indigenous people by facilitating their participation in modern activities.[8]

It is interesting to note how the areas of emphasis in social change
to be achieved through education are profoundly colored by the social and
cultural situations peculiar to each country. In the Philippines the objectives set for education, "to make it responsive to the challenge of
modernization and the goals of national development," were set forth in
the president's executive order creating a presidential commission to
survey Philippine education.[9] In elaborating this concept the Commission
observed, "A society that educates its people must, sooner or later, find
itself a changing society. New social and technological skills for at
least some of the people will develop. Traditional popular expectations
will be subjected to stress from the forces of change; new expectations
will emerge."[10]
A similar theme is found in Pakistan's plans:

Scientific and technological advances have provided the
means of banishing poverty, unemployment, disease and
degrading labour rendered in slavery. . . . Out-dated
institutions which serve no economic and social purpose
should be discarded or reordered.[11]
Economic growth is dependent on the effective use of
the human and material resources of the nation. . . . Of
the two fundamental forms of wealth, the human resources
are clearly more important. . . . It is through the efficient
application of human energy that social capital is created.[12]
Education at all levels is to be expanded and advanced
as fast as required institutions and personnel can be
provided.[13]
The development of manpower resources will be viewed
as an investment in human capital ultimately aiming at
faster economic growth.[14]

If the efforts of the developing countries to meet their educational
objectives, and the results of these efforts, are to be seen in their

correct perspective, it is essential that they be viewed within the ideological framework provided by the concept of the new role of education,
on the one hand, and the social setting in which these efforts were
made, on the other. Two dominant trends seem to emerge from the foregoing analysis: first, it has been social demand that has operated as
the ultimate motive for educational change; and second, education is
now clearly in a state of flux and a constant source of social tension.
No nation is likely to reach a stage of stability as long as the social
demand for education remains unfulfilled.

It is also important to note the fact, often overlooked, that the
educational supply as envisaged in the social demand has both a quantitative and qualitative content, with the latter posing a much greater
challenge, as indicated by the events of the last two decades. As
parameters of educational growth, however, both are important; and both
are complementary as well as competitive, in certain respects. This presents a dilemma to the planner, as we shall see.

However, although the response of the educational system to the
social demand took, by and large, the form of a linear quantitative expansion, as observed by development watchers with justified concern,
this was not the result of conscious planning for quantitative expansion
without regard to quality of education, nor of a planning strategy in
which the claims of quantity were accorded an undeserved priority over
those of quality. Any such simplistic notion would be contrary to the
realities of the situation in developing countries, and abortive as a
basis for planning a development strategy for the future.

The evidence available in government policy documents, national
plans, educational schemes and programs, and the reports of educational
commissions and committees set up by the governments indicates that
the developing countries, especially those in Southeast Asia, have not
only laid great stress on qualitative changes in education but have actually initiated reform measures embracing the entire gamut of educational
activity from the aims, contents, and methods of education to administration, management, and supervision. The developing countries themselves, therefore, view with disappointment and perplexity the shocking
distortions in the growth of their educational systems.

This paradoxical result can be attributed to several factors that
compound the difficulty and complexity of the problem.

First, the targets set in national plans for economic and social
development did not reflect the national aspirations and needs, and
hence failed to motivate education to respond appropriately. As we
shall see later, there is a deepening crisis in development as a whole,
and educational problems are at least partly the product of this crisis.
In all fields, including education, the approach to development planning
has been conventional, unrelated to social realities and needs, and
lacking in insight into the interdependent and interacting relationship
of different sectors. As a result the isolated efforts and investment in
the sector of education proved by and large unfruitful.

Second, the educational systems inherited by most of the developing countries were not designed to meet objectives of economic and
social development of the magnitude to which the developing countries
have committed themselves. For example, in Southeast Asia these educational systems did not grow through an evolutionary process out of the
native systems, since these had actually been supplanted by the systems
created during the colonial period to supply limited numbers of personnel
for the government and commercial offices. The aims, the contents, and
even the media of education were obtained from the society and culture
of the colonial power. Through this highly elitist system a small number
of natives were allowed access to Western education, which, however,
rejected or disregarded all native values and was avowedly committed to
the needs of the ruling power rather than those of the native country.
For example, the philosophy of the new educational system established
in the 1830s in British India, comprising the present Bangladesh, India,
and Pakistan, is candidly explained by the author of the policy, Lord
Macaulay, in the following words, "We must at present do our best to
form a class who may be interpreters between us and the millions whom
we govern--a class of persons, Indian in blood and colour, but English
in tastes, in opinions, in morals and in intellect."[15] In Indonesia, the
Royal Decree of 1892 following the Dutch conquest "divided the natives'
primary schools into first and second class schools, the former being
for the upper classes of the Indonesian society."[16] Soon the new educational systems became symbols of prestige and power associated with
the ruling group, which in the course of time became so pervasive as to
create a wide gulf between the educated class and the masses of the
people, and also between the educational aims and the national needs.
The history of this period, thus, holds the clue to the high prestige of
liberal education, the rigidity of the power hierarchy, and its continuing
influence over the market demand for education, and also the insensitiv-
ity of the educational systems to the needs of the nation. The values
inspiring the goals of national development thus seem to be in a direct
collision course with those originally shaping the existing educational
systems, thus neutralizing much of the reform efforts.

Third, the educational targets have been profoundly influenced by
the concepts and constraints implicit in the capital-intensive economic
growth models transplanted from capital-rich and labor-poor systems,
and thus were far too limited in scope to produce the desired impact on
the educational system as a whole. Even investment in the limited segments falling within the scope of the plan-targets failed to become
critical, and achievements fell far short of objectives, quantitatively
as well as qualitatively. This was partly because of the lack of an
integrated social approach, but largely because of the deficiency in
material and human resources. In most developing countries the investment in education was under 2 percent of the GNP during the decade of
the 1950s, and while it gradually rose during the 1960s, even by the
end of this decade it was still considerably less than what was spent

on the armed forces: U. S. $20 billion was spent on armed forces, com-
pared to U. S. $13 billion on education.[17] Investment in education was
far from commensurate with the goals set for it. The salary structure in
many countries of Southeast Asia clearly placed the educational systems
at a disadvantage in attracting enough able teachers and administrators.

Fourth, some of the reforms have been too fragmentary or too exotic,
unrelated to the needs and realities of the situation and therefore ineffective. An apt example is provided by the new technical institutions, almost in the image of such institutions in the industrialized countries,
which were set up in some developing countries. The investments in
buildings and equipment for these institutions were considerable, but
the trained manpower supplied by them soon turned out to be in excess
of demand. On the other hand, technically trained persons have been
badly needed for many observable tasks; the investment in the facilities
of technical education in agriculture has not touched more than the fringes
of the need. More importantly, the vast manpower resource, grossly
underutilized, has remained completely outside the new plans for educational development, thus at least indirectly preserving the elitist, rigid,
and formalistic character of the existing systems.

Fifth, even where far-reaching reforms were envisaged, as in educational aims, contents, and methods, they have been thwarted by the
gap between policies and actions, ends and means. Some of the nations,
in their desire for rapid and radical educational changes, even envisioned
an altogether new order of education to replace the old system lock,
stock, and barrel. The Education Commissions of both India and Pakistan
were aware of the forces of resistance to change and stressed the need
for an "educational revolution." According to the Indian Commission,

> It becomes evident that the present system of education,
> designed to meet the needs of an imperial administration
> within the limitations set by a feudal and traditional
> society will need radical changes if it is to meet the
> purposes of a modern democratic and socialistic society--
> changes in objectives, in content, in teaching methods,
> in programmes, in the size and composition of the student
> body, in the selection and professional preparation of
> teachers and in organization. In fact, what is needed is
> a revolution in education which in turn will set in motion
> the much desired social, economic, and cultural revolution.[18]

In many countries syllabuses were re-formed, new text books prepared, and teacher training programs expanded. The forces of resistance
seem to have got the better of those of change and reform, however,
demonstrating that the problem is far more complex than generally realized and inextricably bound up in the many variables that determine the
course of a society in transition.

For one thing, those who were supposed to carry out these revolutionary reforms were themselves largely the products of the traditional system, and indeed the foundation on which it rested. Teachers, administrators, parents, and even senior students have the institutional memory so deeply ingrained in them that it has had an overpowering, even if unconscious, influence on their manner of implementing the reforms. Elitism, though much denounced as a colonial heritage, has continued to characterize the growing educational system, with the socially and economically advantaged having a negligible share in its benefits.

Of the many paradoxes seen in a society in transition, none are more frustrating than those stemming from the deep-seated psychological factors that shaped the habits and attitudes of the people during the period of subjection. Ruthless criticism of an existing order exists side by side with resistance to change. Enthusiasm for reform rises and falls in successive waves, generating discussion that is seldom matched by adequate positive action. As a consequence, by the time these reforms had sifted down to the classroom and the pupil through the highly structured bureaucratic hierarchy of the government and the educational administration, the envisaged reforms retained very little of their revolutionary flavor. They had become so transformed in the face of resistance that they were hardly distinguishable from what they were intended to replace.

Resistance seems to be most pronounced where reforms are most needed. One such area, by all accounts, is the system of examination, which has been universally criticized as the cause of most of the ills of the present educational system. Intellectually debasing, with its emphasis on mechanical memory, it has so far been successful in driving out (as in Gresham's Law) better systems of evaluation that emphasized knowledge and creativity.

It is perhaps desirable to dispel the erroneous notion that the existing system is unresponsive to the "economic needs" as indicated by the market demand for manpower. Historically the demand for general education stemmed from the existing largely undifferentiated economic and social tasks and the consequent need for a general education that would qualify the individual for a wide range of general and not so specialized skills. To some extent the opposition to reforming the traditional examination has arisen from an apprehension that other forms of examination would be more difficult to pass and therefore not conducive to economic opportunities. However, more positive evidence is provided by the spectacular rise in the demand for admission to institutions of technical education at various levels. What seems to have gone wrong with the technical institutions is that they have also been by and large pulled into the gravitational orbit of the traditional system and have tended to develop the same rigidity and uncreative, bookish, and mechanical approach that characterized the latter. Thus even the modern sectors of education, although designed on the model of their counter-

TABLE 1.2

Enrollment Growth Rates by Educational Levels and Regions, 1960-66
(number of pupils in thousands)

	1960/61 Academic Year				1966/67 Academic Year				Percentage of Increase 1960-66			
	First Level	Second Level	Third Level	Total	First Level	Second Level	Third Level	Total	First Level	Second Level	Third Level	Total
Africa	18,931	2,115	192	21,238	26,748	3,893	334	30,975	41	84	73	45
Latin America	26,973	3,885	567	31,425	36,653	7,468	978	45,099	36	94	72	45
Asia*	74,645	12,186	1,432	88,261	111,986	21,421	2,911	136,300	50	76	103	54
Developing countries	120,549	18,186	2,191	140,924	175,387	32,782	4,223	212,374	42	80	93	51
World	248,486	63,927	11,174	323,587	311,700	96,713	19,992	428,405	25	51	79	32

*Excluding Japan, Mainland China, North Korea, and North Vietnam.
Note: Figures may not total due to rounding.

Source: Office of Statistics, UNESCO.

parts in the more developed countries, have failed to bring enough vitality into the system to counter the inertia of the traditional sector. It is therefore evident from the experiences of the last two decades that the distortions in the educational growth pattern, which are causing serious concern in the developing countries, occurred not for lack of measures for reforming the educational system but in spite of them, thus providing another dimension to the challenge of evolving a development strategy based on a proper identification of the variables within the educational system, and also the variables outside it that bear on educational and social change.

QUANTITATIVE EXPANSION VERSUS QUALITY

In the above circumstances the planning measures could make very little qualitative change either in the educational system or in its product; what the educational plans did achieve was mostly in terms of physical targets that made the quantitative expansion conspicuous by contrast. Viewed as such, of course, the growth in the numbers of the enrolled was quite impressive, as shown in Tables 1.2 and 1.3. It will also

TABLE 1.3

Comparative Enrollment Ratios at First and Second Levels, 1967/68
(in percentage)

	Enrollment Rates of Primary School Age Population[a]	Enrollment Rates of Secondary School Age Population[a]	Combined Primary and Secondary Enrollment Rates[a]
Africa	40	15	28
North America	98	92	96
Latin America	75	35	55
Asia[b]	55	30	45
Europe and USSR	97	65	85
Oceania	95	30	67
(Arab Countries)	(50)	(25)	(38)
Developing countries	54	23	44
World	68	40	56

[a]Regardless of the school they attend.

[b]Excluding Mainland China, North Korea, and North Vietnam.

Source: UNESCO, Estimates of the Office of Statistics, quoted in World Bank Education Sector Working Paper, September 1971.

appear that the rate of increase in enrollment compared quite favorably
with the rate of growth in Gross Domestic Product, both in total and per
capita, estimated at 5.2 and 2.7 percent respectively during 1961-67.[19]

A closer look at the quantitative gain, however, will reveal that
the enrollment statistics that are so often projected as an indicator of
educational progress hide a number of disturbing facts about quality.

First, even the quantitative gain ceases to be substantial in terms
of the total number of school age children. Even if the age group relevant to the first and second levels of education only is considered,
against 208 million enrolled in the school system 256 million, or over
55 percent, were still outside the system after a generation of educational effort.

Second, of those enrolled nearly 50 percent are in Grade I, and
more than a quarter of them will leave within a year, while over half of
the total number enrolled in the first five grades will leave at different
stages without completing the course. There are of course exceptions,
but these are numerically insignificant. The general tendency inexorably
leads to the swelling of the ranks of the illiterate population.

Third, the number of illiterates still constitutes two-thirds of the
adult population, and it rose by 100 million to 800 million during the
last decade.

With the increase in population even the quantitative gap between
educational supply and demand is widening, to the dismay of most of
the developing countries. However, the problems involved are not
merely those of controlling the wastage accompanying expansion and of
moving faster toward the goal of universal primary education and elimination of illiteracy, although these goals, to which the developing
nations are committed, are extremely important. Bound up with these
problems are the necessity of vital qualitative changes mentioned
earlier, which cuts across the educational sector into other sectors of
national development.

THE CHALLENGE OF THE RESOURCE GAP

The educational task ahead of the developing countries would be
a great challenge by its sheer magnitude, even if they were not hindered
by the constraint of resources. The problem of financing educational
development with their limited resources has in the past proved to be a
major impediment to faster progress.

Difficult as the problem is, it is accentuated by two factors. The
first is historical, the backlog of illiteracy and inadequate schooling;
the second is demographical, the rapid growth of population compounded
by its age structure. In 1970 the ratio of the five- to twenty-four-year
age group exceeded 45 percent in developing countries, compared to
corresponding figures of 30.3 percent in Europe and 37.3 percent in

North America, and is likely to increase slightly by 1980. In absolute
terms the educational burden on the developing countries will be much
greater, since in 1970 the actual population in the same age group was
478 million in the developing countries but only 238 million in Europe
and North America. In financial terms it is still greater, since allowance
must be made for upgrading the quality of the teaching personnel, school
buildings, equipment, and libraries to a reasonable minimum. There
must also be substantial additions to educational expenditure if the 800
million adult illiterates are to be brought under nonformal programs of
education and if extension programs are to be established to update the
education and training of other adults who are deficient in education.
Financially the task is staggering, since the developing countries have
only 12.5 percent of world resources for all the tasks that have to be
done in all sectors of development. According to a study by a UNESCO
team for the Asian region, the estimated cost of achieving even such
modest enrollment targets as 80.2 percent in the first level, 32.55 percent in the second level, and 4.96 percent in the third level by 1980
would involve an expenditure of U.S. $9.3 billion, which is about a
quadrupling of the U.S. $2.9 billion that was spent on education in this
region in 1965.[20] The question of how countries can mobilize resources
of this order for the education sector is, however, bound up with that of
the overall resource gap in the developing countries.

The resource gap affects all sectors. It presents a challenge that
is central to the process of development as such and impedes the very
process by which it is to be overcome, in a vicious circle. The gap
between needs and resources haunts all developing countries, and in
view of the deepening crisis in education and development, this question
is naturally agitating the minds of many. Can the developing countries
do better than they have done in the past in generating resources? There
is also the related question about the allocation of available resources:
What principles should guide the judicious allocation of available resources to various sectors and the establishment of intersectoral priorities? The present crisis is to no small extent the outcome of the lack
of such principles in the application of the scarce resources and the
lack of rationally developed criteria in establishing priorities consistent
with the national development goals. For example, as already observed,
the total investment of the developing countries in education even by
the end of the 1960s was U.S. $13 billion, lagging far behind their
military expenditure of U.S. $20 billion.

DISPARITY IN EDUCATION:
THE MYTH OF EQUAL OPPORTUNITY

Closely linked to the social objectives of justice and equality of
opportunity that are stressed in the national development plans is the

problem of eliminating or at least significantly reducing the disparities in educational opportunities. The problem is, however, much more complex than commonly realized.

The expansion of education already achieved during the last two decades did not prove to be the social equalizer it was expected to be. In this respect the imbalance in its growth was more serious than its insufficient quantity. The proportionately higher rates of growth of the higher levels of education, the unequal distribution of the available educational facilities in each level, and the inverse relationship between the participation of the underprivileged and the enrollment in levels of education widened the existing inequalities. As earlier mentioned, over half of those enrolled in the primary grades dropped out before completing the fifth grade, and two-thirds of the adult population, or the majority of the active labor force, has had no access to education and hence has remained illiterate.

The explanation of this grim paradox appears to lie in a complex set of factors. For historical, social, economic, and political reasons, different regions and social segments have been in different stages of development, some visibly more underdeveloped than others, even within the same developing country. Certain social groups, such as the economically and socially disadvantaged, have continued to lag behind others in educational opportunities.

In Bangladesh, India, and Pakistan, the most populous regions of Southeast Asia, women as a class are among the socially disadvantaged and have fewer educational opportunities. Social beliefs continue to present a formidable block to their equal participation in educational opportunities, and these beliefs are stronger in places that are educationally more backward.

In some countries there are special social groups, such as the lower castes in India, products of the particularistic structures of traditional societies, that because of their socially ascribed inferior status have remained economically and educationally backward, thus presenting a special problem.

The difficulty of the problem in general is accentuated by the gross inequalities in home environments and the existence of the high-fee special private schools that have grown up in places to serve the affluent.

A deliberate policy of educational development aiming at the rapid equalization of educational opportunities suggests itself as an obvious strategy. There are powerful pressures, however, both social and political, for increased attention to the more advanced regions and groups wielding more political and economic power instead, and these are aided by the influence of deep-seated social and cultural factors operating as forces of resistance to change. One result of the influence of such pressure groups is the proportionately larger public expenditure on higher education in countries with low rates of participation in primary education and high rates of adult illiteracy. A recent sample study in Bangladesh[21] showed that in the two areas selected for study over 50 percent of the children of the primary age group were not enrolled in primary schools at all and that 70 percent of those enrolled dropped out before completing Grade 5 due to economic and social disabilities. To the extent that this reflected the national trend, the growing public expenditure on higher levels of education involved at least partly the transfer of resources from the poor to the rich. This is illustrative of the situation prevalent in the developing countries in general because their fiscal systems are substantially dependent on indirect taxation, the burden of which is also shared by the poor. The challenge here is much more than one of evolving a planning strategy to create more educational opportunities faster to benefit the underprivileged; if the goal of equality of opportunity in education is to be realized, it is also necessary to identify and eliminate the factors within the economic and social institutions that tend to aggravate the disparity in education. This conclusion is also confirmed by some recent studies on affluent societies that have failed to achieve social equality, through creation of equal schooling facilities without adequate measures to overcome the disabilities stemming from poor economic and social environments. In the opinion of Daniel P. Moynihan of Harvard, who was also associated with the U.S. Family Assistance Plan, the problem is clearly bound up with the issue of income redistribution.[22]

THE STAGGERING PROBLEM OF WASTAGE IN EDUCATION

Wastage in the form of dropping out of school prematurely or repetition of grades has assumed a staggering dimension with the expansion of education in the developing countries. I have already mentioned wastage in the first level of education, but its high incidence can be seen in all levels and types of education.

Wastage has been a most frustrating experience for the developing countries: by diminishing the educational output it lowers the rate of return on investment in education. Not only does it increasingly waste scarce resources, but it also slows down the pace of progress to the goal of universal education and reduces the supply of needed manpower of various types. These last two effects have brought this issue to the focus of public attention.

Though the problem appears to be a structural one associated with the internal efficiency of the educational production mechanism, it is not entirely so. There are also larger variables involved, such as the economic status and attitude of the parents, the quality of home environments, the state of public health and communications (particularly in rural areas), local customs and laws regarding the minimum age for employment, and not least the quality of resource input, which depends to a large extent on the share of resources of the education sector. For example, assuming that wastage was completely eliminated or substantially reduced, the large number of additional pupils retained within the school system as a result would require a corresponding supply of additional teachers. Inferentially it may be argued that wastage, while rooted in a complex set of economic and social causes, at least partly measures the number that the present system with its present teacher supply is unable to absorb. This is, therefore, an area that calls for more research in depth, but the problem is a burning one demanding urgent attention.

THE EDUCATED UNEMPLOYED

Another form of wastage that is equally serious for the developing nations is represented by the educated unemployed, the number of whom has during the last decade assumed alarming proportions. Paradoxically, while the development process is dependent on turning out more educated manpower, at the same time it is unable to use an increasing number of those who are educated; this is another serious distortion in the growth pattern. For many of the developing countries, particularly those in South and Southeast Asia, the problem has already become explosive in character. In Ceylon, according to a Labor Force Survey conducted in 1968 by the Department of Census and Statistics, "over 25 per cent of the unemployed comprised persons who had passed at least G. C. E. (0) Level," that is, high school graduates.[23] In India the educated unemployed exceeded 2 million in 1972, constituting about a quarter of the total unemployed.[24] During 1968-69 in Pakistan 250, 000 to 300, 000 educated persons entered the labor market in search of jobs.[25] In the Philippines 33 percent of the college graduates and a larger number of those with one to three years of college were unemployed in 1966-67.[26]

That the problem is partly the outcome of a mismatch between the type of educational output and the type of demand is evident from the concurrent existence of shortages and excesses in the supply of trained manpower in certain areas, but the rising incidence of unemployment even among those with education of a technical or professional type both at the second and third level indicates that it is, in fact, a part of the much larger problem of the employment of the vast labor force.

As a result many countries in the region have found that even a modest development of the hitherto neglected technical education sector resulted in a surplus stock. India, with a population of over 500 million, has had to halt the further growth of her weak technical education and keep it under review at the reduced annual intake of 18, 000 in degree courses and 27, 000 in diploma courses.[27] In the province of North Sumatra in Indonesia it has been estimated that about 60 to 70 percent of the graduates of technical institutions are unemployed because there is not enough industry to absorb them.[28] A manpower study in Pakistan undertaken by a UN expert also indicated surpluses in several areas of technical skill.[29] These preposterous results are, however, directly ascribable to concepts and models of economic growth underlying the national plans of these countries.

There are of course many other related issues that concern education. For example, how can economy and education work in concert in generating employment, particularly through research and innovation in the field of labor-intensive technology, conducive to increased productivity and employment, particularly in the rural sector, or through supply of skills aiding self-employment? Looking into the future, is it possible to improve the technique of forecasting manpower requirements and the input-output coefficients of economic growth so as to make these forecasts good for periods as long as those of the "lead-time" in education? If not, what remedies are available for meeting the transition disequilibria? What measures are called for to correct the present known imperfections in the labor market and structures of salaries and incentives, to the extent the latter are responsible for the rise in the number of the educated unemployed?

RAISING THE EFFICIENCY OF THE EDUCATIONAL SYSTEM

The relation of wastage to the internal efficiency of the educational system has been briefly mentioned as a quantitative problem. However, another kind of wastage more serious from the viewpoint of human development, though less tangible, may occur and probably has constantly been occurring because the aims, contents, methods, and everything else that presently goes into education as inputs are not adequate to the best development of the innate powers of an individual to live a full and useful life as a person, as a family member, as a citizen, and as a worker.

The aims of education, as well as its curricula, and the values, attitudes, knowledge, and skills that education is expected to develop, are of course inspired by the national goals of human, economic, and social development, which in turn will be profoundly changed under the influence of the products of the system. The various educational inputs, including students, teachers, and various parts of the education's production mechanism, act and react on one another. The efficiency of the production mechanism is heavily dependent on the quality of the human resource, influenced by the social and economic environment of students and teachers, the habits and attitudes they bring with them, and the incentives within and outside the system that motivate them. These major variables are not so tangible as the physical inputs, such as housing, equipment, books, and laboratories, but if anything they are more important in the proper articulation of the system.

The human dimension in the production function of education makes educational systems fundamentally different in certain aspects from systems concerned with nonhuman products. First, even assuming that the aims, contents, and methods of education are reformed in an appropriate manner and that all modern aids to education are available and used, the education-industry will still remain labor intensive. Second, the differences in the innate abilities and potentialities of students will be reflected in the product quality, and the more efficient an educational system is the more sensitive it should be to these individual differences, unlike nonhuman systems, in which quality control is achieved through standardization. Third, human raw materials are not a passive input; they play an active role on the quality of the final product by their will and effort, and the skill and knowledge they learn in one stage will aid them in acquiring other skills and knowledge at a later stage. Thus in a rapidly expanding educational system the quality control presents an enormously difficult and complex task. It should be stressed here that if the rapid growth of population adversely affects the quantitative task, its effect on the qualitative task can be devastating, seriously eroding the poor resource base of a struggling education sector. Quality improvement is therefore a problem that faces many difficulties not found in other sectors of development and raises many issues central to social decision and policy prescription.

THE GROWING KNOWLEDGE GAP

Questions relating to the efficiency of the educational system are of course crucial to the maximization of educational benefits, and they lie at the very heart of educational development. Viewed in global context, however, the problem has another dimension stemming from the knowledge explosion, which has created a wide gap between the poor and the rich countries in the stock of knowledge. Scientific knowledge is growing exponentially in the industrial countries; such indicators as the output of research papers, the number of scientists and engineers, and the consumption of energy indicate that science and related activities grow so rapidly that scientific knowledge doubles itself in some 10 to 15 years. The number of science journals, 1,000 in 1870, is now 100,000, and is likely to rise to 1 million by the year 2000.[30] According to all indications the time between basic discovery and its application is also continually diminishing. The developing countries lag far behind in this knowledge race, and the gap is widening.

THE GENERATION GAP

The generation gap presents a new challenge to both education and society. Historically it has been the source of the ferment impelling the youth to challenge old values, thus supplying one of the elements of dynamism for social change and progress. In this context the ferment was not unwelcome, and even appreciatively characterized as "divine discontent."

In recent decades the generation gap has, however, come to signify a new youth phenomenon associated with unrest, alienation, rebellion, and violence. In the developing societies, now in transition with the sources of conflict located in their many archaic and obsolescent institutions, youth activism is regarded as an inevitable and endemic social malaise.

The social and economic situation in the developing countries is indeed a fertile ground for discontent and unrest. With the growth in the number of the educated, articulate, and idealistic youths wearing the reformers' mantle, poised against a monolithic and rigid social structure, the situation is ever volatile, and if anything accentuated by both education and the authorities. When it is uncreative and unrelated to the realities of life, education sharpens awareness of the many disadvantages of the underprivileged without providing the skills and motivation to overcome them. The authorities, entrenched in anachronistic institutions and traditions inherited from a colonial era, are stubborn and unresponsive to the needs of the people.

In such a situation grievances, the raw materials of protest and activism, are indeed most easy to find, for use not only by those who are aggrieved but also by others who become the standard-bearers. A survey of a series of violent outbreaks of student unrest in different parts of India reported:

> But those who spoke of the economic unrest . . . and the
> struggle that students waged against poverty did not them-
> selves seem affected by it. They had idealized the situ-
> ation, fitted it into their conception of a society tainted
> by corruption and ill-practices and perhaps thought it was
> somewhat pointless and weak to study in such a changeful
> era. Maybe their ideas are not wholly realistic but what
> is important is that these notions are deeply entrenched in
> their minds and the education they get does nothing to
> remove them. [31]

Education and the authorities are also often in conflict because of their negative approach to social problems. Educational institutions operate in isolation away from the social milieu, except when they are forced into the vortex of it by student activism. The authorities rely on an outmoded edict that teachers and students remain apolitical, honored more in the breach than in the observance. Teachers and students work in a climate of frustration, being unable to relate themselves to goals of development that in many cases have no direct relevance to their life. Not infrequently the lack of motivation is also due to the unhealthy campus climate bred by inadequacy of staff and resources,

and more importantly by lack of clear commitments to values. A large
proportion of teachers and students is morally and intellectually in a
state of flux, literally drifting with the tide.

The victims of some of the protests have been the educational
institutions themselves, and the causes have been far from lofty.

> Briefly, there have been many ugly strikes and demonstra-
> tions—often without any justification—leading to violence,
> walk-out from classrooms and examination halls, ticketless
> travel, clashes with the police, burning of buses and cin-
> ema houses, and sometimes, even manhandling of teachers
> and university officers.[32]

Sometimes, however, the causes of these protests can be found
in the structures, procedures, and practices within the educational system itself. Many of these are totally inappropriate in the present times,
such as misuse of punishment, overcrowded classrooms, lack of recre-
ational facilities, and veto over students' union decisions.

Youth activism, far from being limited to the developing countries,
has in recent years emerged as a world phenomenon, symbolizing the
power of the youth, a new element to reckon with on the part of those
who wield power. In some countries, particularly in the developing
world, the legitimacy of this power has been established on the basis
of the initiative and leadership provided by the students during national
crises, as in Bangladesh and Thailand. Even some of the affluent countries are accepting a readjustment in the institutional structures to admit the youths to the power-sharing process, for example, by lowering
the age of enfranchisement or by allowing representation to students in
the decision-making apparatus of a university. It is, however, doubted
by some if these desirable reforms will go far in rooting out the causes
of the increasing proneness to violence, which is viewed by them as a
malaise afflicting the present generation of youth.[33]

A recent survey of the campuses in the United States, however,
disclosed that the alienation of the youths was not so much from disre-
spect for, or difference from, the views of their elders or from a greater
swing to the radical left as from causes of youth activism that lie deep
within the structure of the society.[34] There are also striking parallels
between the basic manifestations of this activism in the affluent and in
the developing societies. In both it is in essence a crisis in values
caused by the generation gap. This crisis arises from the forces inherent in social structures that operate to preserve outmoded values,
underlining the failure of both the society and the education system to
adjust themselves to the changing needs of contemporary life.

What is disturbing, however, is that the recourse to violence as
a means of bringing about the desired social changes and the attendant
disruption of campus life undermine the very values that institutions of
higher education are intended to preserve. Beyond the immediate material

loss, this violence seriously impairs the goals of educational, economic, and social progress.

The Indian Commission on Education and National Development, while noting with concern the trend towards a progressive deterioration of the situation, observed that

> the responsibility for the situation is not unilateral--it is not merely that of the students or parents or teachers or State Governments or the political parties--but multilateral. All of them share it, together with many factors in the objective situation and no effective solution is possible unless each agency responsible for the malaise does its own duty. Some of the remedies for students' unrest, therefore, go beyond the education system. But even if we leave them out, there are two major things that the education system itself can and must do: remove the educational deficiencies that contribute to it and set up an adequate consultative and administrative machinery to prevent the occurrence of such incidents.[35]

It is thus evident that a new challenge has appeared in the generation gap, and both society and education will have to change considerably and move together to be able to meet it. The new problems relate to the various components of the educational process, and viewed as human development they can be as numerous as there are individuals within a system, embracing the whole spectrum of their life at home, in school, and in society. All of these interacting problems are formidable, and at the center of them lies the problem of infusing a new motive force of creativity and dynamism within the educational system that will make it more responsive to each nation's social and economic objectives by adapting it to the changing needs of the developing society through a continuous process of renewal and regeneration.

It has been a matter of deep concern to the developing countries that these problems, difficult and complex as they are, have seemed to be unaffected by reform efforts within the educational sector. It was, however, observed that these problems were interwoven into the much larger web of economic and social problems, which was beyond the direct control of the educational sector as such. The solution to these problems, therefore, presents a task that the education sector by itself cannot accomplish, as amply demonstrated by the experience of the last two decades. The need for an intersectoral approach and a new growth strategy is, thus, clearly indicated.

NOTES

1. See The Preliminary Report of the Bangladesh Education Commission (1973) and The First Five-Year Plan of Bangladesh (1973-78) (1973); the national development plans current in 1974 of Burma, Ceylon, India, Indonesia, Malaysia, Pakistan, Philippines, and Thailand; Government of India, Report of the Education Commission, 1964-66; Government of Pakistan, Report of the Education Commision (1960), Pakistan's New Education Policy (1971); Report of the Presidential Commission to Survey Education in the Philippines (1970).

2. Philip H. Coombs, The World Educational Crisis: A Systems Analysis (New York: Oxford University Press, 1970), p. 20.

3. The Interim Report of the Bangladesh Education Commission, May 1973, pp. 1-13; The First Five-Year Plan of Bangladesh (1973).

4. Third Five-Year Plan of India (1961-66), p. 573.

5. Ibid., p. 1.

6. Quoted in Government of India, Report of the Education Commission (1964-66), p. xiii.

7. First Five-Year Plan of Indonesia (1969/70-1973/74), p. 9.

8. Second Five-Year Plan of Malaysia (1971-75), p. 222.

9. Report of the Presidential Commission to Survey Education in the Philippines (1970), p. iii.

10. Ibid., p. 1.

11. First Five-Year Plan of Pakistan (1955-60), p. 2.

12. Second Five-Year Plan of Pakistan (1960-65), p. 329.

13. Ibid., (Preface).

14. Fourth Five-Year Plan of Pakistan (1970-75), p. 105.

15. H. Sharp (ed.), Selections from Educational Records, Part 1 (1781-1831) (Calcutta, 1920), p. 116.

16. M.S. Huq, Education and Development Strategy (Honolulu: East-West Center Press, 1965), p. 13.

17. Economics Bureau, U.S. Arms Control and Disarmament Agency, World Military Expenditures 1969 and Related Data for 120 Countries (Washington, D.C.: U.S. Government Printing Office, 1969), p. 11.

18. Report of the Education Commission, op. cit., p. 9.

19. World Bank Annual Report (1973), pp. 82-83.

20. UNESCO, An Asian Model of Educational Development (New York: United Nations, 1966), p. 72.

21. Taherul Islam, Social Justice and Education System of Bangladesh (Dacca: Dacca University Bureau of Economic Research, 1973).

22. Daniel Patrick Moynihan as quoted by Godfrey Hodgson in "Do Schools Make a Difference," The Atlantic Monthly (March 1973), p. 45 (footnote).

23. Five-Year Plan of Ceylon (1972-76), p. 5.

24. The Report of the Committee on Unemployment and Under-employment, as quoted in The Times of India (December 1972).

25. A. Jozefuwicz, Pakistan National Commission on Manpower and Education Research Study No. 5, the Commission, 1970, p. 62.

26. Report of the Presidential Commission to Survey Education in the Philippines (1970), p. 39.

27. India's Fourth Five-Year Plan (1969-74), pp. 363-64.

28. Peter A. Slors, "Some Bottlenecks in Indonesia's Educational Structure, with a View on Its Future," mimeographed (Djakarta: Department of Education and Culture, Board of Educational Planning, January 12, 1971), p. 8.

29. A. Jozefuwicz, "Probe into the Question of Unemployment among the Educated Youth," (Karachi: National Manpower Council, UN Manpower Planning Project, July 1968), pp. 15-19.

30. Report of the Education Commission, op. cit., p. 718.

31. "The Unquiet Campus: Indian Universities Today," A Statesman Survey, 1960, p. 9.

32. Report of the Education Commission, op. cit., p. 536.

33. John P. Willson, "Reform and Hysteria in Higher Education," Modern Age, 15, no. 3 (Summer 1971), 280.

34. The New York Times, April 17, 1972 ("Changing Values on Campus": Report of a Survey conducted by Daniel Yankelovich, Inc. for John D. Rockefeller 3rd. Foundation, 1972).

35. Report of the Education Commission, op. cit., p. 537.

2

THE ROOTS OF
THE CRISIS

The crisis in education stems from a crisis in development as a whole. Many of the problems are rooted in a complex set of interrelated and interdependent economic, social, and political factors universal in character and some of them with international dimensions.

The present chapter analyzes the major global factors operating outside the sector of education but profoundly influencing the course of its development. This will provide the necessary perspective to the search for a new strategy of educational development as an integral part of overall national development.

GENERAL BACKGROUND

The decades of the 1950s and 1960s represent a new era in the history of planned development and a generation of development effort. During this period the development movement spread to the entire Third World, comprising the emergent nations of Africa, Asia, and Latin America, with two-thirds of the world population. The Third World urge for progress was reflected in the commitment of these nations to planned development, and the resulting national plans are unique as blueprints of the most exciting social and economic experiments ever undertaken in the history of human endeavor.

What has indeed been most striking is that the upsurge of enthusiasm and the efforts generated by the new development movement have been shared by the richer countries as well, as thousands of individual scholars and specialists became participants in this movement.* The

---

*The number of foreign experts and volunteers working in developing countries and nationals of developing countries studying abroad in 1968 alone has been estimated at 180, 000.[1]

climate in which this worldwide movement was launched was one of unprecedented enthusiasm.

Several factors appear to have operated in producing this climate. The most evident among them was, of course, the mood of the nations. The emergent nations were determined to move forward, make sacrifices, and subject themselves to the discipline implied in planned development. For the rich nations, with the scars of the World War II still fresh, development of the Third World appeared to be a worthwhile venture as an investment in the future security of the world. Two other concomitants encouraging the richer nations were apparently the success of international cooperation in achieving the spectacular recovery of the war-ravaged countries in Europe and of Japan and the new prosperity of all the industrialized countries during the postwar era. With the advent of the United Nations Decade of Development commencing from 1961, the movement received an added impetus and an official international footing.

The backdrop of the development movement in the countries of the Third World and in Japan, however, presented contrasting scenes sharpened by some major social, economic, and cultural differences. The implications of these differences in the type of growth model and also in the time path of development turned out to be much more far-reaching than realized at the launching of the development movement. Their full significance appears to have been obscured by the high expectations raised in the industrialized countries by the prospect of harnessing the untapped natural resources and the vast manpower reservoirs available in many of the developing countries and in the developing countries by the prospect of application of the rich stock of knowledge, skill, and resources already stored in the industrialized countries through advances in science and technology.

However, these expectations were based on a number of unrealistic assumptions, and inadequate attention was paid to the factor endowments and other important economic and social variables deeply influencing the growth process in the developing countries. For example, the fallacy of borrowing capital-intensive growth models from the industrialized countries for use in societies in which capital is scarce and labor abundant, and in which the prevailing social stratifications rule out the free interplay of market forces, was too apparent to be missed by any objective observer. Some economists, including Gunnar Myrdal,[2] drew pointed attention to the futility of using planning concepts that were unsuited to the conditions of the developing societies, though without much effect on their fellow economists and the policy makers.

In the early years of planning objectivity was clouded by the belief that science and technology could perform the same miracles in the developing countries as they had accomplished in the industrial countries. While the usefulness of science and technology in modernizing production methods is beyond question, the fact remains that the political and economic structures of the world are at present so hindered by national policies and biases that they do not permit the free flow of

capital-based technology from the countries in which it is in plentiful
supply to those in which it is scarce. This has been the most important
deterrent to the growth of the modern sector at a pace fast enough to
reduce poverty and unemployment. The total external aid, the bulk of it
being loans, to the entire developing world was barely $15 billion in
1970, compared to military expenditures of over $180 billion by the
developed countries in the same year.

By 1970 many crisis spots had begun to appear. The developing
countries came under severe stress from constraint of resources, distortions in intersectoral growth, declining growth of external aid, diminishing of their share in external trade, mounting debt-servicing liability,
rising unemployment and underemployment, inflation, declining real
wages, growing inequalities in income, and rapidly increasing population
below the poverty line. Meanwhile the erosion of the value moorings and
the sharpening of the conflict between the claims of "growthmanship"
and social justice have become a serious threat to their very social and
political stability. The decade of the 1960s closed and that of the 1970s
opened under the shadow of a deepening crisis.

THE ANATOMY OF ECONOMIC GROWTH

Viewed in statistical terms and judged by the rate of growth in
gross domestic product, the performance of the economic sector of the
developing countries appears to be impressive. Between 1950 and 1969
the GDP of the developing countries as a whole grew at an average
annual rate of about 5 percent, which seemed to compare favorably with
that of the industrial countries in the early stages of their development.
This performance was due to no small extent to the policy of investment
in those subsectors of the economy that were expected to yield the best
return most quickly, though they were not necessarily the most important
to ultimate economic viability.

Moreover, a closer look will reveal that the favorable growth rates
were more apparent than real. In the first place, as Table 2.1 will show,
they were largely neutralized by the growth in population, a trend which
has continued to plague the developing countries in the absence of
rational population policies with the high priority they deserve.

In the second place, the average conceals great disparities in
income and wealth even within countries. What is most disconcerting
is that the per capita rate of growth in GDP in 70 percent of the total
population of the third world was only 2 percent or less. Thus the net
increases in annual income of the majority of the population in the
developing countries were really quite insubstantial, hardly exceeding
$2. At this rate of growth the prospect of relieving the abject poverty
in which the population of most of the countries lives a subhuman life
appears to be too distant to have any hopeful significance. These are

TABLE 2.1

Average Annual Rate of Growth in Gross Domestic Product, 1961-70
(in percentage)

	Rate of Growth in GDP			1961-70 Population			Rate of Growth in GDP per Capita		
	1961-65	1969	1970*	1961-65	1969	1970*	1961-65	1969	1970*
All developing countries	5.1	6.3	5.9	2.6	2.6	2.6	2.5	3.6	3.3
Africa	4.4	5.4	5.1	2.4	2.6	2.6	1.9	2.8	2.4
East Asia	5.5	9.1	7.1	2.8	2.8	2.8	2.6	6.1	3.2
South Asia	3.4	4.5	4.8	2.5	2.4	2.4	0.8	2.1	2.3
Middle East	7.5	8.2	5.1	2.9	3.1	3.1	4.4	5.0	2.0
Southern Europe	7.3	7.7	5.9	1.4	1.5	1.5	5.8	6.1	4.3
Latin America	4.9	6.3	6.6	3.0	3.1	3.1	1.9	3.2	3.4

*Preliminary

Source: World Bank Annual Report, 1971.

important facts thrown up during the 1950s and 1960s, which clearly
warrant a reexamination of the goals of economic growth and planning
strategy.

SECTORAL GROWTH

Neither the gross domestic product nor the gross national product
tells us much about the growth process, the plan-strategy and its effect
on different sectors, however. An idea about the dynamics of growth
and the role and potential of different sectors in development can, however, be obtained from an analysis of the past performance of the major
sectors.

Agriculture

Although agriculture forms the largest sector of the economy of the
developing countries, it was assigned a low priority in the plan-strategy.
In the initial years of development the progressive decline in agricultural production was indicated by the fact that while the developing
countries exported 14 million tons (net) of food grains annually during
the 1930s they imported 10 million tons (net) of food grains annually
during the 1960s. Imports of food grains were especially high in 1966
and 1967 following failure of the monsoon rains in South Asia for two
successive years.

Happily the situation underwent a dramatic change with a major
breakthrough in food production popularly known as the "Green Revolution" in a number of countries as Table 2.2 will show. This spectacular
growth was made possible by a reorientation of the plan-strategy, with
the higher priority it deserved assigned to agriculture, accompanied by
price incentives for farmers and improved seeds, fertilizer, and farm
machinery and better irrigation and easier credit. The most critical
contribution was made by the new high-yield (dwarf) varieties of wheat
and rice developed in Mexico and the Philippines, respectively.

The "Green Revolution" highlighted the importance of the skill,
research, and technology component of external aid and the possibility
of creating favorable conditions through conscious planning to overcome
resistance to change. Contrary to common belief, the peasant farmers
responded enthusiastically to the expectations of larger returns and,
overcoming the barriers of time-honored custom and tradition, came forward to try the new seeds and the new technology including the use of
fertilizer, pesticides, and tube-well irrigation. This success holds out
the hopeful prospect of a similar breakthrough in other sectors of development through research and new technology, thus indicating an important direction the planning strategy may follow to open up new

TABLE 2.2

Average Annual Growth Rates in Food Production, 1951-69
(in percentage)

Country	1951-60	1967-69
Burma	2.5	6.7[a]
Ceylon	2.7	8.4[b]
India	3.3	6.2[a]
Malaysia	5.7	14.7[c]
Pakistan	1.6	6.4[a]
Philippines	3.1	8.0[c]

[a]1968 only.

[b]1967 only.

[c]1969 only.

Source: Report of the Commission on International
Development (New York: Praeger Publishers, 1969), p. 28.

possibilities of fruitful development through the cooperation of education
and other sectors.

The "Green Revolution" has clearly demonstrated the potential of
the agriculture sector for further growth. It is the beginning of a process
that can be extended to the entire agriculture sector, and aided by diversification of crops it can vastly increase both productivity and employment opportunities. Since 60 to 80 percent of the labor force is employed
in agriculture and nonagricultural sectors can absorb no more than a
small fraction of the annual addition to the labor force, agricultural
development should be oriented to labor-using methods of improving
agricultural productivity.

It should, however, be borne in mind that the "Green Revolution"
has not yet touched more than a small fringe of the vast agriculture
sector. In the second place urgent reforms in the existing land laws,
which favor large farmers, are necessary to ensure that the mistakes of
the industrial policy are not repeated through premature mechanization[3]
in the agricultural sector, impeding the fullest exploitation of its
employment potential. The strategy of extending the benefits of the
Green Revolution to the entire agriculture sector also has important
implications regarding the role of the education sector, not only through
research or future supply of manpower trained in the new technology,
but equally through training of the labor force already employed, to

cope with the new technology. Thus a high priority for agriculture and input including the educational input constitute the cornerstones of a planning strategy to spark off an agricultural revolution, a precondition for economic takeoff and a viable base for educational growth.

Industry

The manufacturing industry, which to all practical intents and purposes has been the focal point in the plan-strategy of the developing countries, showed a ratio of growth of over 7 percent per annum during 1950-67. The corresponding rate of growth for the world as a whole, excluding communist countries, was about 6 percent. There can be no valid comparison with the present growth rate in the industrialized countries, however, since the developing countries started from a very low base.

The contribution of this sector has doubled in Asia, ranging from 15 to 20 percent of national income. In Latin America its share in national income is between 15 and 30 percent. The emphasis of the industrial development policy of the developing countries has largely been on the production of import substitutes. Two-thirds of all consumer goods needed by them are now produced within the regions, besides about 40 to 50 percent of the intermediate goods and 20 to 30 percent of the capital goods.

While the importance of rapid industrialization of the developing countries to a balanced restructuring and growth of their economy can never be minimized, in the past the growth model was based on a capital-intensive technology without due regard to the options available in the choice of technology to maximize both productivity and employment. Moreover, industrial growth was promoted through a policy of large subsidies in the form of preferential exchange rates, tax rebates, export bonuses, and high tariff protection. The impressive performance in import substitution was based on a production policy of preference for luxury goods over wage goods. The result in most countries was concentration of wealth in a few hands, accompanied by an increase in the tax burden and the prices of essential commodities, hurting the ordinary man and accentuating the detrimental effects of the growing income disparities. Thus the policy of industrial development and plan-strategy both directly contributed to the distortions in the growth pattern that now cause deep concern in the developing countries.

One of the most urgent needs in the industrial sector, with an important bearing on education and research, is the exploration of the possibility of stepping up industrial growth through labor-intensive technology, production of wage goods, and exploitation of the local materials, with the twin goals of maximizing employment opportunities and increasing real wages by making wage goods more plentiful and cheaper.

Social Overhead

Investment in roads, railroads, power, and rapid communications during 1948-67 has resulted in some improvement of the infrastructure that served as the basis of development. The annual railway growth rate during the period ranged from 2.9 percent in passenger traffic to 4.4 percent in freight traffic. Past experience, however, indicates the vast potential of labor-intensive methods in developing roads and the economic advantages of water transport in riparian areas.

The annual growth rate in the production of electric power during 1951-67 was 10.5 percent, indicating a seven-fold increase in Asia, a five-fold increase in Africa, and a four-fold increase in Latin America. The policy in the development of power was oriented to the needs of industries and urban consumers. As a result, while the supply of power still lags behind the rapidly growing demand of the industrial and urban sector, the role of power in the vast agriculture and rural sector is insignificant. The potential of electrification in the modernization of the rural sector and the creation of employment in this sector can, however, hardly be overstressed. The existing imbalance in power sharing between the two sectors seems to be a major reason for the underdevelopment of agriculture and rural industries, thus adversely affecting both employment and the utilization of trained personnel in this major sector of economy.

Public Health

The most significant gains in the social services sector appear to be those achieved in the area of public health, demonstrating the effective use of applied sciences. The rise in the life expectancy to about 50 years (with wide variations among the developing countries) was faster than expected, contrary to the general developmental trend of performance falling short of expectations. Malaria was virtually eliminated. The number of deaths due to epidemic diseases was substantially reduced.

The improvement in life expectancy, with the yet uncontrolled growth in population, has produced one of the dilemmas of development, however. It has tended to neutralize correspondingly the gains in economic growth and accentuate the problems of education and employment, at the same time underscoring the paramount role of education, both formal and nonformal, in evolving and implementing a rational scheme of population control.

The therapeutic health services, though considerably enlarged, were still very inadequate as shown in Table 2.3. It will thus appear that the health sector is still extremely underdeveloped and represents

TABLE 2.3

Number of Inhabitants per Physician

	1952	1966
All developing countries	5,100	3,600
Africa	11,800	9,200
South Asia	6,600	5,200
East Asia	11,800	7,400
Southern Europe	3,000	1,150
Latin America	2,100	1,800
Middle East	4,800	3,300
Industrialized countries	880	750

Source: Report of the Commission on International Development (New York: Praeger Publishers, 1969), p. 41.

one of the most depressed areas in the growth pattern. The development needs of this sector clearly deserve more attention and have important implications for education in the size of the demand for trained manpower and also the design of the courses of training for meeting these needs, as we shall see later.

International Trade

An important indicator of economic growth is the growth of exports. During 1953-68 exports from the developing countries grew at 4.7 percent per year, while twenty countries increased their exports by more than 8 percent per annum. Impressive as this performance may seem to be, the fact remains that the world trade as a whole grew faster by an average of 6.9 percent, and the share of the developing countries steadily declined from 27 percent in 1953 to 17 percent in 1970. The growth in world exports and the relative shares of the developing and the industrialized countries during the last decade is shown in Table 2.4. Even in primary products, the share of the developing countries declined from 54 percent to 42 percent. In contrast the industrialized countries more than doubled their share in world exports. Chief among the reasons why this trend in world exports has been unfavorable to the developing countries are (1) trade liberalization in the postwar period was aimed principally at expanding trade among industrialized

countries; (2) the economic policies of some of the developing countries
had the effect of discouraging exports, another cause of the distortions
in the growth pattern; (3) the neglect of agricultural development resulted
in the food imports mentioned earlier; (4) the inability of some of the
developing countries to change the structure of their exports gave them
a rapidly declining share of exports of food and agricultural raw materials
(halved by 1966-67); (5) great advances were made in developing syn-
thetic materials to replace the agricultural raw materials formerly
exported from developing countries. All of these trends indicated the
lack of appreciation in developing countries of the value of research
input in economic growth.

The decline in the share of the developing countries in the export
trade has grave implications. It means a setback in the future rate of
growth, since export earnings are the principal source of foreign exchange, being nearly four times as large as the flow of aid and private
investment. It adversely affects countries dependent on international
division of labor, in particular the smaller ones, since trade in a deeper
sense is "an engine of growth." It also adds to the problems of debt
servicing.

Thus the techniques used to plan economic growth have proved
to be detrimental to the long-run economic interest of the developing
countries and have retarded their progress toward self-reliant
economies.

TABLE 2.4

Growth in Exports
(F.O.B. in millions of U.S. dollars)

	1961-65	1969	1970
World	157,508	272,590	312,010[*]
Industrialized countries	106,862	193,140	224,700[*]
Developing countries	31,854	49,640	54,160[*]
	(20%)	(18%)	(17%)

[*]Provisional

Source: World Bank Annual Report, 1971.

INTERNATIONAL AID

The international dimension of the development effort can be seen
in the flow of aid from the international development community through
bilateral or international arrangements. The important part played by
international aid in development is often stressed and rightly so. As
observed earlier, the reliance placed on external aid in the growth
models was far greater than warranted by the realities of the world situation, however. In the first place, the external aid formed rather a
small fraction of the total investment in development, although it made
it possible for the developing countries to import part of the much-needed
machinery, equipment, and raw materials for industry and fertilizer,
pesticides, irrigation equipment, and other materials for agriculture.
External aid in recent years has financed about 10 percent of the investment in development but 20 percent of the imports.[4] In the second place,
the contribution of international aid to development through the sharing
of the knowledge, skill, and technical know-how that the advisers,
consultants, and personnel trained abroad carried with them was also
of inestimable value to the developing countries.
    As observed above, aid is only one of the components of the flow
of external resources to the developing countries, the major component
being export earnings, and part of it is used for debt servicing. The
total flow of external resources falls into two categories: (1) official
development assistance, including grants and multilateral contributions,
bilateral loans, and other official aid, and (2) private assistance,
including direct and portfolio investment and private export credits.
The pattern of the total flow of external resources under these categories during 1965-70 is summarized in Table 2.5.
    It will appear that while the total annual flow of resources
steadily increased in absolute volume from $10.36 billion to $14.71
billion during 1965-70, the official development assistance increased
at a slower rate, from $5.87 billion to $6.81 billion during the same
period, registering a decline in 1968. Remarkably, the increase in the
total flow was accounted for largely by the increase in the private flow.
This increased the proportion of hard loans and hence meant a larger
burden on the developing countries in debt servicing.
    Both the total flow and the total official flow of resources as the
share of GNP declined during 1965-70, from .78 percent to .74 percent
and from .48 percent to .40 percent respectively. This indicates that
by the end of the 1960s the rate of progress toward reaching the United
Nations' target of 1 percent of the combined national incomes of the
industrialized countries actually showed a decline. Unless this trend
is reversed immediately it seems unlikely that the United Nations'
modest target of international aid flow can be attained, although it
does not appear that there is anything magical about this 1 percent
of GNP or that even if this target is reached any spectacular results

TABLE 2.5

Flow of External Resources from DAC[a] Countries to Developing Countries and Multilateral Institutions, 1965-70
(in billions of U.S. dollars)

	1965	1966	1967	1968	1969	1970[b]
Official and private	10.36	10.28	11.24	13.06	13.68	14.71
Official alone	6.17	6.45	7.01	7.05	7.21	7.95
Private alone	4.18	3.83	4.23	6.01	6.47	6.76
Official development assistance	5.87	6.07	6.62	6.32	6.62	6.81
Grants and multilateral contributions	4.07	4.08	4.33	4.02	4.31	4.41
Bilateral loans	1.80	1.99	2.29	2.30	2.32	2.40
Total flow as share of GNP (in percentage)	0.78	0.78	0.43	0.78	0.75	0.74
Official flow as share of GNP (in percentage)	0.48	0.46	0.46	0.43	0.39	0.40
Official development assistance of GNP (in percentage)	0.44	0.43	0.43	0.38	0.36	0.34

[a]DAC = Development Assistance Committee of the Organization for Economic Cooperation and Development. DAC countries are Australia, Austria, Belgium, Canada, Denmark, France, Germany, Italy, Japan, Netherlands, Norway, Portugal, Sweden, Switzerland, United Kingdom, and United States.

[b]Preliminary. (The final statistics published in later reports do not materially alter this picture or its conclusions about trends.)

Source: World Bank Annual Report, 1971.

can be achieved. It may be noted here that the performance in Europe
and Japan was the outcome of a much larger rate of investment than this,
under considerably more favorable conditions. The trend of investment
reflects the changing mood of the nations, and the importance of this
change of mood to the future of our global society is indeed most disturbing. In marked contrast, the investment in arms is rising and has
already exceeded $180 billion,[5] compared to $15 billion spent on aid
in 1970. In this connection the following observation of World Bank
President Robert McNamara is very significant, particularly in view of
his experience as a former U.S. Secretary of Defense:

> Let us look for a moment at this question of resources.
> For the so-called security of an ever spiraling arms race,
> the world is spending $180 billion annually and the figure
> steadily goes up.
>   Four years ago in a speech in Montreal, I tried to
> point out that more and more military hardware does not
> provide more and more security. There is a point of
> diminishing returns beyond which further financial ex-
> penditure on military power does not yield increased
> returns and does not provide greater strength. . . .
> most of the nations . . . are beyond that point of
> diminishing returns.[6]

Considering that the developing countries are now using as much as 20
to 30 percent of their export earnings for debt servicing, as against 10
to 12 percent regarded as normal, there is evidently a need for stepping
up the flow of international aid on easier terms and for enlarging the
scope and character of international trade arrangements to allow the
developing countries to increase their share in the world exports at
mutually beneficial rates.
    In view of the change visible in the mood of the nations certain
facts, though well-known, need to be reviewed. The benefit of aid to
recipient nations is generally recognized, but its benefit to the donor
countries tends to be overlooked or underestimated. In the first place,
to the extent that aid takes the form of goods and services transferred
from the donor countries to the recipient countries, as is generally the
case, it means an enlarged market for the goods produced in the donor
countries and hence increasing employment opportunities for their
nationals. In the second place, since the major part of the aid is in
the form of loans repayable by the recipient countries, it gives the
donor countries a command over additional goods and services after
the stipulated period, so that aid does not involve any permanent loss
of wealth and may even improve the economic positions of the donor
countries by increasing their shares of world wealth through enlarged
world trade and necessary adjustments in the international division of
labor. The crucial importance of aid lies in the fact that if it is given

and used for genuine development it helps produce more, which means more to share within the world community, to the benefit of both donors and recipients.

The fruitfulness of aid, as clearly demonstrated by the experiences of the last two decades, depends on two basic factors, the quality of the aid determined by the purpose and conditions and the ability of the recipient country to put it to its best use. According to the findings of the Pearson Commission aid has been least effective where it has been provided primarily because of political considerations. In like manner, aid given for military reasons means a diversion of valuable external resources from vitally important national purposes such as fighting poverty, hunger, disease, and illiteracy to building up armies of a size that poor countries do not need and that they cannot afford; in many cases defense has consumed a very large part, in some countries over 50 percent, of the national revenue budget. Another tragic result, perhaps not intended, of the bolstering of the armed forces has been the emergence of military dictatorships in some countries, retarding or even reversing political developments conducive to the social changes essential for rapid development. External aid with a predominantly political or military component also proved to be a major cause of the imbalance in the growth pattern plaguing many countries, at least in some cases endangering security and stability within and outside the nation. The Report to the President of the United States from The Task Force on International Development headed by Rudolph A. Peterson gives the following breakdown of U.S. foreign assistance by purpose for fiscal 1969:[7]

	Millions of dollars	Percent
Security	3, 396	52
Welfare and emergency relief (not including private assistance)	368	6
International development (not including private investment)	2, 706	42

In gratifying contrast, one component of aid that yielded a benefit out of all proportion to its monetary value was the human component, represented by the ideas, knowledge, and skill of the consultants from abroad and also the teachers, students, and others trained abroad who participated in the development efforts. "In 1968 alone, there were over 100, 000 experts and volunteers working in developing countries, financed under official programs, and over 80, 000 students and trainees were studying in the industrialized countries."[8] In addition nearly an equal number consisted of consultants, analysts, and engineers engaged in preparing and implementing capital projects and of experts and trainees supported by private organizations.

This two-way flow of human capital greatly stimulated development and served as a catalyst at least in some cases to create a climate of boldness and willingness to experiment. Foreign experts teamed up with trained nationals of the developing countries in the exciting quest for change. The path of progress was far from smooth and a process of trial and error was inevitable, but aid in this shape appeared to be a novel enterprise shared by the nations in their common effort to create a better world. The component of aid specifically applied to education did not, however, exceed 10 percent of the total aid and was as low as 3 percent in Asia. Considering the catalyzing effect of training and research on both economic and social development, it appears that the aid component that was the richest in quality remained the poorest in quantity and availability. In retrospect it may be argued that many of the flaws in the growth pattern might have been avoided if the aid policy had been education-oriented and if more reliance had been placed by the developing countries on labor-intensive technology and technological education oriented to the development and use of such technology.

THE POPULATION EXPLOSION

During the past decades, one of the most serious and intractable impediments to faster progress has been the population explosion. With the levels of fertility remaining more or less constant there was a heavy concentration of children under 15 years of age. As a result nearly one-half of the population in Asia was in the low production and high consumption age groups of under 15 and over 65. The other half of the population was in the productive age group of 15 to 64 but not fully employed.

The population crisis arises from the fact that despite the increasing efforts of the developing countries in population control, their populations tend to grow faster than those of the industrialized countries, thus neutralizing a substantial part of the gain achieved by their economic growth. This is illustrated in Table 2.6.

The rate of growth of the population of the developing countries exceeded the United Nations projection of 1951 by 1.2 percent by the mid 1960s, due largely to the success of health measures adopted to reduce the mortality rate, thus underlining one of the dilemmas of development. At the present rate of growth the population in the developing countries would double itself before the end of the present century, thereby doubling the need for food, clothing, housing, education, and health services. Thus a terrifying dimension is added to the task of development, since the developing countries, which could not achieve in 20 years a rate of growth sufficient for meeting even the basic economic and social needs of the present population, will be required in the next 30 years to grow enough to provide for the needs

TABLE 2.6

Rate of Average Annual Real Growth and
Share in Gross Domestic Product, 1961-70
(in percentage)

	1961-65	1968	1969	1970*
Developing countries				
Total GDP	5.1	6.2	6.3	5.9
Population	2.6	2.6	2.6	2.6
GDP per capita	2.5	3.5	3.6	3.3
Industrialized countries				
Total GDP	5.2	5.5	4.8	3.4
Population	1.2	0.9	1.0	1.0
GDP per capita	3.9	4.5	3.7	2.4

*Provisional.

Source: World Bank Annual Report, 1971.

of double that population. The implications of the situation are therefore
most grave for the future of the nations and the quality of life in the
next generation if effective measures are not taken to check the growth
of population. Among these measures the most important and also the
most urgent are a well-designed and adequate program of education in
family planning and enlargement of the size of the family planning program itself to enable it to reach all areas and all segments of the population. This will naturally involve corresponding expansion in the supply
of trained personnel to operate the programs.

Here is another challenging educational task that is highly relevant to development needs and that will call for efforts both inside and
outside the formal education system, involving both the school and the
community in mutually reinforcing roles.

UNEMPLOYMENT

Among the problems that had assumed disturbing dimensions by
the end of the 1960s, the most alarming was that of unemployment in
general and unemployment among the educated in particular. A paradox
of the decade was that increased investment in development was accompanied by increasing unemployment and underutilization of human
resources, thus giving rise to one of the most socially and politically

40

EDUCATION, MANPOWER, AND DEVELOPMENT

TABLE 2.7

Unemployment and Underemployment in Developing Countries,
Excluding Mainland China

	Level in Millions		Level in Percent	
	1970	1980	1970	1980
Fully employed	504	592	75.3	70.5
Underemployed	130	200	19.4	23.8
			24.7[a]	29.5[b]
Total employed	634	792	94.7	94.3
Unemployed	36	48	5.3	5.7
Total labor force	670	840	100.0	100.0

[a]Percentage of the total number underemployed and unemployed
in 1970.

[b]Percentage of the total number underemployed and unemployed
in 1980.

Source: Robert McNamara, Address to the Board of Governors of
the World Bank, September 27, 1971, p. 11.

explosive distortions in the pattern of economic growth, with its far-
reaching impact on other sectors, particularly education. The developing countries suffer also from inadequacy of statistics and considerable
ambiguity in the concept of employment and underemployment. The
indications, however, are that the equivalent of 20 to 25 percent of the
entire labor force is at present unemployed in the developing countries.
Thus it will not be incorrect to say that "failure to create meaningful
employment is the most tragic failure of development."[9]

The outlook for the future appears to be even grimmer. It is estimated that the labor force throughout the developing world is likely to
grow even faster during the 1970s than it did in the 1960s, by 2.3 percent annually on the average. The impact of the population explosion
during the last two decades can also be seen in the vast increase in
the labor force, resulting from the fact that nearly 50 percent of the
total population of the developing world is under 15 years of age.
Population planning, however sound and effective, is unlikely to make
any decisive impact on the unemployment problem in the near future,
since the children who will constitute the labor force then are already
born. The magnitude of the problem is indicated in Table 2.7.

Beyond question the present inadequate rates of growth cannot
absorb the increase in the labor force already caused by the growth in

population, and the situation is bound to get worse. For example, India's fourth five-year plan envisages the creation of 19 million new jobs; but 23 million new workers will be seeking jobs, thus adding another 4 million to the number already unemployed.

It is erroneous to think that an acceleration of the growth rate by itself can provide the solution to this problem, on the analogy of the already industrialized countries, where full or nearly full employment and rapid economic growth go together. For example, Venezuela and Jamaica enjoyed average annual growth rates as high as 8 percent between 1950 and 1960, but at the end of the decade unemployment was higher in Venezuela and remained just as high in Jamaica, even though 11 percent of the country's labor force had emigrated during the period.

> What this means is that in addition to expanding their growth rates, the developing countries must adopt national policies promoting the right balance between capital and labor-intensive activities, and between the supply of skilled and unskilled workers so as to maximize output through full utilization of the total labor force.[10]

It should be possible to generate more employment through a dynamic and flexible economic policy, with appropriate use of labor-intensive technology and an educational system properly geared to this aim. One of the pitfalls of development planning in the past was the distortion of factor prices with a view to the overstimulation of capital-intensive and labor-saving technology, ending in failure to create adequate employment opportunities.

> Such technology is readily available in the industrialized countries, and there has been a tendency for the aid-giving agencies and foreign contractors to transfer it without modification. . . . Concessional interest rates, overvalued exchange rates, and differentiated tariffs reduced the private cost of the imported capital equipment, while market wage rates overstated the real cost of labor. [11]

Even where the rate of growth was above the average of 5 percent, in the nonagricultural sector, output grew faster than employment. One of the chief causes, for example in Pakistan, was that "the Capital-labor ratio, i.e., the value of fixed capital per man-year of employment . . . is higher than the country's factor endowments seem to indicate as socially desirable. In quite a few cases it has been found to be higher than in Japan."[12]

The development experience of the last two decades has provided many lessons. One of the most socially significant lessons is that the social cost of chronic and mounting unemployment is very high. "Let

there be no doubt: social costs are real costs. And once human hope-
lessness and frustration have been pushed beyond the breaking point,
social costs can erupt into catastrophic economic costs as well."[13]

DISPARITY IN INCOME AND WEALTH

Among the many anomalies and distortions observed in the pattern
of growth, none has been more disturbing than that the gap between the
per capita incomes of the rich and poor nations has been widening instead of narrowing, in both the relative and absolute sense. On a
regional basis this gap between the rich and poor nations was in the
ratio of 16:1, but if the countries at the apex and at the bottom of the
range are considered the disparity is as wide as 40:1.

What is most ironic is that the development effort of the 1950s
and 1960s has produced a similar trend of income disparity between the
rich and poor within the developing countries themselves. "In many of
them the share of total income going to the richest 5% of the families
is larger than the share of the poorest 60%, and in one of the largest
Latin American countries, it is almost twice as great."[14]

The pattern of income disparity in South and Southeast Asia is
illustrated by Table 2.8, which is based on a recent study. The fact
that per capita income in the first four countries in Table 2.8 is below
$100 leads to the distressing inference that the bulk of the population
in these countries lives on a much smaller fraction of $100 than shown
in the table and therefore marginally, between bare subsistence and
starvation.

The blatant inequalities in income and wealth arising from the
relentless pursuit of economic growth underline one of the most serious
pitfalls of the past planning strategy and are naturally treated with deep
concern by the developing countries in their recent plans. For example,
Ceylon's current five-year plan (1972-76) stresses the need "to reduce
social tensions by the elimination of wasteful consumption and by
redistributive measures . . . to raise the living standards of the low-
income groups by improved housing and sanitary facilities."[15]

India's fourth five-year plan noted as two of its major concerns
the reduction of concentration and diffusion of wealth, and improvement
in the condition of the common man and weaker sections, especially
through provision of education and employment. Pakistan's fourth five-
year plan (1970-75) identified the imbalances and distortions that had
emerged over the past 20 years and expressed concern over the rise in
prices, decline in real wages, increase in landless labor, and accen-
tuation of inequalities in income, pointing out that luxury consumption
highlighted the gulf between the abject poverty of the "have-nots" and
the ostentatious living of the "haves." It was noted in the plan that
the inevitable consequences were the sharpening of the conflict between

TABLE 2.8

Share of Bottom Sixty Percent of Population
in Total National Income

Country	Percent of Income
Burma	36.00
Ceylon	27.47
India	36.00
Pakistan	33.00
Philippines	24.70

Source: I. Adelman and C. T. Morris, "An Anatomy
of Patterns of Income Distribution in Developing Nations,"
Final Report (Mimeographed, Northwestern University,
1971).

economic growth and social justice and unprecedented political upheav-
als caused by the social and economic confrontations.

The four-year plan of the Philippines (1971-74) also stresses the
need for "a more equitable distribution of wealth." The economically
more affluent Malaysia is also concerned over the problem of income
disparity, and its second five-year plan (1971-76) emphatically states,
"We need to ensure at the same time that there is social justice, equal
sharing of income growth and increasing opportunities of employment."[16]
Among its other objectives the Indonesian plan (1964-70, 1973-74) is
"directed towards creating a just and prosperous society based on
Pantja Sila."[17]

POLITICAL TRENDS

The events of the 1950s and 1960s in the developing countries
have demonstrated that the most powerful single element influencing
the character and course of development is the political power structure,
and yet the political variables seem to have received the least attention
in the national development plans.

While some measure of centralization in national planning has
been not only inevitable but desirable, the degree of centralization
observable in planning has been in a way a reflection of the highly
centralized political power structure in the developing countries.

These countries, in most cases starting from scratch, did not
seem to have much political option in the initial stage, and concentration of political power in the hands of those who had emerged as

leaders during the freedom movement was a logical corollary. Many of these patriotic leaders were earnest about the democratic participation of their people in the affairs of the state at various levels, and constitutional and other legal measures indicated efforts towards decentralization of power through the creation of political institutions at the provincial and local levels.

These measures were not, however, taken in concert with the devolution of adequate powers in local planning and development. There were efforts to involve the people in development through their participation in planning and plan implementation, but such efforts were limited to a few experimental communities. By and large the effect of these measures on the national life was no more than a ripple, while the currents of power lay deeper and were unaffected. The evolution of the much-needed political institutions conducive to change, growth, and development was in several cases arrested or slowed down by the frictions produced by continuing power struggle, leading in some cases to the rise of personal or military dictatorships.

However, the factor that most directly affected the pace and pattern of development was the policy followed by many of the developing countries, irrespective of their form of government, of investing more heavily in the military (over 50 percent of the national budget in some countries) than in education and health. The most striking paradox of the last two decades was that they proved to be decades of military development more than of economic and social development, with the emerging trend of increasing poverty, greater inequalities, and greater military strength.

If the pitfalls of the past decades and their grave consequences are to be avoided, and if the development efforts are to be more productive and fruitful, the development strategy must be informed by the objectives of development and by an insightful recognition of the political, economic, and social realities of life in the developing countries. The role of education has to be seen in the context of this overall strategy.

NOTES

1. Report of the Commission on International Development (New York: Praeger Publishers, 1969), p. 51.

2. Gunnar Myrdal, Asian Drama (New York: Pantheon Books, 1968) and The Challenge of World Poverty (New York: Pantheon Books, 1970).

3. Report of the Commission on International Development, op. cit., p. 60.

4. Ibid., p. 73.

5. Robert McNamara, Address to the Board of Governors of the World Bank, September 21, 1970, p. 22; and World Bank Annual Report 1971, p. 61.

6. Ibid., pp. 22-23.

7. Task Force on International Development, Report to the President of the United States (Washington, D.C., March 4, 1970), p. 7.

8. Report of the Commission on International Development, op. cit., p. 51.

9. Ibid., p. 58.

10. Robert McNamara, Annual Address to the Board of Governors of the World Bank, September 29, 1969, pp. 15-16.

11. Report of the Commission on International Development, op. cit., p. 59.

12. S.R. Bose, "Green Revolution and Agricultural Employment under Conditions of Rapid Population Growth: The Pakistan Problem" in Employment and Unemployment of Near East and South Asia, Vols. 1 and 2, Ronald G. Ridker and Harold Lubell, eds. (Delhi, Bombay, London: Vikas Publications, 1971), p. 542.

13. McNamara, September 1969, op. cit., p. 16.

14. McNamara, September 1971, op. cit., p. 13.

15. Five-Year Plan of Ceylon (1972-76), p. 12.

16. Second Five-Year Plan of Malaysia (1971-75), p. vi.

17. First Five-Year Plan of Indonesia (1969/70-1973/74), p. 9.
The "Pantja Sila" is an Indonesian term meaning "five principles" and refers specifically to the "Five Principles of the State" underlined in an address of the President of Indonesia to the Preparatory Committee for Indonesian Declaration of Independence. The five state principles are: divine omnipotence, humanitarianism, nationalism (United Indonesia), democracy, and social justice.

3

**THE DYNAMICS OF
DEVELOPMENT AND
EDUCATION**

The analysis undertaken in Chapter 2 of the growth patterns in the developing countries during the 1950s and 1960s indicates serious imbalances in development and describes the many formidable problems that have bedeviled the path of education and development. Although development is a complex process involving numerous interacting forces, the plan-policy adopted in most countries has been extremely narrow in conception and design. The villain is not the stress that has been laid on economic growth, which is clearly a prime need, but the shortsighted strategy of concentrating investment on modernizing a tiny industrial sector to achieve this goal, while ignoring the other factors in development.

THE CHANGING CONCEPT OF DEVELOPMENT

There are, however, indications of a growing awareness within the developing countries and the international development community of the need for a reappraisal of the goals and strategy of development. This rising awareness was echoed in the following observation by the president of the World Bank, Robert McNamara, in his address to the annual meeting of the board of governors on September 27, 1971:

Development has far too long been expressed in terms of
growth of output. There is now emerging the awareness
that the availability of work, the distribution of income,
and the quality of life are equally important measures of
development.
Although this is gradually being accepted in theory,
it has yet to be translated into practice by either the
developing countries or the suppliers of external capital.

46

It is toward this broader concept of the entire development process that the World Bank is moving.[1]

The aim of this chapter is to widen our view of development and to
consider the related role of education in the context of the overall objectives and dynamics of development.

The use of the term "development" in its current sense began with
the emergence of the nations of the Third World. Though development is
not infrequently identified with economic growth—and the tendency to
interpret it so still persists—it is recognized as a multidimensional concept by both the developing nations and the international development
community.

The essential elements in the concept of development and their
implications for the national governments and the international development community are spelled out in the resolution of the United Nations
General Assembly proclaiming the beginning of the Second United Nations
Development Decade on January 1, 1971.[2]

The principal objectives of development as stressed in the United
Nations proclamation are (1) a minimum standard of living consistent
with human dignity; (2) sustained improvement in the well-being of the
individual; (3) sharing of benefits by all; (4) more equitable distribution
of income and wealth; (5) a greater degree of income security; (6) expansion and improvement of education, health, nutrition, housing, and
social welfare; and (7) the safeguarding of the environment.

These objectives of development embrace the whole gamut of a
nation's economic, social, and cultural life, and progress towards their
realization cannot be measured entirely by the rate of economic growth
or by any other single indicator.

In this context a number of incorrect notions should be dispelled.

First, it is erroneous to label all the countries of the Third World
as poor countries, as is often done to distinguish them from the more
developed countries, which are characterized as rich. There are some
countries in the developing world that are as rich as, and even richer
than, some of the countries in the more developed world, on the basis
of per capita income, but the level of living of the people in these
countries does not measure up to the standard reached by the people
in the more developed nations. A country may be rich actually or poten-
tially, but it remains underdeveloped if its standard of living is underdeveloped, since this implies that the social, economic, and political
institutions are also not developed well enough to sustain the well-
being of the people at a sufficiently high level. In other words, man
remains both the end and agent of development.

Second, changes in social structures and values are also implicit
in the process of development. Historically the translation of the concept of a fuller life for the people as a whole into reality is a comparatively recent and epoch-making social phenomenon. What has existed
as a noble and inspiring human goal in the minds of philosophers and

thinkers has become realizable through advances in science and technology in a number of countries. These countries are all highly industrialized and also most advanced in education, science, and technology. Some scientists, social scientists, and planners tend to associate development with the social structures found in these countries, hence the emphasis on scientific and technical education, capital-intensive investment, market economy, the use of the universalistic and achievement criteria in resource allocation and work evaluation, and life styles based on a high level of consumption. The degree of emphasis laid on these different factors, however, varies according to the school of thought and its discipline orientation.

THE ECONOMISTS' APPROACH

Economists with a classical orientation look upon development as a process of transformation of a "traditional society" into a modern one. The "traditional society" is heavily dependent on agriculture, with little or no access to science and technology or an inability to make any systematic use of them. Its transition to the status of a "modern society" is characterized by a buildup of social overhead capital, a spate of technological developments in both agriculture and industry, and recognition by the political power of the value of modernization of the economy.[3]

During the period of transition the developing societies recognize the need for progress, introduce changes in the educational system, even if on a limited scale, and create infrastructures in the form of banks and other economic institutions to mobilize capital, stimulate investment, widen the scope of commerce, and encourage the establishment of modern manufacturing concerns. The most important phase in the development process is the takeoff stage, which makes a real breakthrough by overcoming the barriers to steady progress and setting into motion a chain activity toward sustained growth at an accelerated rate. Industries grow rapidly, and a large part of their profits is ploughed back into production in setting up new plants, expanding existing ones, employing more workers, and raising the demand for supporting services and for other goods, thus leading to the growth of more industries and to increasing urbanization. The new class of entrepreneurs also grows in size, exploiting hitherto untapped resources and using new technologies in production, and thus provides further impetus to economic growth.

The takeoff stage is followed by a long interval of sustained progress, even though some fluctuations may be experienced, and the countries move towards economic maturity. Modern technology is extended to all economic activity. Investment rises, enabling the rising output to outpace the growth in population. The economy at this stage demonstrates its capacity to move beyond the original industries of the takeoff period and set up more sophisticated industries, with a simultaneous development of the technological and entrepreneurial skills necessary to produce whatever is wanted.

The next stage is a phase of economic growth marking a shift towards durable consumer goods and services. Attainment of economic maturity increases the real per capita income so substantially that the individual consumption is no longer confined to basic food, shelter, and clothing. The proportion of urban to total population rises, with more people employed in services and skilled jobs. A further extension of modern technology in production is no longer a paramount need in these societies, and more of the national resources are available for allocation to social welfare.

This is the generalized pattern of growth that has been followed by the industrialized countries of the West and by Japan. The stages in the growth pattern are not so clear-cut, however, that the characteristics of one stage cannot coexist with those of another, nor is the length of the interval between any two stages necessarily the same; in fact the two stages may shade into one. For example, Canada and Australia did not have to wait for the stage of maturity before entering the stage of high mass consumption. The economists' view of the development process is thus primarily based on an analysis of the characteristics of the process of economic growth.

The economists' accent is on "modernization" as the path to development. This implies increasing industrialization, and increasing use of capital-intensive technology, both of which the developing countries clearly need. In like manner the developing countries must also accept increasing specialization, which is both a cause and result of technological change. Simply stated, technology is the application of scientific and other organized knowledge to specific tasks, which as a result become divided and subdivided into component parts requiring specialized knowledge. In this way the tasks are performed more efficiently by those who possess the specialized knowledge. These economic and technological changes are all desirable, but they must connect meaningfully and realistically with the overall economic and social structures of the developing countries, which are characterized by a small supply of physical capital and a large supply of human capital, indicating an economic profile vastly different from what is assumed to be the case by some of the economic planners. For model building, they often idealize a modern society in which enlightened self-interest and a market economy are assumed to create pressures on the economic system for maximizing productivity. These assumptions are, however, not borne out by reality.

In the first place, the industrialized countries include some in which modernization was achieved through planned development and full use of manpower with complete state control of the economy. Even in those that are committed to free enterprise and market economy the role of the state in economic development has considerably changed.

Employment, price, and income have emerged as areas of increasing
concern to the state. For example, in the United States the services of
the federal, state and local governments now represent 20 to 25 percent
of all economic activity, far exceeding the share of government in the
socialist democratic countries of Sweden and Norway and comparable to
that in Poland, a communist country.[4]

In the second place, a major feature of economic and technological
change in the modern capitalist countries is the rise of large industrial
corporations, which depend on planning and strategies not dissimilar to
those in socialist systems,[5] since the process of the market economy
is no longer relied upon to produce the result and a considerable part of
what was formerly the domain of market economy has been overrun by a
system of planning.[6] It will thus appear that both the modern large cor-
poration and the modern apparatus of social planning are really two
variants of economy's response to the same need in two different social
systems.

Both economic systems and technology have been created by
people to be their servants and not their masters. A developing country
should look upon technology as a means to an end, and this end is
product maximization relative to the country's resource position and
social realities. It should opt for a technology that will enable it to
use its human and material resources to the best advantage at that point
of time. Its growth models should aim at a series of such short-run
equilibria, based on changing technology, to move the country towards
realizing its full potential of development. This will naturally imply a
pragmatic approach to changes in economic institutions, based on
feedback. For example, if a growth model based on market economy
operates to increase the impoverishment of the people and concentrates
the wealth in the hands of a few in a developing country, as observed
in Chapter 2, the need for a change of the model is clearly indicated.

All too often in the past, growth rates were used as the yardstick
in the choice of plan-models and also in the evaluation of plan performance, regardless of their effect on employment and social justice. The
emerging concept of "net economic welfare" (NEW) now being advocated
by some leading economists underscores the inadequacy of GNP as a
dependable measure of real economic growth.

One of the benefits of a higher growth rate is claimed to be a
wider range of choices available to the people. This is not necessarily
so, however, and depends very much on the structure and components
of growth. If the higher growth rates are mainly due to value added in
such wasteful fields as production of arms, expansion of armed services, production of luxury goods, gambling, and the like, the society
would be better off with a lower growth rate than with these goods and
services and their socially baneful effects. In like manner when the
choice is between two models, one with a higher growth rate but lower
employment and greater disparity and the other with a lower growth rate
but higher employment and less disparity, the second model is clearly

the better one and should be preferred. The energy crisis has brought into focus another major variable determining the quality of growth, namely the energy-efficiency of the technology used in production and in sustaining the level of consumption. In other words, the quality of the growth of the GNP is extremely important and must be taken into consideration along with the quantity of its growth. As already mentioned earlier, the concept of the parameters of growth also needs to be enlarged to keep in proportion the major objectives of development. The indicators of growth should include not only how much is produced, but also what is produced and how it is produced; not only how much is saved and invested, but also how it has been saved and invested. Social cost must be added to economic cost and social gain to economic gain in order to keep the growth picture in its correct perspective.

THE POINT OF CONVERGENCE OF ECONOMISTS, PSYCHOLOGISTS, AND SOCIOLOGISTS

Psychologists and sociologists view development as essentially a process of psychological and sociological change. The psychologists contend that propensities to save and invest and other habits and attitudes conducive to growth are not economic but psychological variables.[7] Some economists also openly recognize the value of linking economic theory with psychological and sociological analyses in building plan-models.[8]

Based on an analysis of the social structures of modern industrialized countries, some studies have attempted to uncover value attitudes conducive to economic growth, associating it with a social structure including the following characteristics: (1) human resources allocated on the basis of universalistic criteria of efficiency and ability and not by particularistic criteria of race, creed, caste, family, clan, or color; (2) increasing division of labor or "specificity" of a person's relation to others; (3) evaluation of individuals by their achieved and not ascribed status, that is, in terms of what they can do and not of who they are; (4) concern of the "elite" and ultimately the people with the common or national good rather than with their own private ends; and (5) an objective and rational approach to means and ends.[9]

An interesting point of convergence of the economists, psychologists, and sociologists in their analyses of the growth process can be seen in the stress laid on technological change accompanying increasing application of scientific knowledge and a greater division of labor, with more individuals concentrating on more specific tasks with increasingly specialized knowledge so that the tasks are better done. This is clearly the central aspect of the dynamics of growth and indicates the direction that the mutually supporting processes of development and education will have to follow in the developing countries. It should, however, be noted that the value attitudes and structural differentiation in the psychological and sociological analyses appear to be based on idealized pattern variables widely different from the actual social norms of the people. Besides, it is far from clear how to determine empirically whether or not the characteristics of a social structure, like stress on "achieved" as opposed to "ascribed" status, are reflected in the attitudes of the members of that social structure in a given society.[10]

In the second place, the characteristics of modernization stressed in these analyses are presented in such a way as to suggest that they were to be found in the same degree in the Western countries in their own initial stages of modernization. It would be more correct, however, to view them as the product of a historical process that did not follow the same course even in all industrial countries. The value of the universalistic and achievement criteria as incentives to growth and productivity and to the process of modernization can hardly be overstressed, and there is clearly a need for building into planning strategy a mechanism for their increasing application. It is not, however, correct to think that the rate of development can be related to the rate of modification in the value attitudes and social structures as cause and effect in any known way.[11]

THE ROLE OF EDUCATION IN DEVELOPMENT

What we do know is that development involves a complex process of social change, dependent on the components of technological change, specialized knowledge, division of labor, and appropriate social structures and values. The "mix" of these components has taken different forms in different industrialized countries and even in the same country at different times, and therefore it does not lend itself to any absolute policy prescription but needs to be adapted to the conditions peculiar to a country.

Thus, assuming the goals are known, planning has the role of directing the desired social change by (1) identifying and defining the tasks involved, (2) using the educational sector to provide technology and specialized knowledge to perform these tasks, (3) estimating, mobilizing, and allocating the human and material resources required to perform the tasks in a rational manner, (4) creating the required economic, social (educational and cultural) and political institutions, (5) modifying values and attitudes for motivation and introducing innovations at crucial points, and (6) projecting and evaluating the consequences of change.

Education interacts and is interdependent with the process of development. Social structures, policies, and goals exert their influence on the education sector, as on other sectors, while the education sector influences economic and social development by inducing change in technology through the systematic application of scientific and other knowledge, in skills and specialized knowledge for specialized tasks as a consequence of their division and differentiation, and in values and attitudes to provide the necessary incentives for increasing productive efficiency. The net change in growth is the result of the productivity of the new technology and skills, assisted by changes in values and attitudes and reduced by the dysfunctionality that is caused by obsolescence in both technology and skills.

Although the role of education is crucial in the process of development, this role is a part of the sum of the interdependent and interacting roles of the various sectors of the society. The determination of the relative value of these roles in quantitative terms presents the most formidable challenge to research in planning and development. The need to identify, as precisely as possible, the tasks implied in the goals of development, both in quantitative and qualitative terms, and then to determine the respective roles of education and other sectors in performing the tasks, is clearly indicated. Planning strategy will therefore have to pay more attention to local planning and the microanalytical approach instead of depending entirely on centralized macroanalytical techniques as it has in the past.

A number of studies are available, with both the macroanalytical and microanalytical approach, on the economic value of education and the matching of its supply and demand; some of these studies are examined in the following chapters. The experience of the 1950s and 1960s has, however, demonstrated the danger of overdependence on planning models based on theoretical analytical reasoning that is relevant to economic or cultural situations in industrialized countries and divorced from the social realities in developing countries.

HUMAN AND SOCIAL VALUES

There are many elements in the concept of development that do not lend themselves to quantitative measurement and hence tend to be understressed compared to those that do; yet these are an integral part of the value system inspiring the goals of development and therefore need to be brought within the ambit of development planning. For example, freedom, equality, human dignity, and social justice raise important issues related to the quality of life. Only a part of quality of life is dependent on economic growth, in other words; the rest of it encompasses the vast area of human and social development, which education through the ages has tried to explore and serve. Throughout history the quest for a "good life" has inspired new thought and action, and the changing concepts of good life, though not reduced to plan blueprints, have profoundly influenced social institutions and value systems.

As a matter of fact, quality of life is central to the very concept of education, since education is a process of qualitative change which develops those specific innate qualities that enable an individual to lead a full and productive life as a person, a worker, and a member of a family and a society. Social values have traditionally been featured so prominently in education that until recently educational planning was almost entirely oriented to the objectives of social development. Even in the industrialized countries the economic goal of education received wide recognition only with the increasing dependence of industrial growth on scientific and technological knowledge since the late 19th century.

The influence of social values on education is rooted in the tradition of hundreds of years, in which education was the privilege of an elite group. The members of this group were either scholars dedicated to knowledge or clerics dedicated to religion, both frowning on worldly goods, or else the wealthy gentry. Education was primarily sought for knowledge, and any other benefits flowing from it were regarded as incidental. The distance between the educated elite and the uneducated workers reflected the distance between the cultural and economic aims of education.

This influence of tradition still lingers and is a powerful force of resistance to the changes in the social structures and values that are necessary for gearing education more effectively to the goals of development. The low value attached to manual labor and the high value attached to formal liberal education, the polemics over the general versus technical contents of education, and the question of selective versus liberal access to higher education are some examples of the continuing influence of this anachronistic tradition. Even in the industrialized societies, where the close link between technology-based industrial growth and education is an accepted order of life, the debate over the goals of education is far from over. There are still large communities of scholars who deplore the value that has come to be attached to the economic goal of education. There are clearly signs of deep concern within the academic communities of large American universities over the fact that scientific research has become so dominated by the economic goal that social values are overshadowed.[12] Such a concern is not altogether unjustified; the growing ferment among the youths, the rising incidence of antisocial activities, the expanding pockets of poverty, the increasing environmental pollution in many of the industrial countries, and above all the hazards of an arms race, indicate the need for more balanced goals of education and development in the more developed nations as well.

Though the developing countries have as yet far to go in the process of industrialization and though their present problem is one of having the economic goal of education properly reflected in the educational system, their plans should take note of the emerging problems in the industrial countries. Technical and vocational education needs to be duly stressed, but this does not imply that general education should be understressed. As we shall see later, education is not divisible into separate compartments according to social and economic ends. What goes under the name of general education, if properly designed, is really the skill to learn other skills and the ability to observe, analyze, reason, and cope with the environment. These are the qualities needed for success in a vocational role as well as in a social role. In like manner the social objectives of education cannot be realized if the educational system is deficient in the specialized knowledge needed to increase production enough to advance the social objectives. General and technical education, far from being mutually exclusive, are closely interrelated and interactive. The problem lies in designing a system of education articulated by elements of both in the right proportion.

Within the social system and its subsystems there are many economic and social blocks to the translation of any set of goals into practice. The serious distortions in the growth pattern during the 1950s and 1960s were an evidence of the existence of these blocks and also of the slow rate of change in the basic social structures and values essential for overcoming them. From the experience of several countries there is also evidence that the tension and instability created by economic disparity and social injustice cannot be eliminated or contained for long by merely stressing ideological (political, religious, or cultural) values.

NATIONAL PLANS AND SOCIAL OBJECTIVES

The current development plans of most countries in South and Southeast Asia therefore rightly assign a great importance to the reorientation of the plan-strategy to give due weight to the social objectives of development. The plans also seem to recognize directly or implicitly the role of education as an instrument of social change, through equalization and expansion of educational opportunities in promoting occupational and social mobility, creating a sense of social concern and civic responsibility, and instilling cultural and moral values.

The recently published First Five-Year Plan of Bangladesh (1973-78) opens with the following words: "The state of Bangladesh is founded on the four basic principles of democracy, nationalism, secularism and socialism";[13] and stresses the constitutional pledge to ensure the establishment of an egalitarian society in which the toiling masses are emancipated from all forces of exploitation and all citizens enjoy equal opportunity.

Ceylon's five-year plan is "primarily geared to correct the serious gap which has today arisen between the needs of the people and exploited resources. In social terms, the plan seeks to upgrade hitherto neglected strata of Ceylon Society—the unemployed, the urban and rural poor, the landless labourer, the wage-earner and the small peasant."[14] The emphasis on educational change, to quote from the plan, "belongs to the overall strategy for the entire economy."[15]

An investment of 172 billion rupiah in the social field, including education and health, is envisaged in the Indonesian first five-year development plan (1969/70-1973/74). The plan-targets in education are, among others, to raise the enrollment in the primary age group (7-12 years) to 80 percent in 1973, compared to 63 percent in 1967, and to stress community and adult education to be organized around schools.

In light of the experiences and observed trends of recent years, India's fourth plan underlines:

> The most notable lesson is that current tempo of economic activity is insufficient to provide productive employment to all, extend the base of social services, and bring about significant improvements in the living standards of the people. [16]

The plan also suggests more comprehensive planning, that is, with more attention to the social aspects of development and greater control of resources than has been attempted in the past, with a view to attaining the objectives of equality and social justice. It reiterates one of the principles of the second plan as the basis of a long-term strategy for development:

> The task before an underdeveloped country is not merely to get better results within the existing framework of economic and social institutions, but to mould and refashion these so that they contribute effectively to the realization of wider and deeper social values. [17]

The specific role of education in achieving these social objectives, as indicated in the plan-targets, is

> to provide at the first stage free and compulsory education up to the age of 11 and to the extent resources of the states permit to cover the age-group 11-14. . . . Emphasis is being laid on vocationalization of education at the secondary stage and on the provision of part-time and correspondence courses. [18]

The investment in social services and related programs, including health and education, has been raised from Rupees 16, 970 million in the third plan to Rupees 35, 600 million in the fourth plan.

The second Malaysia plan (1971-75) places special importance on social development as a part of the new strategy "in which national priorities are reordered and efforts intensified to deal with economic and social problems confronting the country. Economic policies and development will be considered in their relationship to social development in general and the overriding need for national unity in particular, "[19] as warranted by the problems and needs of a multiracial society and inspired by the principles of "Rukunegra" (proclaimed on August 31, 1970), aiming at "a united, socially just, economically equitable and progressive Malaysian nation."[20] In this context the plan recognizes the need for "the formulation of education policies designed to encourage common values and loyalties among all communities and in all regions; the cultivation of a sense of dedication to the nation through services of all kinds; the careful development of a national language and litera- ture, of art and music."[21] The plan views education as a "major com- ponent of the search for balance in the development process"[22] and underscores the need for ensuring that "Malays, other indigenous people and the poor of other races have greater access to higher edu- cation."[23] The allocation for education and health has been raised in the present plan to 1, 067 million Malay dollars, or over 14 percent of total public sector investment, from 752 million Malay dollars in the previous plan (1966-70).

The social objectives also feature prominently in Pakistan's fourth plan. Commenting on the performance of the previous plans in the social sector, the plan said:

> One of the main inadequacies of our development process is the neglect of social sectors. It is true that the pro- vision of social services has not fulfilled the needs or aspirations of the people; and the shortfall in resources during the Third Plan was accompanied by severe cuts in social sector programmes.[24]

The plan charted out the following strategy to meet the claims of eco- nomic and social objectives:

> The choices open before the nation do not always dictate a sacrifice of growth objectives, in seeking greater social justice. The challenge for economic management during the Fourth Plan would be to identify and move along the path where these objectives coincide. However, when there is conflict, much greater emphasis has to be placed on con- siderations of social justice. Economic growth is a means and not an end in itself.[25]

In Pakistan's fourth plan the major mechanism for promoting social welfare took the form of programs to provide "social services, either free or at a subsidized rate"[26] in education, health, family planning, housing, and environmental control. Resources allocated for these services amounted to 27 percent of the total plan investment, compared to 20 percent in the past. The target in primary education was set at raising the enrollment to 66 percent of the age group in 1974-75, com- pared to 51 percent in 1969-70, and an adult education program with a

work-oriented approach was for the first time adopted on a national
basis, with a plan-target of educating 2.5 million adults by 1974-75.

The Philippines has a fairly wide base of education and has already
achieved universal enrollment at the first level. Her four-year development plan (1971-74) is geared to "rationally derived targets to meet
manpower requirements of national development."[27] As such it is
envisaged that "Basic Schools instruction and citizenship training will
be afforded to all children of elementary school age to prepare them for
a place in society"[28] and at the second level "for higher education or
for gainful employment . . . according to social needs and individual
capacities."[29]

The adequacy of the measures envisaged in the national plans of
South and Southeast Asia to expand and equalize the opportunities of
education to promote the goals of economic and social development will
be examined in Chapter 7. There is clearly awareness of education's
role in economic and social development throughout the region, but it
cannot be said that the plans show a comparable degree of awareness
of the role of education in political development, which is of vital importance not only to the stability of a nation but also to the reorientation
of the political structure to the needs of the people and their participation in development.

POLITICAL FACTORS AND DEVELOPMENT

As observed in Chapter 2, the political factors involved in the
decision-making process of planning and development are by far more
important than commonly realized and often overshadow other factors,
including considerations of economic and social viability. Policy prescription is finally the concern of the authority at the apex of a political
structure that in many countries is highly centralized and also wields
great influence on the implementation process down the line, thus
virtually determining both the shape of the plan-policy and its outcome.
Such a centralized authority is far removed from the people and constantly in danger of losing the national perspective and becoming unresponsive to the people's needs and aspirations. Where channels of
communication through participatory elective institutions do not exist
or have ceased to be effective because of influences such as corruption,
factionalism, or coercive pressures, the plan-policy and the growth-
path chosen may ultimately lead to disaster instead of development as
happened in Pakistan in 1971, or to an eruption of violence and traumatic changes in the power structure as seen in Thailand and more
recently in Ethiopia. Political development is, thus, an imperative
that cannot be overlooked without imperilling the goals of development,
and in this the role of education is indeed crucial.

ECONOMIC VERSUS SOCIAL DEVELOPMENT

In addition to restructuring the political institutions to ensure effective decentralization of both political and economic power, education must also be redesigned to provide the knowledge, the skill, and above all the qualities of character for effective participation of the people in these institutions and in planning and plan implementation at local levels. The social, political, and economic life of most of the developing nations stands so eroded by corrupt and unethical practices that the value to the development process of social and political education to instill among the people the qualities of honesty, integrity, and sense of public duty and national purpose is far greater today than ever before. To stimulate a shift towards a better balance between economic and social development, a proportionately greater expansion of education, health, and other social services will be necessary. This change in strategy, however, need not necessarily mean a contraction of the economic sector, as suggested in some of the plans.

In the first place, the current plans predict a considerable increase in the total investment in development. In the second place, a closer look will show that such a notion of conflict seems to stem from the concepts and assumptions underlying the growth models used in the past. One of these assumptions was that the marginal rate of saving was higher for higher incomes; this is incorrect, since the marginal rate of saving is related to a given income distribution. According to the report of the panel of economists on Pakistan's fourth plan,

> a redistribution of income changes one's saving because of a change in one's own income as well as of others particularly of those whose consumption pattern one tries to emulate. Taking this into account it can be theoretically established that a more egalitarian income distribution may well increase rather than decrease aggregate saving even if savings were purely voluntary. On top of it, austerity drives and forced saving measures are likely to be more successful politically if the sacrifice is shared equitably by all sections of the society.[30]

It may also be noted that the entrepreneurial profit is often erroneously considered to be the only criterion to predict the rate of saving and investment. However, workers also save at a rate that is not insignificant, and such savings can be greatly stimulated through institutional facilities like provident funds and insurance.

> If the less capital-intensive projects do not have a lower profit but a larger wage income because of the higher

output/capital ratio, and there are institutional arrangements
to increase the savings from the wage income, total savings
generated from a given amount of capital may be even larger.[31]

It will thus appear that the ends of social justice can be promoted through
reduction of income disparity and that increased employment can be created through more investment in less capital-intensive projects, without
any detriment to economic growth.

The issue also has to be considered in terms of the development
objectives, which are invariably related to a country's value system. If
the ultimate objective of economic development is to create a progressive
democratic society in which all individuals have equal opportunities of
self-development, there is clearly no basic conflict between growth and
social justice. The choice of a development framework will of course
have to be guided by these ultimate objectives of development and their
underlying values. As the panel of economists associated with Pakistan's
fourth plan observed,

> It should be recognized that in term of ultimate objectives
> and in the context of Pakistan, development of car assembly
> plants, coca-cola bottling plants and growth obtained from
> efficient advertising machines cannot produce the same
> results as larger production of food and clothing. Some of
> the industries have developed in the name of import substi-
> tution which can only be sustained with the help of con-
> tinued luxury consumption of a privileged class. . . .
> Social justice considerations have to be built in the basic
> production structure of the country.[32]

Pakistan provides the most striking case study of tragic consequences
flowing from a growth model that is based on the strategy of a relentless
drive for growth, overriding the considerations of social justice to
individuals and regions.

The realities of development experience clearly warrant an objective reappraisal of the goals of development, and there are also important
value issues that need to be taken into consideration. For example,
what is a full and good life in terms of the physical, intellectual, moral,
and aesthetic well-being of an individual living within a society, and
what style of life and of production and consumption does it imply?
Also, considering the resources that are not renewable and the ecological hazards accompanying the production technology necessary to
sustain a given style of life, what consideration is due to the interests
of future generations in choosing and following a present style of life?
These are issues that the developing countries need to take into careful
consideration in reexamining the goals of economic and social development that they set before them during the 1950s and 1960s, and in
determining the goals of future development.

While limitations of resources and existing social and economic inequalities make these questions urgent in the developing countries, there is also a growing recognition that they are highly relevant for the developed countries.

As observed in Chapters 1 and 2, the fountainhead of inspiration for the development movement was the belief that with access to modern science and technology the emergent countries of the Third World could attain a level of living comparable to that achieved in the industrial countries. It was also assumed that their development effort would be aided by the world community through the sharing of both knowledge and resources. The experience of the 1950s and 1960s, however, indicates that the disparity between the less developed and the more developed countries has widened. At the present rate of growth some of the developing countries may in 60 or 70 years achieve a decent level of living, but not the affluence and the wide range of choices enjoyed by the industrialized countries in their present state of development. During that period if the more developed countries can maintain a rate of growth even approximately equal to the present rate, they are likely to move up further in the scale of growth. The flow of aid has also fallen far short of expectations both in quantity and quality. Therefore it would be unrealistic for the developing countries to plan a development oriented to the life styles achieved in the Western industrialized countries, even if a Western life style were desirable as a goal.

However, it is not correct to interpret the quality of life in terms of the life styles of the industrialized countries, since these are the product of a complex evolution influenced by their respective cultural, social, and economic institutions and values and therefore not identical in all of the industrial countries; nor are all the components of these life styles relevant to the quality of life. Although it is true that never before has any economic system achieved such a high level of living as now found in the industrialized countries, it does not necessarily follow that the level and style of consumption is the proper measure of their social merit and quality of life.

Indeed, there is much in the style of production and consumption of the West that detracts from the quality of life. Rapid depletion of nonrenewable resources and environmental pollution, two major trends observable in the industrial countries, have already become causes of grave concern. The present rate of production uses up resources so rapidly that it endangers the future well-being not only of the coming generations but also of the present generation. According to the noted American physicist Ralph E. Lapp, a Nobel prize winner, "We are using up our energy at a fantastic rate and exploration rates for oil and gas are lagging far behind the consumption."[33] The energy crisis was so great in his country, he warned, that by 1985 the public might beg utility companies to build nuclear power plants rather than condemn them as polluters. As a matter of fact the industrial countries appear to have been overtaken by the energy crisis much faster than indicated in this warning.

LIMITS TO GROWTH

The sense of danger is further heightened by the dark forebodings that there are limits to growth and that the technology on which the affluent industrial societies rest is unlikely to continue to advance at a rate necessary to sustain the present tempo of growth and thus avert the crisis. Many view this as a global crisis resulting from a complex set of factors and becoming a predicament for all mankind. The central and long-term problems are identified as the arms race, environmental deterioration, the population explosion, and economic stagnation.

Drawing on a global model developed by Jay Forrester of the Massachusetts Institute of Technology,[34] an international team of experts headed by Dennis Meadows investigated the five basic world factors that determine and therefore ultimately limit growth, namely population, agricultural production, natural resources, industrial production, and pollution.[35] Among the findings of this study the most startling and disturbing is that if the present growth trends in world population, industrialization, food production, and resource depletion continue unchanged, the most probable result will be a rather sudden and uncontrollable decline in both population and industrial capacity within the next 100 years.

According to this study it is not enough to hold the population in check in order to avoid the overshoot and collapse of the industrial system; if population is held constant after 1975 (by equalizing the birth and death rates, but the remaining variables of industrial output, food, and services per capita continue to grow exponentially, the eventual depletion of nonrenewable resources will cause a sudden collapse of the industrial system.

Though the Meadows study is based on a computerized model using a sophisticated technique, it is not free from the limitations inherent in such models, as the authors admit. Moreover, the model developed in this study for stabilizing the growth system, though claimed to be a world model, is actually more relevant to the industrialized countries, in the present state of disparity between them and the developing countries in level of industrialization and consumption. It has, however, important implications for the developing countries. In the first place, the rate of population growth is much faster in the developing countries than in the industrialized ones. As such, the need for stabilizing population growth at the zero rate by equalizing the birth and death rates within the shortest possible time is of greater urgency in the case of the developing countries.

In the second place, development should not be identified with the industrial growth and life styles to be found in the industrialized countries. On the contrary, as highlighted in this study, some aspects of the growth pattern of those countries are now posing a threat not only to their future but to the future of global stability and progress. In the long run it would therefore be imprudent and even perilous for the developing countries to emulate the growth pattern of the industrial countries. Instead they should seek an equilibrium between capital and population, between agriculture and industry, and between the demands of economic growth and social justice, according to their own values and social realities.

In the third place, as newcomers in industrialization the developing countries can avoid many of the problems now facing the industrialized countries as a consequence of their indiscriminate industrialization and lack of a rational consumption policy. They can gain enormously through the choice of an industrial policy that avoids concentration of industries and promotes technologies that are energy-efficient and capable of collecting and making use of waste products for recycling, reducing the rate of depletion of resources, increasing product lifetime, promoting easy repair, minimizing the capital depreciation rate, and safeguarding the environment.

In the fourth place, the educational and cultural contents of development emerge as goals with endless possibilities and none of the risk factors involved in the drive for industrial growth. The crisis overshadowing the industrialized countries is primarily the result of the concept that progress is based on higher productivity in terms of industrial growth and greater consumption, regardless of their effect on the quality of life. There is, therefore, a need to redirect technological advances towards significant improvement in the quality of life.

Thus if quality of life is the central goal of development it will imply (1) the satisfaction of the basic material needs such as food, shelter, and clothing; and (2) availability of surplus production and leisure for intellectual and cultural pursuits to enrich the life of the individual and the community.

While developing countries must seek economic growth until the basic needs of their people for food, shelter, and clothing have been met, the level of growth necessary to meet these needs will have to be determined by them according to their own values and not those of the industrialized countries. Another guiding consideration will be the surplus production available for intellectual and cultural pursuits.

In sum, economic growth is not by itself an objective of development, but rather a means to an end, which is man's well-being. The industrialized countries have already reached a stage, which the developing countries will eventually reach, when their well-being is better served by maintaining a state of equilibrium between growth of capital and population.

Such a nongrowing state has through the ages been envisioned by many thinkers, philosophers, economists, and biologists.[36] This state of equilibrium does not, however, imply stagnation in the progress of human society; on the contrary, it means that the level of economic growth already attained is sufficient to meet the physical needs of life. Further growth of the society from this point will be made along the path of progress towards new heights of intellectual, cultural, and social well-being, rather than by wasteful consumption. The energy crisis, which has impaired the life styles in the industrial countries, underscores the wisdom of a shift to new value moorings to subserve rationally conceived life styles. The ancient philosophy of "plain living and high thinking," if heeded, could make this world a better planet to live on, with the prospect of a better life for the people of all the nations of the world.

It is imperative for each developing country to elect a design of growth and a life style for its own social and economic development, according to its own values and resources. By the same token, the design of its educational system will also have to be consistent with its goals and values, along paths to be charted according to its needs and resources. The most pervasive goal to inspire both designs, according to the analysis in this study, should be the development and utilization of human resources. The degree of success in achieving this goal will be the primary measure of the effectiveness of the plan-strategy in both development and education.

NOTES

1. Robert McNamara, Address to the Board of Governors of the World Bank, September 27, 1971, p. 29.
2. International Development Strategy: United Nations Action Programme of the General Assembly for Second U. N. Development Decade (New York: the United Nations, 1971), pp. 2-3.
3. W. W. Rostow, The Stages of Economic Growth (Cambridge University Press, 1960), pp. 1-11.
4. John Kenneth Galbraith, The New Industrial State (New York: New American Library, 1968), p. 14.
5. Ibid., p. 19.
6. Ibid., pp. 34-35, 37.
7. G. M. Meier and R. E. Baldwin, Economic Development (New York: John Wiley and Sons, 1957), p. 23.
8. W. A. Lewis, Theory of Economic Growth (London: George Irwin, 1955).
9. For example the following works: Max Weber, The Protestant Ethic and the Spirit of Capitalism (New York: Charles Scribner's Sons, 1930); M. Weber, Theory of Social and Economic Organization (New York: Oxford Press, 1907); T. Parsons, The Social System (Glencoe, Ill.: The Free Press, 1957); B. F. Hoselitz, International Congress of Studies on the Problems of Underdeveloped Areas, "Sociological Approach to Economic Development," (Milan: Museo della Scienza e della Tecnica, 1954).

10. David C. McClelland, The Achieving Society (Princeton:
D. Van Nostrand Co., 1961), p. 17.

11. S. N. Eisenstadt, Modernization: Protest and Change (Engle-
wood Cliffs: Prentice-Hall, 1966), p. 146.

12. John Kenneth Galbraith, The New Industrial State, op. cit.,
p. 301.

13. First Five-Year Plan of Bangladesh (1973-78), pp. 1-2.

14. Five-Year Plan of Ceylon (1972-76), p. 21.

15. Ibid., p. 17.

16. Fourth Five-Year Plan of India (1969-74), p. 13.

17. Ibid., p. 2.

18. Ibid., p. 19.

19. Second Five-Year Plan of Malaysia (1971-75), pp. 2-3.

20. Ibid. The "Rukunegra" is a Malay term for national ideology.
The five basic principles embodied in the Rukunegra as proclaimed on
August 31, 1970 are: belief in God, loyalty to kind and country, up-
holding the constitution, the rule of law, and good behavior and morality.

21. Ibid., p. 3.

22. Ibid., p. 44.

23. Ibid.

24. Fourth Five-Year Plan of Pakistan (1970-75), p. 9.

25. Ibid.

26. Ibid., p. 12.

27. Four-Year Development Plan of the Philippines (1971-74),
p. 179.

28. Ibid., p. 185.

29. Ibid.

30. Planning Commission, Government of Pakistan, Report of the
Panel of Economists on the Fourth Five-Year Plan (Islamabad, 1970),
p. 43.

31. The Economic Commission for Asia and the Far East, United
Nations, Economic Development and Human Resources: ECAFE Growth
Studies, Series No. 3 (Bangkok, 1966), p. 13.

32. Report of Panel of Economists, op. cit., p. 121.

33. The Washington Post (April 13, 1972).

34. See Jay Forrester, World Dynamics (Cambridge, Mass.:
Wright Allen, 1971).

35. Dennis Meadows et al., The Limits to Growth (New York:
Universe Books, 1972), p. 11.

36. For instance: Plato in Laws (350 B. C.); Aristotle in Politics
(322 B. C.); Malthus in An Essay on the Principles of Population(1798);
John Stuart Mill in Principles of Political Economy (1857); Harison
Brown in The Challenge of Man's Future (New York: Viking Press, 1954);
E. J. Mishan in The Costs of Economic Growth (New York: Praeger Pub-
lishers, 1967); Harman E. Dalyim in Toward a Stationary-State Economy
(New York: Holt, Rinehart, and Winston, 1971).

In planning towards the goal of balanced and well-integrated national development, the developing countries are much more advantageously placed in terms of technical knowledge and of experience than they were even in the early 1960s. In the early years of development the specter of poverty loomed large, practically overshadowing all other problems; the most formidable impediment to development appeared to lie in severe limitations of resources and the strategy that seemed to follow was to focus attention on economic growth. This line of reasoning is quite understandable and remains substantially valid even in the conditions of the present decade. Where the planning strategy went wrong during the past decades, however, was in its myopic concept of development and its equally blurred vision of the interacting forces of development.

As observed in the foregoing chapters, the plan-strategy was based on a growth model in which product growth was used as the sole indicator of development, regardless of its social cost and without any more balanced emphasis on investment in physical and human capital. To all intents and purposes the role of human capital in development was totally ignored, as well as the pervading social context that lent special importance to it.

One reason for this, of course, was that skill in the technique of development planning was a scarce commodity in those early years, and the developing countries were almost entirely dependent on external aid for this critical service. They do not appear to have realized that capital-intensive technology was a part of the total economic and social structure of the industrial states evolved in the West over a period of time and that it would not fit countries that were differently structured economically and socially. Growth models were literally taken from one set of social conditions and transplanted into another, without attention to their differences in important variables of growth and apparently without much perception of the interlocking character of these variables. There was also a lack of realization that the fruits of modern agriculture and modern industry could be harvested only through adequate investment in human beings.[1]

The most striking weakness in the planning strategy of the developing countries was the inadequacy of the growth models followed in the developing countries even in order to maximize economic growth, to which these models were supposedly oriented. In the opinion of a contemporary British economist, one of the lessons of the past years of development is that during the early postwar period emphasis was erroneously placed on investment in material capital without due regard to the creation of a labor force both equipped with the necessary technical skills for modern industrial production and also properly oriented to the acceptance and promotion of economic and technical change.[2]

THE CONCEPT OF HUMAN CAPITAL

Empirical research in various countries, a substantial part of which has been carried out in the United States, sparked by the pioneering work of Theodore W. Schultz, has indicated that the part of the measured growth in advanced countries that cannot be accounted for by increases in labor and capital, as conventionally measured, can be explained by human capital or the quality of labor input, representing the productivity of investment in education and in training the labor force.

New and exciting possibilities have thus been opened up, both in economics and in education, with the emergence of the concept of human capital and the application of the methods of economic analysis to the determination of its role in production. The general notion that education was not entirely consumption and that it had a valuable investment component could be found in some form or other in the works of many of the earlier economists, such as Adam Smith, David Ricardo, John Stuart Mill, and Alfred Marshall. However, human capital as an economic concept received its first clear recognition in Irving Fisher's highly abstract theory of capital, in which the human component is considered, as well as physical capital. In this theory the degree of "liquidity," that is, the degree to which the physical entity embodying the capital stock can be freely bought and sold, is not regarded as an essential criterion of capital. Schooling is a kind of capital formation, since investment in schooling implies investment in a potential future source of income. Here the capital formed was human, since the capital stock yielding future income was embodied in human beings.

The most important single feature distinguishing human capital from physical capital, however, is that control over the human capital remains vested in the individual embodying the capital, regardless of the source of investment. A related concept, of relevance to education and society, is that of intellectual, or knowledge, capital, which once created is a free good in the sense that its use by one individual does not diminish its availability to others. Intellectual capital is both a part and a product of investment in human capital and an important input in the production of new physical capital through technological change. Thus the concept of human capital involves a whole set of interacting factors that operate to produce a multiplier effect on the growth process.

The revolution touched off by the concept of human capital and the concept of education as an investment in human capital has not yet gathered enough strength to sway the bulk of the fraternity of the economists brought up in the English neoclassical tradition, which has no room for the notion of human capital and which continued to dominate the theory and policy of growth. This tradition was strengthened by the General Theory of John Maynard Keynes and its subsequent variants, such as, for example, the conversion of the Keynesian short-run equilibrium into the Harrod growth model.

The most striking feature of Keynesianism and the growth models inspired by it is that they view labor not as an active agent of production but as a passive agent, depending for its employment on a high enough rate of investment and particularly of investment in the production of physical producer capital. Apart from its outstanding contribution to economic theory, Keynesianism also contains an important lesson: it demonstrates the need to relate economic theory to a changing society and to seek constantly for new concepts that enable the tools of economic theory and analysis to fit the changing social phenomena and thus survive obsolescence. However, there is increasing evidence that the conception of capital (physical) investment as the key variable in the economic system and the assumption of a homogeneous labor force of a given quality that underlie the Keynesian theory are open to serious limitations. The long-term growth theories that sprang from the Keynesian theory and explained growth in terms of physical capital and its rate of income have also suffered from the same inherent limitations. It became evident after World War II that physical capital worked its miracles only in lands where there were many qualified people who knew how to use it, such as in the Marshall Plan countries and in Japan. The econometricians were also intrigued by the discovery that their old aggregate capital-output ratios were not behaving properly. For the period covering the late 1920s through the 1950s in Western Europe and Japan, they could account for half or less of the national income growth by conventional measures.[3]

The concept of human capital, therefore, continues to attract increasing attention from the economists. The literature produced on the economics of education during the 1950s and 1960s was considerable (as many as 800 items are listed in Mark Blaug's bibliography on the subject[4]) and shows a confluence of interest on such vitally important aspects as the economic value of education, the contribution of education to past economic development in advanced countries, and the role of education and increased investment in education in the planned development of less developed countries.

Let us briefly examine the findings of selected studies on the economic value of education in their bearing on planned development, keeping in view different aspects of education.

Contrary to the traditional belief that all education is consumption, many of these studies have underscored its important investment component. Education in the sense of service through schooling has both of these properties because of its role in developing the innate abilities of a person to live a full personal life as an individual and as a member of a family, and economically productive life as a worker, and a socially useful life as a citizen. The consumption aspect can be seen in those elements of education that yield present satisfaction to the individual, such as being able to read, solve a mathematical problem, appreciate a poem, or carry an experiment to a successful conclusion. Many elements in education yield benefits in the future through acquisition of knowledge and skill; these represent the investment aspect of education.

What is satisfying as present consumption in education may also serve as future consumption because present education also serves as the foundation of future education and is capable of unlimited repeated use to yield similar future satisfaction. Thus to the extent that education, even as a consumption good, yields future satisfaction, it enhances future real income. These satisfactions, though too intangible for measurement and inclusion in the computation of the GNP, are nevertheless a part of the real income accruing to the individual and in some cases to the society.

The productive capacity of labor is predominantly a produced means of production representing the human capital, created largely by investment in education. Even if the numerous social benefits of the education of an individual that accrue to the family, the neighbors, the employer, the coworkers, and the society are excluded from consideration, from the purely economic point of view the role of human capital and the important part played by education in its formation lends a new dimension to education in planned development. The history of industrial countries indicates that as the society advances in the scale of industrial development its growth rate becomes increasingly dependent on that of education, science, and technology.

THE EXPERIENCE OF THE UNITED STATES

In the development of the concept of capital formation by investment in education, a major breakthrough was achieved through the outstanding study of Theodore W. Schultz, based on an analysis of empirical input-output series linked to investment in education in the United States.[5] In this study Schultz measured among other things the value of student time as a labor input in the educational process. The study showed that earnings foregone as a measure of student input accounted for half of the total cost of secondary and higher education in the United States and that the total investment in human capital formation from 1900 to 1956 rose from 9 percent to 34 percent of the total investment in physical capital. Using the investment in the schooling of people in the labor force and the rate of return earned on this investment as the basis of his computation, Schultz found that the former, expressed as a stock of capital in 1956 dollars, amounted to $180 billion for 1930 and $535 billion for 1957; therefore the increase in the stock of capital between 1929 and 1957 was $362 billion.

An important assumption underlying this estimate was that all of the cost of education was an investment in future earnings. Schultz prepared three estimates of return on these investments; the lower two estimates showed a return of 9 percent and 11 percent. Applying these two rates to the increase in capital stock of $362 billion, he obtained slightly less than $33 billion, or $40 billion as the growth in the national income from education. This amounted to either 16.5 percent with 9 percent as the rate of return or 20 percent with 11 percent as the rate of return of the total growth on the basis of an increase of $200 billion in the national product.

The findings in the Schultz study supported those of Edward F. Denison's study based on historical comparisons, which attributed 21 percent of the economic growth in the United States between 1929 and 1957 to education.[6] A more recent work by Denison has confirmed these results for several Western countries.[7]

It may be noted that the Schultz study was limited to formal schooling, including "activities that are an integral part of the teaching and learning of students"[8] and excluding other educational functions such as research, the discovery and cultivation of potential talent, and nonformal schooling. Fritz Machlup tried to fill this gap by measuring the cost of all types of education in the United States, including education on the job, in the home, in the church, and in the armed services as well as the cost of formal schooling, special schooling, public libraries, and other educational programs. His estimate of the total cost of education for 1956-57 was over $60 billion, or 12.9 percent of the adjusted gross national product.[9] Jacob Mincer, in his study of on-the-job training, estimated the amounts invested in such training of males in the United States labor force at $5.7 billion in 1939 and $12.5 billion in 1958, both stated in 1954 dollars.[10]

Gary Becker developed a theory to cope with the problems of investment in human capital, and among his conclusions were the following: (1) Earnings being the gross of the return on human capital, some persons may earn more than others by investing more in themselves. (2) Learning, both on and off the job and in other activities, appears to have the same effect on observed earnings as education, training, and other traditional investments in human capital.[11] This highlights the economic value of nonformal education, which has a special significance for the developing countries because they have a large labor force lacking in education and skill.

As I have already mentioned earlier in this chapter, several studies made during the 1950s discovered an increase in the national product that cannot be explained by man hours and traditional capital. Moses Abramovitz estimated the rate of increase in the net national product in the United States since 1870 at 3.5 percent per year, of which 1.7 percent was attributable to labor and capital in the conventional way and 1.8 percent, or more than half of the increase, unaccounted for.[12]

A study by John W. Kendrick, limited to the private domestic economy of the United States for the period between 1899 and 1953, estimated the increase in real product at 3.3 percent per year, of which the increase in the conventional investment of labor and capital was 1.6 percent, while 1.7 percent, or more than half of the increase, remained unexplained.[13]

In a study reported by Robert M. Solow in 1957, the unexplained residue was estimated at 87.5 percent of the increase in output per man-hour in the United States between 1909 and 1949.[14]

The unexplained residue discovered in all of these studies is substantial and cannot be dismissed as mere windfalls or quasi-rents of labor. The logical inference to be drawn is that at least a large part of this residue is a return on investment in skills and related abilities.

These studies also clearly demonstrate the inadequacy of a concept of capital in which the human component is left out. The Nobel prize winning American economist Simon Kuznets, noted for his contribution to the concept of national product, also pointed out the narrowness of the traditional concept of capital and the need for broadening it to include investment in human beings.[15]

These studies on the stock of educational capital and the return from investment in education, though directly related to the American situation, provide a valuable insight into the dynamics of the formation of human capital through investment in education. Briefly stated, they have the following implications for development planning:

1. In an industrial country that has already attained a high level of schooling, although much schooling is still needed to maintain it and also the industrial system, its value diminishes as a source of further economic growth. However, in a country in which the level of education is low, if the level of schooling is raised substantially and rapidly it becomes a substantial source of growth, assuming, of course, that the education provided is of the type and quality most relevant to economic growth. This important assumption often seems to be overlooked, especially when the economic value of education is discussed out of its social context, as if the economic value of any type of education were the same.

2. From the viewpoint of educational capital stock, each year of high school added per worker adds more to the capital stock in the labor force than each year of elementary school added.

3. On the other hand, the rates of return on investment tend to diminish with the rising levels of education and investment in the high school stage and then rise slightly in the college stage.[16]

4. A general assumption in most economic analyses is that all expenditures on schooling are in the nature of investment in producing and earning capabilities. Burton A. Weisbrod points out in his study other aspects of schooling, some to the benefit of the student and his family and some to the benefit of other individuals and families in the community. It is thus evident that not all of the benefits that accrue to a student become part of his earnings, as in the case of preparing his own income tax return. What can we then infer from estimates of return to expenditure on education, based on the assumption that all of it is investment? According to Theodore Schultz the answer is:

> A great deal really, provided the limits to the information
> are always taken into account. In the case of a college
> education, when a rate of return based on total costs is
> as high as that on alternative investments, it follows that
> the greater the consumption captured by others, the larger
> the underinvestment. . . . In the case of elementary
> schooling, the rate of return is higher than on alternative
> investments, and the consumption component accruing to
> the student and his family is large, and the benefits cap-
> tured by others is, also, large.[17]

5. The various types of advanced professional education, such as engineering, medicine, dentistry, nutrition, agriculture, technology, and law, are predominantly considered as investments in productive capabilities in the United States. A similar presumption exists in the developing countries, except in the field of law, where the supply of graduates far exceeds the demand. As regards general college and high school education in the United States (not concentrating on voca- tional education), it is estimated by Schultz that

> schooling contributes substantially to consumption, and the
> benefits captured by others are not small. As a working
> assumption, one-half to three-fifths of the costs of high
> schooling is invested in production capabilities that
> increase future earnings that accrue to students.[18]

6. In countries with high incomes, though those with schooling up to the eighth grade earn less than those with more schooling, the difference, even if considerable, is not so large as "to produce on the much larger costs, a rate equal to the high rate realized on what is invested upon the completion of the elementary grades."[19]

7. In the absence of adequate information about key variables it cannot be precisely stated whether a parallel proposition would be valid for low income countries. It would be necessary to consider whether or not there are employment opportunities for children of school age; whether the structure of wages is favorable; and whether reliable

information is available. There is, however, "a strong presumption with respect to many countries that are thought of as being quite poor that the best 'pay-off' in terms of production and earnings to people is in more and better elementary schooling."[20] Perhaps it would be more appropriate in the context of the situation in the developing countries to say "more and better elementary schooling relevant to the needs and realities of life in the developing countries," which might imply contents and methods of elementary education that are substantially different from those of the rich countries.

8. The inclusion of "earnings foregone" in the cost of education has been a subject of some controversy; the objections seem to arise at least partly from the traditional concept of capital. The concept of earnings foregone as clarified in the Schultz study provides "a key explanatory variable of a large set of behavior observed empirically."[21] It is a hypothesis that needs to be tested in the light of conditions actually prevalent in a country, however. In many developing countries even children of primary school age are employed to supplement family earnings, and the concept of earnings foregone by them because of their enrollment in school reflects an economic reality. At the same time lack of employment opportunities, as indicated by growing unemployment in most developing countries, is also an important qualifying factor that cannot be overlooked. If earnings foregone are excluded from cost, then at least in the industrial countries the result is a reduction in the estimated stock of educational capital and a corresponding increase in the rate of return on the investment in education. In any event the bearing of this issue on educational planning in developing countries seems to be rather marginal.

9. The contribution of research to growth in the United States has a message of special significance to the developing countries. The history of the development of the United States shows a dramatic transformation in the relationship between educational and economic growth from a smaller to a greater degree of interdependence, and the industrial sector has become more dependent on education and science rather than the reverse. The establishment of land-grant colleges was a recognition of the value of applying advanced knowledge to the fields of agriculture and industry to promote growth. Agricultural research as a whole is suggested by one estimate to yield a return at the rate of 35 percent a year.[22] Though the contribution of research to growth was not included in the study by Schultz, he did point out that half of the basic research in the United States was conducted within educational institutions, if measured against the quantitative expenditures on total research. Following an indirect method of allocating what remained after he had accounted for all of the elements he had identified and measured, Denison estimated that more than 18 percent of the growth in the national product between 1929 and 1957 was due to what he called "advance of knowledge."[23]

Finally, as a country advances in economic growth, the indications are that there is a better recognition of the economic value of education and a greater degree of dependence on education, including science, for sustaining and promoting the rate of growth.

10. The studies so far discussed, while throwing new light on the relationship of investment in education to productivity, do not indicate the factors determining the changing demands for education. Attempts to examine the changes in demand have been made by economists and manpower specialists through projections of manpower needs based on past trends, in many cases on the assumption of very rigid demand structures at a given level of national income. Another approach to this admittedly difficult task can be seen in studies to determine correlations among indexes of human resource development (like school enrollment by levels and by types of education curricula in higher education and by expenditures on education), proportions of the population in selected occupations, participation rates in basic health services, and national income. A composite index is used in these studies for classification of countries.

In this class is the well-known 1963 study by Frederick Harbison and Charles Myers, which underscores the importance of secondary, higher, and nonformal education and training on the job, based on an analysis of data relating to 75 countries, thus providing useful clues to development planners.[24]

The study by Walter Galenson and Graham Pyatt, prepared for the International Labor Office in 1964, was highly sophisticated technically and fell more appropriately into the class of the aggregate production function studies like those of Schultz and Denison. Investigating the determinants of growth in labor productivity in 52 nations over the period 1951-61, the study uses capital input figures, adjusted to allow for improvements, along with indexes of labor quality. However, as in the case of the Harbison and Myers study, the enrollment data are used as education variables while the educational characteristics of the labor force are not. Lead education variables are derived from the enrollment rates of a previous period. The study attributed only 9 percent of the variation in the growth of labor productivity (in all countries under study taken together) to the physical capital investment ratio taken by itself, ranging from 20 percent in wealthy nations to 5 percent in the poor ones.[25]

Among studies based on cross-national comparisons, the 1963 study by M. J. Bowman and C. A. Anderson has some special features because it was not based on simple cross tabulations of literacy rates vis-a-vis per capita incomes. It reached some interesting conclusions; some that are especially relevant to developing countries are

(1) an apparent threshold effect of something like 40 per cent adult literacy, as a necessary but not sufficient condition of economic emergence, (2) negligible income effects

of proportions of the adult population with secondary
schooling once those with primary schooling were taken
into account (excepting countries with over 90 per cent
literate), and (3) . . . the world-wide emphasis upon
education both as an instrument variable in public policy
oriented to growth and as a national prestige symbol is
producing a situation in which schooling must almost
inevitably lead economic development rather than
following on it.[26]

This last observation seems to be borne out by the historical
developments if quantitative growth of education is taken as the indicator. As demonstrated by the events, however, this seems to mask
many important issues seriously affecting both educational and economic
growth.

THE EXPERIENCE OF THE USSR

A striking example of rapid economic progress achieved through
planned development was provided by the successful transition of the
USSR from an underdeveloped economy to a self-sustaining one within
less than two decades. The aims of development were naturally influenced deeply by the new ideology of the Russian nation.

Karl Marx had stressed mastery of the tools of production as the
key to the improvement of man's lot. While advocating revolution to
achieve the final social goals, he was, however, emphatic that the
best solution was to unite the man and the citizen and the individual's
private and social capacities.[27]

Under Lenin and Stalin the marriage of ideology and economic
interest found expression in the launching of an ambitious program to
eliminate illiteracy and educate the proletariat and peasantry throughout
the Soviet Union. During the "planning era" commencing in 1927, the
USSR began to plan in terms not only of "material product balances" but
also of "labor balances." These plans represented the first deliberate
attempt to relate the output of the schools to the manpower needs of
developing industry and resulted in the construction of a comprehensive
"manpower and education plan" for the entire nation.[28]

Among the numerous studies undertaken in the USSR on various
aspects of the economics of education, the classic and best-known one
is that of Academician S. G. Strumilin, which was based on an empirical
enquiry into the relative influence upon the skill level of a group of
Leningrad workers in the metal trades of age and length of work experience, formal education, and on-the-job training. His findings were:

Even simple literacy (achieved after one year of instruction)
raised the productivity of labor of workers by 30 per cent on

the average, while a year on the job experience of illiterate
lathe workers raised their qualifications and output by no
more than 12 to 16 per cent per year.[29]

He also estimated the return from investment in primary and secondary education.

The labor productivity of the persons having had 4 years
of schooling exceeds that of illiterate persons by 43 per
cent, the labor productivity of persons having secondary
education by 108 per cent, and of persons having university
education by 300 per cent respectively.[30]

Since then studies in the USSR in this field have grown rapidly.
S. G. Strumilin, in a 1962 article in Economicheskaia gazeta, reported
as follows:

In 1960 the total national income in current prices equaled
146. 6 billion rubles (according to later data this amount
was revised to 145 rubles). Not less than 33. 7 billion, or
23 per cent of this, can be ascribed to the raising of the
qualifications of the population.[31]

It appears that in the initial period of planned development of the
USSR the prevalent thinking (similar to that of some of the planners and
policy-makers in developing countries during the past decades) was that
investment in machines was the most decisive factor in development.
However, the difficulties experienced with untrained workers operating
the machines and the findings of the research pioneered by S. G. Strumilin
led to a reorientation in the plan-policy, with large dividends recorded
in the 1962 article by Strumilin mentioned above.
   In this context it may be noted that 75 percent of the Russian
population in 1917 could neither read nor write. During 1920-39 more
than 57. 5 million illiterate and 38. 5 million semiliterate adults finished
schools or courses in reading and writing, compared with about 31. 5
million finishing four-year elementary schools and seven-year junior
secondary schools in the 12 years from 1924 to 1935.
   The economic value of education and research is especially underscored in V. E. Komarov's study in the following terms:

The development of productive potentials also requires large
expenditures on education and scientific research, and
these expenditures should be given a prime place, in as
much as physical capital, no matter how it is expanded or
perfected, cannot produce anything without people.[32]

V. A. Zhamin, recor of the Moscow State Pedagogical Institute, in
a study based on Strumilin's methodology but with adjustments to take

account of the new wage scales that were introduced in industry in 1960 and 1961 and also to include agriculture, reported that

> Approximately 27 percent of the national income in 1962 can be ascribed to investment of resources in education and the consequent increase in qualifications of labor.[33]
>
> Workers who have nine to ten years of education generally master new techniques twice as quickly as their colleagues who have only six or seven years of education.[34]

A study based on a large-scale sample survey at the Vladimir Il'ich factory in Moscow conducted under the auspices of the Laboratory of Economics of Education at the Moscow Lenin Institute yielded some interesting results partly quoted below:

> From the replies given in 392 special questionnaires, it appeared that in order to advance one salary grade, a metal worker spends an average of five years, if he has five to six years of education; but with seven years of education he needs little more than three years. To advance one salary grade with an eight-year education requires from two to three years, but with a ten-year education in most cases a year or in rare cases only a half year.[35]

The existence of a high degree of correlation between the duration of general education and the production norms underlined in the above ✓ study finds further endorsement in the following report of I. I. Kaplan, based on a study of 1,243 workers in the Dynamo and Vladimir Il'ich factories:

> For most workers the percentage by which production norms were fulfilled rose proportionately with the level of general education. For example, among tool fitters in Skill Grade IV with five years of working experience those with Grade 8 education fulfilled their norms for the shift an average of 35 percent more than those with only Grade 5 education. The production norms with full secondary education exceeded those of workers with grade education by 25 percent.[36]

> Another interesting finding of this study was that

> as general education levels of workers increase, the quantity of nondefective output noticeably rises and the amount of tool breakage falls.[37]

There was also a direct relationship identified in this study between the educational level of workers and the time taken by them to

master new types of work. The effect of general education on the learning of new skills, as well as on management ability and attitudes toward
work, thus appears to be much greater than recognized in the national
plans of the developing countries. Of course, an important caveat lies
in the meaning of general education, which in the Soviet context implies
contents and methods of education substantially different from those of
general education prevalent in many of the developing countries.

THE EXPERIENCE OF JAPAN

Since the Meiji Restoration in 1868, the striking progress made
by Japan in her transition from an underdeveloped economy to the rank
of one of the most advanced nations of the world has given her a unique
place in Asia. Both in her economic development and in her spectacular
recovery after World War II, Japan's achievement is rightly attributed
to the human factor as represented by her educated and trained manpower.
    A study by the Japanese Ministry of Education that was based on
the analytical technique devised by Theodore Schultz indicated that

> though in 1960, the value of the stock of educational capital
> was 18 percent (7, 110 billion yen) of the value of the stock
> of physical capital (39, 800 billion yen), it yielded propor-
> tionately greater return. During 25 years from 1930 to 1955,
> the increase in the educational capital was estimated to
> have contributed 25 percent of the increase in the national
> income, i. e. , 70 percent of the 37 percent increase in the
> national income. [38]

Not only does this study by an Asian industrial country lend support to the findings of similar studies elsewhere, but the historical
experience of Japan in developing her educational and economic systems
seems to have a significant message for the developing countries, which
find themselves torn between the conflicting demands on their scarce
resources of the economic and social sectors.
    The Meiji era was indeed unique in Japan's history, beginning
with the Emperor's Charter Oath in 1868 which, among other provisions,
required that knowledge should be sought throughout the world. The
policy of using education as a catalyst for progress in Japan became
further evident from the Government Order of Education in 1872, which
in its preamble underlined the role of education as the key to success
that no man could neglect. The goal enunciated in this code was that
"there shall, in future, be no community with an illiterate family or a
family with an illiterate person."[39] This was indeed a bold decision
and one of great vision on the part of an emperor, put into sharp relief
by the historic coincidence that about the same time the elected parlia-

ment of a democratic country (England in 1870) enacted a law with a goal
that was similar. In Japan this order marked the foundation of the modern
educational system, which subsequently went through several phases of
development, such as systemization during 1886-97, consolidation
during 1899-1916, expansion during 1917-39, wartime reorganization
during 1940-45, and finally reconstruction and democratization during
1947-62.[40]
       It should perhaps be stressed here that the far-reaching educa-
tional measures taken in the early Meiji era were not directly linked to
economic growth but laid the foundation on which the country's economic
system was built.
       The diffusion of elementary education improved the quality of the
Japanese people's skills, modernized their thought, and enabled them
to participate successfully in modern economic activities. The rapid
recovery of Japan from socioeconomic collapse after World War II and
its subsequent prosperity were made possible through the accumulated
efforts of prewar education. The successful role played by education
in economic development in Japan should be

       attributed to the effort of the people who had restricted
       consumption and invested money thus in education. That
       the rate of educational expenditures to national income in
       Japan was among the highest (5 per cent) in the world
       substantiates this statement.[41]

       It will appear from Table 4.1 that during the first half-century the
emphasis in Japan was on elementary education. By 1915 universal enrollment in elementary school was accomplished and stress was laid on
expansion of secondary education. It was only after World War II that
upper secondary education and higher education took rapid strides under
the new educational system.
       An important increase in the supply of the needed high-level man-
power for economic development during the Meiji period was caused by
government programs to send students abroad for advanced study.
       As mentioned earlier, though a farsighted policy of investment in
educational development accounted for Japan's economic growth it was
not based on any formal plan to fit the supply of education to the manpower needs in the economy. The first such manpower development
policy was prepared in 1960 as a part of long-range economic development plans by the Economic Deliberation Council. Nevertheless the
responsiveness of Japan's educational system to her changing economic
needs was amply demonstrated by the high rate of return on the investment in education reported in the Ministry of Education study covering
the period 1935-55 referred to at the beginning of this section.
       The contribution of the basic education provided on a nationwide
scale lay in that it prepared "young workers academically, and to some
extent psychologically for the training programs being established by

TABLE 4.1

Historical Trend in the Percentage of the
Appropriate Age Group Enrolled in
Each Educational Level in Japan

Year	Elementary	Secondary	Higher
1875	35.2	0.7	0.4
1885	49.6	0.8	0.4
1895	61.2	1.1	0.3
1905	95.6	4.3	0.9
1915	98.5	19.9	1.0
1925	99.4	32.3	2.5
1947	99.8	61.7	5.8
1965	99.8	86.2	14.6
1969	99.8	87.8	16.7

Source: Research Division, Ministry of Education,
Government of Japan, Education in Japan: a Graphic
Representation (Tokyo: the Division, 1971).

many industrial and commercial concerns."[42] This is in contrast with
most countries in South and Southeast Asia, in which there was no corresponding effort on the part of industrial and commercial concerns.

Japan's economy has progressively become stronger through technological changes assisted by appropriate educational changes, but the
growth pattern did not develop the serious distortions observed in the
developing countries in the form of a large unemployed or underemployed
labor force. Short-run disequilibria between the supply and demand of
educated manpower did, however, occur in certain fields, such as the
humanities and social sciences during 1913 and 1956, thus at least
partly accounting for the socialist and anti-conservative movements.

The overall employment situation has on the whole maintained a
steady level, and it has shown a rapid upward thrust since 1960 as a
result of Japan's continuing high growth rate, until Japan is now faced
with a shortage of labor. The present economic situation and the outlook for the future are noted in Japan's New Economic and Social Development Plan (1970-75) as follows:

Japanese economic growth rate rose further from the second
half of the 1960's due partly to the inflationary trends in
the world economy, but mainly because the structure of the
Japanese economy further strengthened. . . . In regard to
the labor situation, a noticeable shortage of labor became
apparent from the beginning of the 1960's but at present

this labor shortage is not so serious as to impede the expansion of national economy.[43]

In the plan stress is also laid on implementing

measures for the improvement and expansion of scientific and technological education in conformity with the innovation of technology.[44]

The chief contribution of the studies that have been briefly discussed in this chapter lies in the application of analytical tools to the study of a subject that was until recently considered too elusive for such analytical treatment. They have opened up a new horizon in the concept of capital and the possibility of using investment in education as a parameter of growth instead of allocating resources to the sector of education on a residual basis as has hitherto been the practice, using the rate of return on investment in education as the basis of resource allocation. This is an exciting possibility, but the task is extremely difficult in view of the wide range of variables that are involved, including the element of externality in the benefits and the psychological content of investment in human beings. The difficulty is compounded by the fact that the analytical tools, though becoming increasingly refined, are as yet far from perfectly developed, and the empirical data within the developing countries are still too inadequate.

However, the message that these studies have for the developing countries is extremely important in planning the future strategy for development. It may be summarized as follows:

1. Human capital formed by education has proved to be an active agent of economic growth. In the United States, in the USSR, and in Japan, the productive value of educational investment was found to be higher than that of physical capital for the periods under study.

2. In all three of these countries, although they followed different growth-paths, economic growth, increasingly based on sophisticated technology, has become heavily dependent on education and science, with research playing a key role in development.

3. This stage has, however, been reached in these countries through a process of continuous readjustment of the economy to the new technology without serious long-term disequilibria in the use of physical and human capital resulting in any significant unemployment, except during the rare periods of abnormal economic crises.

4. The productivity of the investment in education reported in the three countries should, however, be viewed in the context of the social situation in each of the countries and therefore, of the aims, contents, and methods of education prevailing there and related to the economic and cultural life of the country.

5. It would not be correct to infer that investment in any type or level of education regardless of the social and economic needs in a

developing country would be productive. Nor would it be correct to imply that investment in education alone, even if it is in scientific and technical education, would automatically result in increasing the national product, independently and regardless of investment in physical capital. As a matter of fact, an important and challenging task will be to evolve a growth strategy in which investment in education is combined with investment in physical capital in a mutually compatible ratio to maximize product without leaving the available stock of human capital unutilized.

6. Some of the studies in the USSR have also brought into focus the value of general education, which in the USSR has a substantial content of mathematics and science. The value of a well-designed and well-articulated general education lies in the fact that it develops skills to learn other skills and the ability to analyze and solve problems and cope with a new situation. While a high priority is rightly assigned to the development of technical education in the developing countries, it is important that the value of general education should not be under-stressed either. There is, of course, clearly an urgent need for restructuring the general education which now suffers from many deficiencies. The conditions in most of the developing countries also seem to warrant a fusion of general and technical education, including agricultural education, starting at the primary level, as we shall discuss in Chapter 8.

7. The experience of the USSR indicates further that a fairly satisfactory fit between education and manpower needs is possible, with occasional distortions as reported in some of the studies, while ensuring development and utilization of all available manpower. If the large unemployed and underemployed segment of the labor force in the developing countries is to be educated fully and productively utilized, investment in both educational and economic development will have to be planned as integral and interacting parts of the overall national plan, to enable these sectors to move forward in a mutually supporting manner through a series of short-run adjustments to changing technology to a final stage of maximum productivity.

NOTES

1. Theodore W. Schultz, "Investment in Human Capital," American Review, 51 (1961), pp. 1-7.

2. H. G. Johnson, "Towards a Generalized Capital Accumulation Approach to Economic Development" in Residual Factors and Economic Growth (Paris: OECD, 1964), pp. 219-25.

3. M. J. Bowman, "The Human Investment Revolution in Economic Thought," Sociology of Education, 39 (1966), pp. 111-38.

4. Mark Blaug, Economics of Education: A Selected Annotated Bibliography (Oxford: Pergamon Press, 1970).

5. Theodore W. Schultz, The Economic Value of Education (New York: Columbia University Press, 1963), p. 44.

6. Edward F. Denison, "Education, Economic Growth, and Gaps in Information," Journal of Political Economy, 70, suppl. (October 1962), p. 127.

7. Edward F. Denison, Why Growth Rates Differ: Post-War Experience in Nine Western Countries (Washington: The Brookings Institution, 1967).

8. Schultz, The Economic Value of Education, op. cit., p. 3.

9. Fritz Machlup, The Production and Distribution of Knowledge in the United States (Princeton University Press, 1962), pp. 103-107.

10. Jacob Mincer, "On-the-Job Training: Costs, Returns, and Some Implications," Journal of Political Economy, 70, suppl. (October 1962), p. 57.

11. Gary Becker, "Investment in Human Capital: A Theoretical Analysis," Journal of Political Economy, 70, suppl. (October 1962), pp. 48-49.

12. Moses Abramovitz, Resource and Output Trends in the United States since 1870 (New York: National Bureau of Economic Research, 1956), Occasional Paper 52.

13. J. W. Kendrick, Productivity Trends: Capital Labor (New York: National Research Bureau, 1954), Occasional Paper 53.

14. Robert M. Solow, "Technical Change and the Aggregate Production Function," Review of Economics and Statistics, 84, no. 3 (1957): 312-20.

15. Simon Kuznets and Elizabeth Jenks, Capital in the American Economy: Its Formation and Financing (Princeton University Press, 1961), p. 390.

16. W. L. Hansen, "Total and Private Rates of Return to Investment in Schooling," Journal of Political Economy, 71 (1963).

17. Schultz, The Economic Value of Education, op. cit., p. 57.

18. Ibid., p. 58.

19. Ibid., p. 59.

20. Ibid., p. 61.

21. Ibid., p. 66.

22. Ibid., pp. 39-40.

23. Denison, Why Growth Rates Differ, op. cit., p. 27.

24. Frederick Harbison and Charles Myers, Education, Manpower, and Economic Growth (New York: McGraw-Hill Book Co., 1963).

25. W. Galenson and G. Pyatt, The Quality of Labour and Economic Development in Certain Countries (Geneva: International Labour Office, 1964).

26. M. J. Bowman, "The Human Investment Revolution in Economic Thought," in Economics of Education I, ed. M. Blaug (Baltimore: Penguin Books, 1968), p. 125.

27. Karl Marx and Friedrich Engels, "The Communist Manifesto," in Arthur P. Mendel (ed.), Essential Works of Marxism (New York: Bantam Books, 1961), p. 29.

28. Harold J. Noah (ed. and trans.), The Economics of Education in the U. S. S. R. (New York: Praeger Publishers, 1969), p. vii.

29. Ibid., p. 101, quoted by I. I. Kaplan, "The Influence of Education on Labor Output in the USSR."

30. S. G. Strumilin, "The Economic Significance of People's Education" (Leningrad, 1924), quoted by M. I. Makhmoutov, "Problems of Financing Investment in USSR," in Investment in Education, Report of UNESCO Regional Seminar of Finance Ministers, held in Bangkok, April 1964 (Bangkok: UNESCO Regional Office for Education in Asia, 1967), p. 347.

31. S. G. Strumilin, in Economicheskaia gazeta, no. 14 (1962), quoted in Noah, op. cit., p. 5.

32. Quoted in Noah, op. cit., p. 156.

33. Ibid., p. 6.

34. Ibid., p. 9.

35. Ibid., p. 8.

36. Ibid., p. 108.

37. Ibid.

38. M. S. Huq, Education and Development Strategy, p. 91.

39. Quoted by Don Adams in Education and Modernization in Asia (Reading, Mass.: Addison-Wesley Publishing Co., 1970), p. 35.

40. Government of Japan, Ministry of Education, Research Division, Education in Japan: A Graphic Presentation (Tokyo, March 1970), pp. 16-17.

41. Government of Japan, Ministry of Education, Japan's Growth and Education (Tokyo, 1963), p. 9.

42. Adams, op. cit., p. 54.

43. Government of Japan, Economic Planning Agency, Japan's New Economic and Social Development Plan 1970-75 (Tokyo: Government of Japan, 1970), p. 2.

44. Ibid., p. 83.

5

EDUCATIONAL PLANNING:
APPROACHES TO
DIFFERENT MODELS

An important result of the rapidly growing number of studies on the investment aspects of education that are discussed in Chapter 4 is the exploratory exercises being carried further afield in translating the findings of these studies into educational planning models. The task, of course, involves many difficulties stemming from the fact that the educational process is essentially one of human development, involving the qualities of the body as well as of the mind of the individual and also his life aspects as a person, a worker, and a member of the family and of the society. There are thus many variables affecting the educational process that are intangible and therefore not quantifiable. This human dimension, a fundamental characteristic of the production mechanism of education, distinguishes education from the nonhuman sectors of production and chiefly accounts for the limitations in the application of the analytical tools to educational model-making.

Theoretically speaking, the key principle in building a planning model for education would be, subject to the limitations mentioned above, to gear its production mechanism to operate with maximum internal and external efficiency in meeting the economic and social objectives of a nation through the development of its human resources. External efficiency is indicated by the extent to which the supply of educational output matches the demand, and internal efficiency by the input-output ratio and also by the quality of the output, or in other words by the quality of the entire production mechanism of education.

A mismatch between the educational supply and demand may reflect a lack of external efficiency of the educational system, distortions in the economic and social system, a deficiency in the forecasting technique itself, or a combination of these factors. If the educational system is internally inefficient, this may be caused by any of a whole set of variables, ranging from the aims, contents, and methods of education used or the students, teachers, and other inputs, to interferences in the working of different components and organs of the production mechanism itself, caused by internal or external factors located in the home and in the social environment.

The problems of educational planning are therefore extremely complex, and not all of them lend themselves to quantitative analysis or to the methodology followed in forecasting techniques. The model-making can be approached from the viewpoint of social demand for education, from the viewpoint of economic demand, or from the viewpoint of both. The "social demands approach" amounts to predicting future demand for education by parents and children, ordinarily on the basis of demographic and income trends. Educational planning in France, for instance, closely approximates this approach.[1] The beginning of educational model-making to meet manpower requirements can be seen in efforts to project such requirements according to the forecasts of economic growth over a period of time, thus giving rise to the school of planning based on what is now known as the manpower requirements approach. A second school using the rate of return to investment represents the alternative approach in educational planning. Each of these two approaches has several variants. A third school, drawing on both of these approaches and introducing new variables with a bearing on the quality of education, is now emerging. Some of the models based on these three approaches are discussed below.

THE MANPOWER REQUIREMENTS APPROACH

In the manpower requirements model an attempt is made, on the one hand, to derive the required educational output from a set of economic growth projections and, on the other, to identify the variables that affect the required output of each segment of education. The educational output requirements are based on the forecasts of economic growth and sectoral distribution of output and employment in a given future year. The sectoral distribution of employment is then broken up through a series of computations into a distribution of the labor force by occupation and by level of education. These estimates and the data on the existing stock of educated manpower, less loss due to death, retirement, resignation, and other reasons, are used in creating a plan of educational development to produce the future manpower requirements.

An important assumption implicit in this method is that adequate data are available on the demand side, relating to (1) the number of persons required in the economy in each occupation for a given future year, (2) the present number of persons in each occupation, (3) the annual number of withdrawals from each occupation due to death, retirement, or movement out of the labor force, and (4) the annual number of separations from one occupation and accessions to another as a result of job changes.[2]

In like manner, on the supply side it is assumed that data are available on the existing output of the educational system by the year in question, adjusted for withdrawals and occupational changes. The difference between the required and anticipated stock of personnel in each occupation expected by the target year provides the basis for the computation of the required change in the annual number of graduates from the various levels and types of education. Such a computation further assumes that each occupation is uniquely related to a specific educational background, as indicated by the experience of the industrialized countries.

This method has been used in the preparation of educational plans in a number of countries, such as the USSR and West Germany among the industrialized countries and Kenya, Nigeria, Tanzania, and Zambia among the developing countries.[3]

The manpower approach circumvents a problem that we will discuss later in the rate-of-return method, in estimating shadow prices for resources for which there are no valid market prices. It is not, however, easy to find reliable data on sectoral employment and worker trait requirements in developing countries, and the use of norms applicable to industrialized countries, which is common, can produce highly misleading results. Average performance in each job does not allow the fixing of any uniform standards. It is also hard to estimate manpower needs for lower skills.

It is important to note that the specific targets in detailed manpower forecasting ignore the paths by which such targets are to be reached over time. All changes over time in the numbers of men employed at any given skill are thereby interpreted as shifts in demand, and changes in pay rates are regarded as irrelevant. Considering the long "lead time" in educational manpower, forecasting must have medium-to-long time horizons, with due recognition to the need for adjustments based on "feedback" regarding the pupil-teacher ratio, teacher qualifications, and the possibilities of stabilization between skill acquisition in schools and skill acquisition by other means.

A MODIFIED MANPOWER REQUIREMENTS APPROACH

The model developed by Jan Tinbergen and his associates, a variant of the manpower requirements approach, has several important distinguishing features.[4]

This model is based on a much higher level of aggregation and it achieves considerable simplicity by assuming fixed coefficients in the relationship between the growth of each type or level of manpower and the growth of national income. Unlike the manpower requirements approach, the Tinbergen model takes into account the internal productive relations of the educational system. It also overcomes the problem of linking skills to schooling by defining the manpower categories by educational attainments. It derives a set of required enrollments from "an exogenously given rate of growth" by using two sets of equations. One equation represents the input-output relations of the educational system, or the teachers, equipment, and other input per pupil year at each educational level. The second equation represents the demand for educated manpower in the economy. It was recognized that problems of transition disequilibria were likely to arise under such assumptions, thus indicating the incompatibilities hidden in manpower planning methods in which the time-paths by which the economic and educational systems must travel to bring about equilibrium at the future target date do not receive due consideration. The model uses only secondary and higher education in the equations, on the assumption that primary education presents no impediment to the required expansion of secondary education and production increases in the economy.

The Tinbergen models, like conventional manpower models, disregard costs; strictly viewed, they cannot be treated as social decision models. The simplicity and flexibility of the framework of the Tinbergen models are two of their special merits, but they are also a reason for exercising great discrimination in using them.

The models exclude from their scope such practical questions as, for example, the types of schools and curricula to be expanded or contracted. They have, however, made significant contributions by highlighting some of the difficulties of rapid transition. They have also paved the way for development of programming models that take into account the web of interdependencies in education. They have also stimulated more empirical research in several countries, leading to revision of the models on the basis of a wider range of alternatives in the patterns of adjustment between economic and educational development.

THE RATE-OF-RETURN APPROACH

The rate-of-return model is based on an analysis of the internal rate of return on investment in education through present value-cost comparisons derived from education-age-income data. The aim of this method is to estimate the economic benefits accruing from the costs of schooling, instead of estimating the manpower at various levels of schooling required for a given pattern of economic growth, which is the aim of the manpower approach.

Some of the studies made in a number of industrially advanced countries that estimate the return on investment of various types and levels of education have been discussed in Chapter 4. A comparatively recent study, undertaken in Greece by Harvey Leibenstein, should be

of special interest to other developing countries in view of its bearing
on planning investment in educational development.[5]

In his study Leibenstein used two basic sets of data: earnings
data and data on costs of schooling. The earnings data were collected
through a sample survey of workers in industry and commerce in the
Athens area, including age, years of education, monthly earnings, and
occupation and covering over 2,700 observations for the years 1960 and
1964. He also used as additional data the salary schedules for workers
in public services, as well as information directly obtained from professional organizations.

His finding is that

> it is unclear whether education of the present quality at
> the secondary and higher level considered as a unit can
> have any greater claims on an overall investment budget
> compared with other types of investment. The exceptions
> to the case would be the training for well-established pro-
> fessions such as engineering, chemistry, medicine, etc.[6]

This method provides the basis of the investment-decision theory,
but it has not found a wide acceptance with the planners, mainly for the
following reasons.

1. It ignores the noneconomic and also the indirectly economic
benefits of education. This criticism is equally applicable to the manpower requirements models.

2. The data necessary for this model are not generally available
in the developing countries. Again, the same problem exists in some
degree for the other approach as well and should not be insurmountable.

3. It does not take into account the income effects of ability,
motivation, and family status that interact with the schooling. However,
this problem is also statistically surmountable.

4. It also does not seem to reflect the effects of future changes
in contents and methods in the schooling system and in the pattern of
economic growth, which are important variables affecting the productivity of investment in education.

THE LINEAR PROGRAMMING MODEL

A movement towards at least a partial convergence of the manpower requirements approach and the rate-of-return approach can be
seen in the recent efforts to apply linear programming to educational
planning, using some elements of both planning models.

A good example of this is the model developed by Samuel Bowles
and described by him as "the intertemporal optimizing model of the
educational sector."[7] He computed lifetime earnings estimates from

the raw data from Leibenstein's sample of workers in the
Athens area. The gross income stream associated with each
level of education is a weighted average of the present value
of expected earnings of dropouts, on the one hand, and of
graduates, on the other. The weights here are the fraction
of total admissions expected to drop out or graduate. The
expected earnings of both dropouts and graduates are
weighted average of expected male and female earnings,
adjusted for unemployment and nonparticipation in the
labor force. The foregone earnings-stream for a given type
of school is the present value of the expected earnings of
a graduate of the next lower level, adjusted by sex, unemployment, and labor force participation to correspond to a
typical incoming student.[8]

The model used activities comprising primary school, gymnasium
(first-cycle secondary), lyceum (second-cycle secondary), technical
secondary education, primary school teacher training, and higher education both at home and abroad. It divided the educational sector further
into three categories, namely the humanities and social sciences; physical sciences and mathematics; and engineering and related subjects,
excluding middle technical and assistant-engineer schools.

The estimates of the time profile of earnings and costs take
into account the expected increases in costs per pupil due
in part to increases in teacher-pupil ratios and an anticipated 3 per cent per annum productivity increase.[9]

The model included activities that allowed the educational sector
to recruit additional teachers and assumed that the salary increment
necessary for recruitment to be paid to all teachers and not merely to
those recruited.

Thus, the unit cost of each recruiting activity is the marginal, rather than the average cost. In every case the
recruiting activity was constrained by an upper limit which
was set equal to the number of teachers of each specifi-
cation composing the initial stock of teachers in the year
1961, plus some fraction of the output of individuals
possessing those qualifications throughout the planning
period.[10]

For Greece the most striking results emerging from this planning
model were projected as follows:
    1. rapid growth of second-level education early in the planning
period, followed by a significant expansion of higher education,

2. a change in the enrollment structure within higher education, with decisive shifts towards engineering and related fields,

3. reduction of the dropout rate. In remarkable contrast with a high dropout rate, ranging from 54 percent of the graduates of primary schools to 55 percent of the graduates of the lyceum, by 1974 all successful graduates of a given level of schooling would achieve entrance at the next level. It is also remarkable that

> by the end of the planning period, the derived demand for gymnasium graduates as an input via the lyceum into higher education is sufficiently great to make the maximum feasible continuation rate optimal.[11]

The linear programming and rate-of-return models have one important characteristic in common: both measure the demand for educated manpower by the differences in earnings among various categories of workers without reference to the available supply of labor. However, in the manpower requirements and Tinbergen models, as noted earlier, the demand for educated manpower is determined in terms of the required number of workers, without reference to their relative wages. Thus the demand appears to be totally inelastic in the manpower approach and highly elastic in the linear programming and rate-of-return approaches. Hence the manpower requirements approach, both in the conventional and Tinbergen models, may be regarded as "technological" and the rate-of-return and programming approaches as "economic."

In the manpower requirements approach the basic assumption about the relationship between national income and distribution of schooling implies that the number of workers required by the economy can be derived from the given level of future national income. The choice of occupational and educational input coefficients in a particular sector becomes crucial to the estimation of each type of manpower requirement on an economywide basis.[12] However, this approach does not indicate whether the required occupational composition of the labor force in each sector is average or minimal or whether the required distribution of educational attainments in each occupation is optimal.

An additional difficulty in the use of this method is that the requirement for predicting the rate of growth in labor productivity within each sector in order to determine the required type and level of schooling in the labor force overlooks the fact that one of the main objects of educational planning is actually to influence labor productivity trends, although such efforts have achieved little success even in advanced countries that have had the advantage of dependable historical series.

These difficulties are overcome in the Tinbergen models, in which the manpower categories are defined directly by their educational attainments. In the models originally used by the Netherlands Economic Institute, these estimated relationships between income growth and level of schooling are represented in the requirements for labor of each type. They are represented as demand functions for labor by level of schooling in the models used by Gareth Williams in his study of Greece.[13] However, in these cases some difficulties also arise from the fact that these estimates are based on a cross section of countries at a given point in time and are intended to be used for a particular country over a period of time.

Both the Tinbergen models and the conventional approaches present two additional difficulties. First, it is not shown whether the values that are indicated by the data used in both methods on the observed level of labor input and the composition of the labor force by occupation or educational attainment are optimal. They are implied to be optimal in the Tinbergen equation; otherwise it would be impossible to produce the required composition of workers. In manpower estimates based on the labor input of more advanced countries or more advanced firms within the same economy, the labor input coefficients are presumed to be optimal, though these data, which are historically derived, are presumably the outcome of a process of sub-optimal decision making. If they are not in fact optimal the result will be duplication and aggravation of existing imbalances in the labor market. On the other hand, if the aggregate labor input data used as the empirical basis for Tinbergen equations are regarded as optimal, the question would then arise whether the countries in the sample have any economic need for educational planning.[14]

The second difficulty presented by both versions of the manpower approach arises from the requirement in these models to identify simultaneously both the demand and supply functions for educated labor.

The rate-of-return approach and the linear programming model both assume an equilibrium in the labor market and aim at achieving equilibrium in the human capital market in terms of economic relations between the economy and the educational system.

This assumption does not, however, seem to be realistic in view of the known imperfect structure of the labor market and the chronic labor surplus in most of the developing countries. Even if the educational system is economy-oriented, the assumed equilibrium remains a goal that is sought but rarely realized even in industrialized countries committed to an open economy, as indicated by the income and price control policies in force in several such countries. In the developing countries an additional dimension is added by the necessity of generating employment to absorb the surplus labor, implying a dynamic and continuous adjustment of the educational system to the changing occupational needs over time.

Samuel Bowles, one of the principal authors of the linear programming model, readily recognizes its limitations and observes:

The first is that we must question the degree to which wages of different categories of labor adequately measure scarcities.

Second, even if the wages of each type of labor were always
equal to the value of the marginal product, we would still
have to question the empirical assumption that relative
wages of labor do not significantly depend on the relative
quantities of available labor.[15]

Even where wages roughly measure marginal productivity, it is
hardly feasible to measure precisely the portion of the increment in
earnings that can be attributed to an additional year of schooling rather
than to other factors.

The second problem stems from the shape of the demand curves
for educated labor, implying direct substitution among labor of different
levels of schooling and indirect substitution through changes in the composition of final demand. The result is a considerable amount of substi-
tutability among the various types of labor. It is, however, possible
to check the empirical importance of biases in the results of these
assumptions through a disaggregated analysis if the data on which
labor aggregation functions are available.

MANPOWER VERSUS PROGRAMMING

The two methods indicate important differences in their approach
to the educational system as a supplier of labor, such as, for example,
in the manner in which the cost of an educational program is measured
and the cost related to the choices of an educational policy.

The conventional manpower requirements approach determines
educational requirements from projected income levels and thus does
not explicitly consider the cost at all. Even when costs are computed,
as they were in the Mediterranean Regional Project, this is done after
the framing of the requirement estimates and does not materially affect
the establishment of the enrollment targets.

In the rate-of-return approach the cost of education is measured
in money terms for both social and private costs of schooling, thus
implying that the market valuation of the educational input is an accurate measure of scarcities in the economy. In the Tinbergen and linear
programming models, costs are measured in terms of physical input,
and fixed teacher and student input coefficients are used to indicate
the production function of the educational process, the educational
output being always net of the requirement of the educational system
for its own input. The opportunity costs of operating each activity in
the programming model are based on the physical input coefficients
relating to teachers and students and the shadow prices for these sources
generated by the model itself. Both the Tinbergen and linear programming
models are thus technological in this respect.

Again the models may be classified into "technological" and "economic" categories according to the differences in their basic assumptions concerning the production and demand for educated labor.

The manpower requirements models, including the Tinbergen models, appear to be deterministic, in that they proceed from a given target of national income in deriving the required level of educational development, and the educational plans are not intended to be optimal in the economic sense. The basic principle underlying the rate-of-return and programming models, on the other hand, is one of maximization of national income, subject to the availability of resources.

According to Bowles,

> If, as is quite likely in some cases, the capacity of the economy to absorb particular types of labor is rather limited, we would find that policy prescriptions based on existing scarcities might be inappropriate if carried to any considerable length over a period of time.[16]

Educational planning should therefore be regarded as a continuous decision-making process, rather than a single exercise. Additional information as it becomes available should be used for feedback to the plan in reestimating and resolving the plan-model from year to year, provided, of course, that the rate of acceleration envisaged in the plan is not too rapid.

Another advantage of the second group of models lies in the fact that they do not involve estimation of aggregate quantities requiring more elaborate research and often a complete enumeration, as in the case of the first group of models. The kind of data required for the second group can be obtained inexpensively and quickly even in countries in which the census figures are not available and the system of data collection is still inadequate or underdeveloped.

> Of course, the accuracy of the micro-economic data from sample surveys may be very limited. This is particularly true when we estimate differences between two earnings-streams, for in this case a small error in one stream may create a large error in the estimated present value of net benefits.[17]

THE VALUE OF PRIMARY, SECONDARY,
AND TECHNICAL EDUCATION

The characteristics peculiar to the approach of the models briefly discussed above have important bearing on policy prescriptions. The manpower requirements approach tends to favor second-level education

on the assumption, as in Tinbergen's model, that the supply of labor
with a primary education or less is plentiful. It may be noted that
Frederick Harbison, in his human resource development approach, also
excluded primary education from the indicators of human resource development. On the other hand, the optimal solution of the linear programming model indicated an expansion in primary education and even a
decline in secondary education. This divergence in the policy prescription of the two methods is largely due to the fact that optimizing models
are likely to find primary schooling productive since they explicitly take
educational costs into consideration, unlike the deterministic methods,
and secondary schooling, with earnings foregone included in the educational costs, therefore becomes more expensive than primary education.
In Greece, according to the Samuel Bowles study, one year of secondary
schooling on this basis costs twice as much as one year of primary
schooling; in Nigeria it costs twenty-two times as much. In like manner,
the cost of higher education would be correspondingly much greater.
This is a trend that is supported by the findings of studies on a cross-
section of developing countries, as summarized in Table 5.1. Of course,
conditions in a particular country may vary widely from this trend.

One reason why a rapid rate of growth in secondary education is
stressed in the requirements approach is the absence of choice in the
production of secondary-level skills that is implied in that method.
While recognizing the relative scarcity of middle-level skills, it is
also necessary to note the alternative choices available for the production of these skills, such as on-the-job experience, nonformal training,
and other substitutes for formal schooling.

In respect to technical education, which is recognized in the
manpower approach to the prime need, a different result is yielded by
linear programming; the validity of this result for a particular country
would naturally depend on the stage of industrial development reached
by it. Investment in technical education is likely to be more profitable
in countries with a substantial manufacturing base already created than
in those in which this base is very small and the rate of return on general human capital investment is high, indicating scarcity of high-level
skills for teachers and higher opportunity costs of input.

The level of investment in formal education presents an area of
divergence between the two approaches that is of special relevance to
those countries in which underinvestment in education is apparent even
from a purely quantitative assessment of educational growth. In both
Greece and Nigeria an expansion of the educational sector well beyond
the levels prescribed by the requirements approach was indicated by the
linear programming model. In the case of Greece the rate-of-return
method yielded results similar to those of the requirements approach;
but in the case of Nigeria the former method favored larger investment.
It may be noted here that neither of these two methods seeks to determine optimal expenditure on education, as is the case in the linear
programming, and according to the latter "there are significant economic

TABLE 5.1

Profitability of Schooling in Selected Countries

| | | | Level of Schooling | | |
| | | | | General | |
Country	Concept Used	Date	Primary	Secondary	Higher
Venezuela	Social internal rate-of-return (percent)	1957	82	17	23
Chile	Social internal rate-of-return (percent)	1959	24	17	12
India	Social internal rate-of-return (percent)	1960-61	17	11	8
Colombia	Social internal rate-of-return (percent)	1965	28	20	6
Mexico	Social internal rate-of-return (percent)	1963	25	17	23
Uganda	Benefit-cost ratio (i=.12)	1965	3.70	2.70	0.99
Israel	Benefit-cost ratio (i=.8)	1957	3.48	0.71	0.29

Sources: Martin Carnoy, "The Cost and Return to Schooling in Mexico: A Case Study," unpublished Ph. D. dissertation, University of Chicago, 1964; Arnold C. Harberger and Marcelo Selowsky, "Key Factors in the Economic Growth of Chile" (mimeographed), presented to the conference at Cornell University on The Next Decade of Latin American Development, April 20-22, 1966; Carl Shoup, The Fiscal System of Venezuela (Baltimore: The Johns Hopkins Press, 1959), as reported in Martin Carnoy, "Rates of Return to Schooling in Latin America," pp. 367-68; A. M. Nalla Gounden, "Investment in Education in India," Journal of Human Resources, 2, no. 3 (Summer 1967), p. 352; J. A. Smyth and Nicholas Bennett, "Rate of Return on Investment in Education: A Tool for Short Term Educational Planning Illustrated with Ugandan Data," in George Z. Bereday and J. A. Lauwerys (eds.), The World Year Book of Education 1967 (New York: Harcourt Brace, 1967), pp. 318-19; Ruth Klinov-Malul, The Profitability of Investment in Education in Israel (Jerusalem: The Maurice Falk Institute for Economic Research in Israel, April 1966), pp. 61-66; Marcelo Selowsky, "The Effect of Unemployment and Growth on the Rate of Return to Education: the Case of Colombia," Project for Quantitative Research in Economic Development, Harvard University, Economic Development Report No. 116 (November 1968).

returns to levels of expenditure on education above and beyond those
prescribed by the estimated manpower 'requirements' of the labor force."[18]
In the programming model "the profitability of each educational activity
is evaluated on the basis of shadow prices generated by the system
itself rather than on the basis of market prices."[19]

Another notable study is the 1971 work by J. Alan Thomas on the
application of systems analysis to the educational decision process.[20]
His approach is similar to that of Samuel Bowles and uses complex sets
of input-output matrices and a complicated cost-benefit analysis based
on an identification of sets of intraeducation production functions and
empirical research in educational psychology and educational administration and requiring the design of new empirical studies.

He uses the term "function," in its mathematical and not its sociological sense, to indicate that there is more than one way to produce
education. He is critical of the way in which, from kindergarten through
graduate school, ratios of students to teachers, classrooms, books,
and counselors are often used with little or no empirical or theoretical
justification. In his concept of the production function these ratios
are treated as variables rather than constants, and alternative methods
of allocation of scarce resources are underscored.[21]

The production function concept also serves as a mathematical
basis for decision-making models that facilitate the choice among
alternative solutions to a given problem. Thomas uses the concept of
the production function in examining three distinct types of input-output
relationships reflecting three different approaches, namely that of the
administrator, the psychologist, and the economist, each of whom
looks at the production function from his own point of view.

The analytical tools used for measuring the productivity of the
physical capital are also used in the analysis of the costs and benefits
of the production of human capital; these are called present value analysis and analysis of the internal rate of return.

He employs the "psychologist's production function" in developing
some theoretical approaches to resource allocation in the educational
system. The goal is to advance the development of a management science in education, based on analysis of educational inputs and outputs,
and their interrelationships.[22]

"Value added" is measured in terms of increments in educational
performance. "First, a sample behavior in a given area of curriculum
is observed and measured. Second, by similar means and using the
same subjects, a second sample of behavior from the same curriculum
area is measured after a lapse of time. The performance increment is
the difference between the first and second measures."[23]

Another important assumption implies a production function that
relates output (performance increment) to input (students' time,
teachers' time, equipment including materials and books, and space).

Symbolically this is expressed as

$$p' - p = f(x_1, x_2, x_3, x_4, x_5),$$

where

    p = performance at time t
    p' = performance at time $t+1$
$p' - p$ = performance increment in a single unit of time
    x_1 is student hours
    x_2 is teacher hours
    x_3 is equipment
    x_4 is space
    x_5 represents other, unidentified variables.

"The term 'function' indicates mathematical dependence. The statement, therefore, means that performance increments depend upon (or are related to) inputs of time of students, teachers and others, equipment and space."[24]

The production function in education is, of course, extremely complex, involving a multiplicity of variables in view of the various forces at work within schools and colleges at a given time. "Attempts to improve performance usually involve increasing outputs by lengthening the school day, offering summer school programs, reducing the pupil-teacher ratio, purchasing films, or selecting and buying books. In addition, inputs of improved quality are sometimes substituted for inferior inputs in an attempt to improve outputs."[25]

This leads to the next assumption. "All other things equal, increases in x_1 and/or x_2 are associated with increases in the increment $p' - p$."[26]

Thus, other things being equal, larger amounts of student time, or even of teacher time, will result in increased learning; x_3, the input of equipment, books, and materials, is supposed to be complementary to teachers' time, x_2, the optimal use of material inputs increasing teacher effectiveness. Possible substitutes for teachers' time are such inputs as television, teaching machines, and the like. However, x_4, space, is regarded as "a necessary but not a sufficient condition for learning to occur."[27]

How a mathematical representation of an educational production function can be developed is indicated below:

Select a sample of schools which vary along the input dimension. Through multivariate analysis, determine the relationship, for this sample, between input variations and output increments. Express this relationship in probabilistic terms, as an input-output relationship. The functional relationships are likely to be nonlinear. That is, increases in a given input will not always lead to uniformly proportionate increases in output. For example, the first thousand books in a school library may contribute more than

the tenth thousand books. Hence, estimating input-output
relationships will probably mean estimating the form of the
function as well as its parameters.[28]

The scope for improving the production functions of the educational
system through a search for more efficient methods of instruction and
organization is recognized and stressed in this method. "Some of the
inputs would be spent on search rather than on the production of outputs.
It is likely that the level of outcomes obtained in this way would be
higher than that obtained if all the inputs were directly applied toward
the production of outputs."[29]

THE RELEVANCE OF THE PLAN-MODELS
TO DEVELOPING COUNTRIES

As already indicated, all of these models were built on a number
of assumptions that were not empirically validated, and their analysis
could not proceed without these assumptions. In any case they indicate
an important caveat for the planner. That more empirical research was
clearly warranted to test out these assumptions was demonstrated by
the anomalous result produced by the Tinbergen model when applied to
Greece by Gareth Williams. In his original application of the model
the result was that the secondary enrollment target to be achieved by
the last year of the plan-period exceeded the total population in the
secondary-school age group.

An additional limitation stems from inadequate planning data in
many of the developing countries. However, these models have filled
a vacuum and provide some kind of a measuring and analyzing tool where
none existed before. The later models, for example those of Bowles and
Thomas, are also significantly more meaningful because they carry their
analyses well beyond economics and into education.

There is, however, a clear need for more efforts to improve and
refine the model-building technique. In this area more than in any other,
teamwork involving economists, psychologists, sociologists, scientists,
and educators can be of immense benefit to the developing countries.
Purely theoretical economic analysis can be vastly misleading by creating the erroneous notion that the issues of human and social values
that form an integral part of education can be isolated from those of
systemic efficiency and that the former can be relegated to the background until the latter has produced an economic breakthrough. The
frustrating experience of a generation of development effort based on
this plan-strategy belies such a belief.

The differences in approach of the various models and their underlying assumptions also indicate that it would be imprudent to depend
entirely on any one of them. Used as complementary methods they can,

however, be of great value to educational planning. The results of the manpower requirements models can be checked with those of the rate-of-return and linear programming models. In like manner, the targets obtained through the latter models may be checked and revised in the light of the information produced through studies of manpower requirements. Such a combination is a special necessity in a developing country with an imperfect market economy.

THE NEED FOR EMPIRICAL RESEARCH

The theoretical character of these models and the lack of sufficient empirical research relating to their underlying assumptions will also render it necessary to adapt them to the conditions peculiar to developing countries, particularly those in South and Southeast Asia, where a large agricultural sector and an abundant supply of labor distinguish them from the labor-short, capital-rich, and highly industrialized countries. To fit this picture a modified approach involving corresponding changes in the basic concepts and assumptions in the planning models will be necessary to enable them to bring the entire available stock of manpower within the ambit of both the economic and education sectors.

Such a restructuring of the planning models will also bring them nearer to the development objectives, which concern not only economic but also social and cultural needs. Neither the manpower requirement approach nor the rate-of-return and programming models, taken alone or together in their present form, can fully indicate how much education is needed for a society. As pointed out in Chapter 3, the cultural aims of education are as important as the economic aims, for the society as well as for the individual. As a matter of fact, these aims relate to life aspects that are inseparable, even though the anachronistic notion of an antithesis between work and culture, a relic of the feudal age, still lingers.

Another dimension of the function of education that relates to both economic and cultural aims and that has been brought into the focus of global attention, particularly through the efforts of UNESCO, arises from the concept of education as a lifelong process of qualitative change, implying continuous renewal and regeneration. This function has an important bearing on the production processes of education involving the structure, contents, and methods of education in the developing countries, which are in transition and will have to pass through a series of short-run adjustments to the technological changes necessary for their gradual modernization. The educational plan-models have therefore a special task to perform in the developing countries.

NOTES

1. Raymond Poignant, "Establishing Educational Targets in France" in Planning Education for Economic and Social Development (Paris: OECD, 1963), pp. 205-72.

2. H. S. Parnes, "Forecasting Educational Needs for Economic and Social Development" (Paris: OECD, 1962), pp. 19-22.

3. J. N. Archer, Educational Development in Nigeria, 1961-70: A Report on the Planning and Cost of Development on the Basis of the Ashby Commission's Report (Lagos: Government Printer, 1961); A Report on Manpower, Education, and Training in Zambia (Lusaka: Government Printer, 1966); Calvin F. Davis, High Level Manpower Requirements and Resources in Kenya, 1969-70 (Nairobi: Government Press, 1965); R. L. Thomas, Survey of High Level Manpower Requirements and Resources for the Five-Year Development Plan, 1964/65 to 1968/69 (Dar-es-Salaam: Government Printer, 1965); H. P. Weilmaier, "A Case Study of Educational Planning: West Germany" in G. Z. F. Bereday, J. A. Lauwerys, and Mark Blaug (eds.), Education Planning: The World Year Book of Education (New York: Harcourt Brace & World, 1967); and Nicholas DeWitt, Educational and Professional Employment in the U. S. S. R. (Washington: National Science Foundation, 1961).

4. Jan Tinbergen and Hector Correa, "Quantitative Adaptation of Education to Accelerated Growth" in Kyklos, 15 (1962); Jan Tinbergen and H. C. Bos, "A Planning Model for Educational Requirements of Economic Development" in The Residual and Economic Growth (Paris: OECD, 1964); and Jan Tinbergen and H. C. Bos, Econometric Models of Education—Some Applications (Paris: OECD, 1965).

5. Harvey Leibenstein, "Rates of Return to Education in Greece" in Development Advisory Service, Harvard University, Economic Development Report, no. 94 (September 1967).

6. Ibid.

7. Samuel Bowles, Planning Educational Systems for Economic Growth (Cambridge, Mass.: Harvard University Press, 1969).

8. Ibid., p. 157.

9. Ibid., p. 160.

10. Ibid., p. 161.

11. Ibid., p. 166.

12. Hollister Robinson, A Technical Evaluation of the First Stage of the Mediterranean Regional Project (Paris: OECD, 1966).

13. Gareth Williams, "Planning Models for Calculation of Educational Requirements for Economic Development, Greece" in Tinbergen and Bos, Econometric Models of Education, op. cit., pp. 77-93.

14. Bowles, Planning Educational Systems, op. cit., pp. 180-81.

15. Ibid., p. 182.

16. Ibid., p. 187.

17. Ibid., p. 191.

18. Ibid., p. 203.

19. Ibid., p. 204.

20. J. Alan Thomas, The Productive School: A Systems Analysis Approach to Educational Administration (New York: John Wiley & Sons, 1971).

21. Ibid., pp. 10-11.

22. Ibid., p. 56.

23. Ibid., p. 57.

24. Ibid., pp. 59-60.

25. Ibid., p. 60.

26. Ibid.

27. Ibid., p. 61.

28. Ibid.

29. Ibid., pp. 61-62.

6

THE SOUTH AND
SOUTHEAST ASIA SCENE

Each of the countries in South and Southeast Asia has its own
unique history, culture, values, and goals to inspire and guide the
growth of its social, political, and economic institutions. These
countries also have many economic and demographic characteristics
in common and show striking parallels in the evolution of their
societies.

Though the emergence of many of the countries in this region as
national sovereign states is a comparatively recent phenomenon, they
are heirs to a rich social and cultural heritage, steeped in history that
in some cases goes as far back as several thousand years. All of them
went through a fairly long period of political and economic exploitation
of the masses of the people, either by an alien colonial power or by a
feudal ruling group within the country. Considered in terms of major
social changes, the history of the region seems to fall into three eras.

The first era represents the earliest period and development and
saw the flowering of some of the greatest civilizations, such as the
Aryan, the Indic, the Chinese, and the Muslim, each of which left an
imprint on its contemporary world society as deep as the imprint of
Western civilization on the modern world. During this period social
institutions, including education, were profoundly influenced by values
rooted in religion.

The second era is associated with the social and economic
changes that followed the contact with the West at the beginning of
the colonial period. These changes were most pronounced in education
and in the economy. The economy became geared to the production of
primary goods to feed the industries of Western countries with cheap
raw materials. Now regarded as poor and backward, some of the
countries in this region were once not so underdeveloped, compared
to the countries that now rank among the developed ones.

For example, some of the urban centers of India during the Mogul period were "bigger than the biggest cities in Europe at the same period," and the Indian subcontinent enjoyed a favorable balance of trade, mainly through the production and export of luxury goods, which had unrivalled markets in Europe.[1] The fame of the wealth of this region earned for it the appellation of "the gorgeous East," and inspired the quest that led to the discovery of the Americas and contributed to the preconditions for the industrial revolution in Europe. Thomas Mun, the 17th century English writer, though perhaps somewhat oversimplifying, referred to the world commerce of his day as consisting mainly of the exchange of mineral wealth of the new Indies in the West for the luxuries and refinements of the Old Indies in the East.[2]

Certainly the commerce between the East and the West opened up new markets and resources, thus providing a great impetus to industrial growth in Europe.

> For the East, this was the beginning of a period of stagnation and progressive economic decline. It was reduced gradually to the status of an exporter of its primary products, raw materials, and minerals, and an importer of the finished goods. The two opposite movements thus set into motion by the historical events of the period from about the middle of the sixteenth century to the end of the nineteenth century largely account for the wide gap existing today between the advanced countries of the West and the developing countries of South and Southeast Asia.[3]

The third era is the current one, commencing with the emergence of these countries as national sovereign states after the end of the World War II. It is characterized by spurting activity for their economic and social development. At independence many of these countries did not have more than moderate infrastructures in the form of administrative, economic, and educational institutions. There was, therefore, clearly a need to expand and develop these institutions further to facilitate the transition of these countries from predominantly agrarian economies to at least semiindustrialized economies if they were to achieve self-sustainment. Simultaneously the social and educational institutions had to be transformed to enable them to play their role in changing elitist societies to participatory democracies.

DEMOGRAPHIC CHARACTERISTICS

Among the various regions of the world, South and Southeast Asia stands out for its size, density, and growth and the dependency rate of its population, as shown in Table 6.1.

TABLE 6.1

Population in Selected Asian Countries Compared with that in Selected Industrialized Countries, Midyear, 1968

	Population (in thousands)	Density (per sq Km)	Rate of Growth (in percentage)	Age (Distribution in Percentage) under 15	15-59	60 and over
Asian countries						
Bangladesh	74,000	530	2.5	44.5	49.5	6.0
Burma	26,389	39	2.1	41.3	53.5	5.2
Cambodia	6,557	36	2.4	44.7	51.3	4.0
Ceylon	11,964	182	2.6	40.7	54.0	5.3
China, Republic of (Taiwan)	13,466	374	3.2	45.1	50.7	4.2
India	523,893	160	2.5	41.1	54.1	4.8
Indonesia	112,825	59	2.9	42.1	53.8	4.1
Korea, Republic of (South)	43,470	441	2.8	43.3	51.4	5.3
Malaysia	10,384	31 (67 in West Malaysia)	3.0	43.8	51.6	4.6
Pakistan	60,000	74	2.5	44.5	49.5	6.0
Philippines	35,993	120	3.5	45.7	50.0	4.3
Singapore	1,988	581	2.7	42.8	53.4	3.8
Thailand	33,693	66	3.1	43.2	52.2	4.6
Industrialized countries						
Japan	101,090	273	1.1	26.0	64.0	10.0
France	49,920	91	1.1	25.6	57.1	17.3
United Kingdom	55,283	227	0.5	22.8	60.0	17.2
United States	201,152	21	1.7	31.1	55.7	13.2

Sources: UNESCO Statistical Yearbook 1969 (Paris, 1970); for population of Bangladesh, Planning Commission, Bangladesh, "January 1973 Estimate," First Five Year Plan 1973-78, November 1973; for rate of growth of Burma, Cambodia, Ceylon, China (Taiwan), South Korea, Singapore, and Thailand, UNESCO Regional Office for Education in Asia, Progress of Education in the Asian Region: A Statistical Review (Bangkok: the United Nations, 1969); for rate of growth of the industrialized countries, Economic Commission for Asia and Far East, Economic Development and Human Resources, ECAFE Growth Studies Series No. 3 (Bangkok: the United Nations, 1966), p. 8; for age distribution, UNESCO, An Asian Model of Educational Development (Paris: the United Nations, 1966).

The rate of growth of population constitutes a threat to the pace of growth in the developing world, and this threat is much greater for the countries of South and Southeast Asia because of the size their populations have already reached. During the 1950s the rate of population growth doubled, rising from about 10 percent during the 1940s to nearly 20 percent in the 1950s. If this accelerating rate is allowed to continue unchecked, the population is likely to double itself by the year 2000, thus adding enormously to the already great pressure on the resources of these countries and also to the magnitude of problems in all sectors of development. The problems in the educational sector will, however, be accentuated more than proportionately because of the high dependency rate, which is about 45 percent. An increase of 2 to 3 percent in population will mean a 3 to 4 percent increase in the school-age population.

It may be noted that during the fifteen years from 1965 to 1980 the five- to fourteen-year age group in Europe is expected to remain constant, in North America to increase by 13 percent, and in the Asian region to increase by about 40 percent.

Population control is therefore clearly indicated as central to future development strategy. Many of the countries have already experimented with family planning programs and thus acquired some experience in developing them on an expanded scale. All of their national plans also stress the need for a rapid expansion of the program, but this is apparently not matched by adequate action.

Ceylon's plan (1971-76) envisaged the establishment of family planning clinics in all maternal and child welfare centers. Formerly the program was operated in about 40 percent of these centers, and the effort was considered to be "insignificant in relation to the magnitude of the problem."[4]

India's fourth plan underlined the need for "a strong, purposeful government policy, supported by effective programs and adequate resources of finance, men and materials," in which case the population in the year 2000, which the plan estimated at 890 million, could be "260 million less than what it would be if the present rate of growth continues unchecked."[5] The target of the plan is to protect 28 million couples and prevent 18 million births during the planning period.

Pakistan's fourth plan also placed special emphasis on the family planning program. The aim was to reach 34 percent of the married couples by 1975 and to prevent about 4 million births.[6]

In Indonesia, family planning clinics in operation in 1970 numbered about 226 only. The aim of the program during the 1970-74 planning period was "to prevent 600,000 to 700,000 births by reaching a target of 3,000,000 acceptors (eligible women) regularly visiting the family planning institutions."[7]

Malaysia's 1971-75 plan envisaged a program aimed at reducing the birth rate to 32 per thousand population from the 1971 level of 35 and extending family planning services to the rural areas. The program

goal in terms of acceptors was to reach 600,000 women, with the annual
target rising from 80,000 in 1971 to 160,000 in 1975. The plan estimated that continuing users would rise from 105,000 to about 267,000
by 1975.[8]

The Philippines' 1971-74 plan envisaged government-funded participation in the family planning program at the 1970 levels, though the
total program was expected to be expanded as a consequence of the
growing participation of the private sector. The aim was to reduce the
population growth rate from 3.5 percent in 1970 to 3.2 percent in 1974,
the maximum number of users rising to 780,646, from 142,654.[9]

In all of these countries family planning programs are as yet far
from commensurate with the magnitude of the problem and need to be
stepped up, assigned a much higher priority, and integrated with the
community development programs where such programs exist, with the
fullest use being made of both formal and nonformal education in the
dissemination of population education.

LABOR FORCE, EDUCATION, AND PRODUCTIVITY

The national development plans of the region are replete with
such phrases as "human capital," "the development of human resources,"
"maximization of employment," "socialist, egalitarian, democratic
society," and the like. However, the implications of these objectives
and concepts are not pursued to their logical conclusions in the plan
policies and parameters of growth. The specific increases in allocation
for the social sectors in which education is explicitly or implicitly
included are intended to serve the purpose of moving the countries
towards the desired balance between the claims of economic growth
and social justice. As in the previous plans, educational goals are
set in terms of physical targets without any clear indication how these
targets, if accomplished, will fulfill the stated economic and social
objectives. The extent of productive employment is vaguely noted
without any serious analysis of the required input in terms of specialized knowledge and technical skills needed and the magnitude of the
task involved, in view of the present educational status of the labor
force.

The data available on the education and employment of the labor
force in this region are inadequate. From the data that are available
on the educational status of the labor force, three important characteristics seem to emerge: (1) a high incidence of illiteracy or near illiteracy, such as 72.9 percent in India and 87.2 percent in pre-1972
Pakistan; (2) an extremely low proportion of the population with a post-
primary education, those with a complete secondary education forming
less than 5 percent of the total population; and (3) an especially high
proportion of total illiteracy or inadequate education in agriculture and

TABLE 6.2

Educational Structure of Active Labor Force in Ceylon
by Sector, 1969/70
(in percentage of sector totals)

	Urban	Rural	Estate	Total
No schooling	7	10	43	16
Primary (Grades One through Five)	30	39	48	39
Middle (Grades Six through Ten)	40	37	8	32
Passed O Level	19	13	1	12
Passed A Level	3	1	--	1

Source: Socio-Economic Survey 1969/70, First Round, Government of Ceylon; Matching Employment Opportunities and Expectations, a Program of Action for Ceylon (Geneva, International Labour Organization, 1971), p. 23.

in other allied rural occupations. The prevailing situation is illustrated by Tables 6.2 through 6.4, with data on five countries, which taken together may be regarded as representative of the region.

Several conclusions with a bearing on the linkage between the economic and education sectors seem to follow:

1. Notwithstanding the importance theoretically attached to the value of education as an agent of development, the plan-targets, programs, and implementation measures had been so designed that a vast section of the labor force remained outside the ambit of education.

2. It was unlikely that this picture would alter significantly under these plans, with their emphasis on formal education, since the labor force included in the adult population appeared to be excluded from exposure to education within the formal education system. This underlines a major failing of the present education system, which follows not only the conventional "lock-step" pattern, but also does not offer opportunities for part-time schooling that the large working population in both urban and rural areas could take advantage of on various levels. Thus a critical area of education closely linked to productivity in the entire economic sector seems to have been treated with almost complete indifference in the national plans of the region.

3. Another serious distortion with an important bearing on economic growth is the low participation rate of the large agriculture sector in the post-primary levels of education. It will appear from Table 6.3 that in India, though 131.1 million out of the total labor force of 188.6 million is employed in agriculture, only .3 percent are high school graduates and .1 percent university graduates.

The role of research in development occupies a place of low priority in South and Southeast Asia. There is still an inadequate

TABLE 6.3

Education by Branch of Economic Activity, Selected Countries
(in percentage)

Education	Branch of Economic Activity								
	Agri-culture	Mining	Manu-facturing	Con-struction	Com-merce	Trans-port	Services and electricity	Activities Not Adequately Described	Total
India, 1961									
Illiterate	80.9	79.2	60.4	58.7	32.3	37.5	53.0	—	72.9
Literate without educational level	14.1	14.9	24.5	23.8	37.5	27.7	19.8	—	17.1
Primary to junior basic	4.6	4.4	11.9	10.3	21.7	18.5	13.5	—	7.3
Matriculates	0.3	1.3	2.2	4.8	5.9	10.5	7.7	—	1.7
Intermediate	0.0	0.1	0.4	1.4	1.3	2.6	2.1	—	0.4
Graduates	0.1	0.1	0.5	0.9	1.2	3.1	3.9	—	0.6
Total (in millions)	131.1	5.2	19.9	2.1	7.7	3.0	19.6	—	188.6
Philippines, 1961									
No grade completed	21.4	18.5	15.4	8.1	10.5	4.9	6.4	10.9	16.9
Completed between grades one and seven in elementary school	69.1	61.8	58.8	60.4	54.7	56.3	42.3	65.9	62.8
Completed between grades one and four in high school	8.5	13.6	20.4	26.0	23.8	31.1	20.4	14.0	14.0
At least one year of university	1.0	6.1	5.4	5.5	11.0	7.7	31.0	9.2	6.3
Total (in thousands)	5,617	34	1,114	252	899	322	1,020	122	9,402
Thailand, 1960									
No grade completed	39.3	17.2	33.5	27.9	40.7	12.8	14.9	37.9	37.4
Completed between grades one and four	56.1	72.4	59.9	63.2	50.8	72.6	64.7	58.0	56.7
Completed between grades five and twelve	4.5	10.3	6.4	7.4	7.8	13.4	15.8	4.1	5.5
At least one year of university	0.1	—	0.2	1.5	0.7	1.2	4.7	—	0.4
Total (in thousands)	10,343	29	454	68	744	164	657	219	12,678

Source: OECD, Statistics of the Occupational and Educational Structure of the Labour Force in 53 Countries (Paris: OECD, 1969).

109

TABLE 6.4

Pakistan: Ratio of Civilian Labor Force
by Sectors of the Economy and Education
(per 10,000 employees)

Serial Number	Education	Both Sexes	Male	Female
1	Nil or below primary level	8,723	8,570	9,747
	Agricultural	6,739	6,500	8,338
	Nonagricultural	1,984	2,070	1,409
2	Primary (class V passed) and above	1,277	1,430	253
	Agricultural	681	758	164
	Nonagricultural	596	672	89

Source: "Education and Supply of Manpower in Pakistan 1961-66," Part I, by R.A. Karwanski, Government of Pakistan, Planning Division (mimeographed). Quoted in UNESCO, Progress of Education in the Asian Region: a Statistical Review (Bangkok: UNESCO, 1969), p. 5.

recognition of the fact that the so-called "modern" techniques imported by developing countries have been developed in countries with a very different factor endowment, and as such are often not suited to the factor endowments of the importing country. The need is thus clearly indicated for research in the developing countries to devise techniques best suited to their factor endowments. Bangladesh, the Republic of China (Taiwan), India, Pakistan, and the Philippines seem to have made a beginning in this direction by the establishment of national institutions of scientific and technological research.

Investment in research in countries in the region now ranges from as low as .1 percent to as high as .5 percent of the GNP, not at all commensurate with the task that research is expected to perform. Besides being handicapped by a lack of adequate resources, the quality of research has also in the past suffered from the proliferation of research activities. The limited resources and also the urgency for speedy results make it imperative that research be selective and mission-oriented. Besides assigning a high priority to this critical area in the allocation of resources and stepping up research efforts, it is also necessary to gear the research programs to economic needs. This is a field that offers great possibilities for fruitful cooperation among the countries of the region, as shown by the fine work done by the International Rice Research Institute in the Philippines, which has made "IRRI" a household word in the region.

ECONOMIC GROWTH AND DISTORTIONS IN
THE GROWTH PATTERN

Like most countries in the Third World, those in South and Southeast Asia have also emulated capital-intensive growth models and paid
a terrible social cost for them. Because of demographic and other
economic and social characteristics peculiar to the region, the distortions in their growth patterns were much more grotesque, particularly
in those with a sharply rising population.

As Table 6.5 will show, the growth in the GDP varied from a
little over 3 percent in Ceylon to over 8 percent in the Republic of
China (Taiwan), while the growth of per capita GDP varied from .5 percent to over 4 percent. The growth pattern thus shows a wide variation
within the region. For the major part of this region, on the basis of
population the per capita income is only around U.S. $100 per annum,
which is one of the lowest if allowance is made for the wide disparity
in income distribution.

The GNP also does not measure many factors that vitally affect
the economic life of the people. These are forcefully underscored in
Ceylon's plan: "The trend in GNP does not indicate the growing crisis
in employment, in income disparities and in balance of payments.
Statistics of GNP are insensitive both to distribution of income and to
the virtual stagnation of certain vital sectors of economy."[10]

Another important fact masked by the GNP is that in spite of the
proportionately larger investment in the industrial, or so-called modern
sector, its net contribution to the growth of GDP and employment is only
a fraction of that of the sector of agriculture, as shown in Table 6.7.

It will, however, appear from Table 6.5 that the savings and
investment rates of the region compare favorably with those in the
developing world and also with those of the industrialized countries
in their early periods of development, which are discussed in Chapter 2. Domestic savings financed about 90 percent of the investment
in development. Besides the mobilization of national resources to
finance an increasingly large part of the development program, indicating a trend towards self-reliance, there was a significant increase
in the total development effort, as indicated by the rising investment
shown in Table 6.6.

Agricultural products accounted for 35 to 98 percent of the total
exports from this region. The dependence of these countries on agriculture was, as observed earlier, the outcome of an economic policy
followed for about two centuries during the colonial era. The situation
cannot, however, be corrected by a growth strategy in which investment is concentrated in a small modern industrial sector while agriculture, the main source of growth and also of employment, as shown
in Table 6.7, is not allowed a share in development investment commensurate with its role in growth and employment, as shown in Table 6.8.

TABLE 6.5

Some Basic Indicators of Economic Growth in Selected Asian Countries, 1969

Country	Annual Rate of Growth in GDP	Per Capita GDP (in U.S. dollars)	Rate of Growth per Capita	Gross Domestic Saving	Gross Investment
Bangladesh	4.0	60	0.7	–	–
Burma	4.8	65	2.6	20.7	20.3
Cambodia	5.8	111	2.2	–	–
Ceylon	3.1	129	0.5	12.1	14.5
China, Republic of (Taiwan)	8.1	154	4.5	18.4	19.2
India	4.2	90	1.7 (1968)	8.8	11.3
Indonesia	3.3	95	0.5	–	–
Korea, Republic of (South)	4.9	113	2.3	14.6	20.2
Malaysia	6.1 (West only)	254	3.4	16.0	18.5
Pakistan	6.0	91	3.0	9.7	18.3
Philippines	5.6	164	2.6	17.2	13.2
Singapore	–	449	–	–	–
Thailand	6.1	104	2.9	–	22.1

Sources: International Bank for Reconstruction and Development, World Tables 1971; figures for Bangladesh and Pakistan are from The Fourth Five-Year Plan of Pakistan, (1970-75), except the per capita GDP of Bangladesh, which is from Planning Commission, Government of Pakistan, Report of the Panel of Economists on the Fourth Five-Year Plan (Lahore: Government Printer, 1970), Table 1, p. 2.

TABLE 6.6

Total Investment in Development (Public and Private Sectors):
A Comparison of Past and Present Plans

Country	Previous Plan	Plan Current in 1974
Bangladesh	Taka 3,183.2 million[a] (1972-73 Annual Plan)	Taka 44,550 million (First Five-Year Plan, 1973-78)
Ceylon	—	Rs. 1,420 million (Five-Year Plan, 1972-76)
India	Rs. 104,000 million (Third Plan)	Rs. 534,110 million (Fifth Plan, 1974-79)
Indonesia	—	Rp. 1,059 billion (First Plan, 1969/70-1973/74)
Malaysia	MS. 4,242 million[b] (First Plan)	MS. 13,100 million (Second Plan, 1971-75)
Pakistan	Rs. 29,700 million (Third Plan)	Rs. 35,600 million (Fourth Plan, 1970-75)
Philippines	—	Pesos 4,638 million[b] (new Four-Year Plan, 1971-74)

[a] Based on 1972-73 budget estimates.

[b] Public Sector (Estimated) Expenditure only.

Sources: First Five-Year Plan of Bangladesh (1973-78); Five-Year Plan of Ceylon (1972-76); Draft Fifth Five-Year Plan of India (1974-79); First Five-Year Plan of Indonesia (1969/70-1973/74); Second Five-Year Plan of Malaysia (1971-75); Fourth Five-Year Plan of Pakistan (1970-75); Four-Year Development Plan of the Philippines (1971-74).

TABLE 6.7

Sector Shares in Gross Domestic Product and Employment

Country		Percentage of GDP			Percentage of Employment		
		Agriculture	Industry*	Others	Agriculture	Industry*	Others
Bangladesh	(1972/73)	56.1	8.3	35.6	75	--	--
Burma	(1961)	43.0	18.0	38.0	--	--	--
Cambodia	(1968)	37.7	11.7	40.6	80	4	16
Ceylon	(1968)	38.8	11.6	49.6	49	16	35
China, Republic of (Taiwan)	(1968)	23.1	24.3	52.6	55	16	28
India	(1967)	51.5	14.0	34.5	73	14	13
Indonesia	(1968)	46.1	11.0	42.9	67	8	25
Malaysia	(1968)	30.9	11.1	58.0	51	13	36
Pakistan	(1968)	46.7	11.4	21.9	68	16	16
Philippines	(1968)	34.4	19.1	26.5	58	17	30
Thailand	(1969)	36.1	14.7	49.2	82	4	14

*Manufacturing and mining.

Sources: Employment figures for Indonesia (1961) and Malaysia (1965) are from UNESCO, Asian Model (Paris: the United Nations, 1966); all other employment figures except those for Bangladesh, and all GDP figures except those from Bangladesh, are from IBRD, World Tables, 1971, with the exception of the figure for agricultural employment in the Philippines, which is from the Four-Year Development Plan of the Philippines (1971–74); all figures for Bangladesh are from First Five-Year Plan of Bangladesh (1973–78).

114

TABLE 6.8

Investment in Agriculture as a Ratio of Total Investment
and Share of Employment in Agriculture

	Year	Share of Employment (in percentage)	Proposed Investment in Agriculture as a Percentage of Total Investment
Bangladesh	1972	75	24.0
Ceylon	1965	49	20.0
India	1961	73	17.4
Indonesia	1965	67	30.0
Malaysia	1962	51	26.5
Pakistan	1965	68	13.7
Philippines	1967	58	–

Sources: Share of employment is from IBRD, World Tables, 1971, except in the case of Bangladesh; figures for Bangladesh and all of the proposed investment figures are from First Five-Year Plan of Bangladesh (1973-78); Five-Year Plan of Ceylon (1972-76); Draft Fifth Five-Year Plan of India (1974-79); First Five-Year Plan of Indonesia (1969/70-1973/74); Second Five-Year Plan of Malaysia (1971-75); Fourth Five-Year Plan of Pakistan (1970-75); Four-Year Development Plan of the Philippines (1971-74).

The failure of such a strategy was amply demonstrated during the 1950s and 1960s, not only by the insignificant gain in per capita income but also by the actual decline in the level of living of the majority of the people. The rising unemployment, the inflationary price level, and the fall in real wages, combined with widening income disparity and rapid population growth, aggravated the problems of both poverty and unemployment and made the social and economic confrontations sharper than ever, rocking several countries with political convulsions and ripping one country apart to its very foundation.

THE SPECTER OF POVERTY AND INCOME DISPARITY

Available data on income distribution in the region are as yet far from adequate. According to one study briefly referred to in Chapter 2, the share of the bottom 60 percent of population in the national income was 36 percent in India, 33 percent in Pakistan, and 24.7 percent in the Philippines.

A study on income distribution in India showed a slight decline in the income disparity,[11] but whatever its statistical significance this was hardly of much consequence in alleviating the poverty situation, since the proportion of population with an annual per capita income of U.S. $60 or more was still as low as 11.68 percent of the total population. In fact, poverty has assumed an alarming dimension since 1950. The often-quoted study by Dandekar and Rath estimates the number of people living below the poverty line in India during the 1960s as 40 percent of the population.[12] The Indian Planning Commission, in its recently published paper on the approach to the fifth five-year plan, takes a special note of the rising poverty and admits that persons living in abject poverty constitute between two-fifths and one-half of all population, their number being estimated at over 220 million. If the present strategy of growth were to be relied upon without recourse to direct effective measures to tackle the problems of unemployment and income distribution, projections indicate that it might take another 30 to 50 years for the poorer sections of the people to reach the minimum consumption levels. The Commission also appears to be realistic in its assessment that it would be neither feasible nor desirable to contemplate a waiting period of such duration.[13]

Reliable statistical studies on poverty in Pakistan are not available; inferentially the situation must be worse in view of its wider income disparity. A former chief economist of the government of Pakistan has estimated that "66 percent of the nation's industrial assets, 80 percent of the banking assets, and 79 percent of the insurance assets were controlled by only twenty-two families," all of whom belong to the former West Pakistan.[14] Pakistan's fourth plan records that income distribution had become skewed in the process of economic development. "The symbols of luxury consumption highlighted the gulf between the abject poverty of the 'have-nots' and the ostentatious living of the 'haves.'"[15] The regional disparity, in particular, grew worse, eventually ripping the country apart. The fourth plan admits that the "imbalance in regional income distribution accentuated as

TABLE 6.9

Per Capita Expenditure in Pakistan, 1960-70

	1960/61-1964/65		1965/66-1969/70	
	Development	Revenue	Development	Revenue
East	163.30	73.06	240.00	70.29
West	421.79	261.51	521.05	390.35

Source: Planning Commission, Government of Pakistan, Report of the Panel of Economists on the Fourth Five-Year Plan (Islamabad, May 1970), p. 10.

East Pakistan's per capita income increased at an annual rate of only
.7 percent while in West Pakistan the rate was 2 percent."[16] The
primary cause was the disparate investment, both public and private,
in the two regions, which widened during the 1960s, as shown in
Table 6.9.

When East Pakistan emerged in December 1971 as the independent
state of Bangladesh, it thus started with a backlog of unmitigated poverty, accentuated by an inequitable distribution of growth and a backward economy shattered by the ravages of war.

THE RISE IN UNEMPLOYMENT AND
DECLINE IN REAL WAGES

According to the socioeconomic survey of 1969/70 of the government of Ceylon, the number openly unemployed in Ceylon was as high
as 550,000, constituting 14 percent of the total labor force 15 to 59
years of age. Of those seeking jobs 53 percent had passed the 'O'
Level examination, normally taken after at least ten years of schooling.[17]

During 1951-69 industrial employment in India rose at less than
3 percent per annum, compared to the annual compound rate of 5 percent
increase in factory production. The total number of unemployed, as
indicated by the number of persons seeking jobs who were registered
with the Employment Exchanges, rose to nearly 4.5 million. If allowance is made for the usual underreporting of the unemployed by the
Employment Exchanges, "the number of job-seekers may be placed
roughly at 70 lakhs," or 7 million.[18] The Committee on Unemployment
and Underemployment estimated the number of the educated unemployed
at 2,053,000, including 60,000 engineers,[19] and a recent survey by
the Indian Council of Scientific and Industrial Research reports that
unemployed scientists constituted 21 percent of the educated unemployed.[20] The problem of unemployment assumes a much greater dimension if the vast rural sector is taken into consideration. As many as
17 million persons are likely to remain unemployed by the end of the
fourth plan period.

Real wages and real income suffered a decline in India, due on
the one hand to a rise in the consumer price index from 124 in 1960/66
(1949 = 100) to 213 in 1967/69 and on the other hand to the fact that
the wages of factory workers remained unchanged, in spite of the increase in productivity at an annual rate of 4 percent per year since
1952. Factory labor constitutes only 2 percent of the labor force.

Unemployment in Pakistan in 1964/65 is estimated in its fourth
plan at 7.5 million man-years or 20.4 percent of the total labor force.
The number is of course larger if allowance is made for disguised
unemployment, since the number 36.3 million, which is shown in one
block under "employed and underemployed," is in fact treated as

though it represented only the fully employed. Pakistan's fourth plan
also notes: "Real wages declined by about one-third during the 1960s.
The fixed income groups were hurt by an over-all increase in prices of
about 40 per cent over this decade. The landless labour increased and
there was little gain in the real farm income per head for the small
farmer."[21]

GENERATION OF EMPLOYMENT

The national plans in South and Southeast Asia rightly stress the
ability of the agricultural sector, by far the most important source of
employment at present, to generate additional employment opportunities
and an increase in production. In order to achieve this objective the
plans aim at an expansion of the cultivated area and more intensive
cultivation with improved production techniques.

It is expected that much of the pressure of population on land
can be productively absorbed by taking advantage of the experience of
the "Green Revolution," with more extensive use of the new seeds and
new technology. At the same time such expectations have to be weighed
against the new problems that have come in the wake of the Green
Revolution.

One of them, as pointed out by some critics, is that a new class
of rich farmers is emerging as the main beneficiary of the new agricultural strategy, resulting in increasing mechanization and diminishing
employment.[22] A special committee of the United Nations Food and
Agricultural Organization noted that the introduction of the new high-
yield varieties had greatly reduced the immense food deficits in India
but had resulted in increased social tensions.[23]

These criticisms clearly underscore the need for a careful study
of the possible social and economic consequences of an extended
application of the new technology in agriculture, and adoption of suitable corrective measures where necessary. It is claimed, however,
that there is nothing inherent in the new technology that should necessarily lead to more unequal distribution of farm income or more widespread rural and urban unemployment and that the new technology is
scale-neutral. Its effects on employment might even be slightly positive, with multiple cropping.[24]

The experience of Taiwan indicates the vast potential of agriculture in utilizing the unemployed and underemployed manpower.

The application of the inputs and labor-intensive methods
of cultivation has brought up the average gross agricultural
output per hectare in China (Taiwan) to over seven times
the average for India. Meanwhile, the number of persons
per hectare of farm land in China (Taiwan) is now four

times as great as in India. . . . Thus, the labour-intensive
techniques adopted there do not only provide much larger
employment per hectare of farmland, but also provide employment at a higher productivity per man-year.[25]

Some of the favorable concomitants of a rise in labor productivity
in agriculture are the induced activity in trade and services and also
in urban and rural industries, thus generating new employment opportunities.

It may be noted in this connection that the growth of the modern
nonagricultural sector has provided some outlet for the additional labor
supply in the rural sector but that this has not been adequate to the
need. "While the size of the low and high productivity sectors has
increased in all countries, there has been no significant change in the
deployment of the labour force as between the two sectors in the ECAFE
countries."[26]

It is therefore evident that until the modern nonagricultural sector
has grown to a point where it can absorb the additions to the labor force,
the developing countries in this region will have to depend on agriculture and allied traditional activities for the utilization of the bulk of
this additional labor force. In order to ensure a steady rise in labor
productivity, however, there must be a continuing effort to improve the
production techniques in agriculture. The national plans of most countries recognize this need, though it does not appear to be reflected
properly in their educational programs. The plans also do not indicate
how the sectors of education and agriculture will relate in order to
meet this need within the frame of the overall plans.

INNOVATIVENESS AS AN AID TO EMPLOYMENT GENERATION

Even where the growth strategy is not discriminatory against
labor-using technology, in countries like those in South and Southeast
Asia that have a vast surplus labor supply but a capital scarcity, increased technical unemployment and consequently a lower income per
head may accompany a higher level of labor productivity. The situation
can be materially altered through capital-stretching, to enable more
workers to be employed per unit of stock.

The innovativeness demonstrated by Japan in this direction is
indeed most striking. The device of operating the imported plants to
their fullest capacity by running them at rates far in excess of the
practice in the United Kingdom and the United States stands out as
the simplest but perhaps quantitatively most significant example of
the Japanese innovativeness. In many industries, including mining,
the Japanese have made a rational response to their different factor-
endowments by preferring the use of labor to that of machines if the

same work could be done manually. For example, instead of mechanical conveyor belts, human conveyor belts were devised. In like manner, packaging and inspecting were often done by hand.

An extremely ingenious "capital-stretching innovation of which much use was made in historical Japan is what might be called the plant-saving variety."[27] For example, in cotton weaving "most of the yarn was 'put out' to farm households, with individual looms in farmhouses and worksheds. But, even in the modern factory style spinning industry, preparatory and finishing processes were carried out largely at the cottage level."[28]

The Japanese economic wisdom in exploiting the complementarities between the many small labor-intensive operating units and the large industrial management is at the root of the survival of domestic industry on a subcontracting basis.

> The traditional merchant middleman, as a representative of the subcontracting unit, served as both supplier and market for the goods to be worked up domestically. A specialization of functions between work-shops, even between the members of a given family developed. One roof economies could be achieved in this fashion (by using cheap labor in cooperation with old-fashioned machinery at the workshop level), while economies of scale could be achieved in financing, purchasing and merchandizing stages.[29]

Unfortunately, in South and Southeast Asia the great potential of the tradition of labor-sharing by the members of a family has not been exploited in the same manner in industrial development. Instead the growth technique that was selected undermined employment, increased poverty, and gave rise to industrial slums polluting the environment and denying the urban poor even the free goods of fresh air and pure water.

Ironically enough, the sector of agriculture in the subcontinent showed an imprudent haste in becoming capital-intensive with official encouragement, and even more so in the wake of the Green Revolution. The preposterous lengths to which this irrational policy has been carried are dramatically illustrated by the fact that "until recently farmers in labor-surplus Pakistan and India paid much less for a 35 horsepower tractor than did the farmers in labor-scarce Iowa."[30] There is thus a need for an employment-oriented growth policy in agriculture as well.

DIRECT ATTACKS ON THE PROBLEMS OF POVERTY AND UNEMPLOYMENT

The current national plans of several countries also envisage the generation of employment opportunities through the use of labor-intensive techniques with relatively small increase in investment, in implementing projects of rural construction, farming, and household industries.

The philosophy underlying rural works programs is that the surplus labor in rural areas can be utilized for capital formation, thus strengthening the rural sector with the help of the very factor that is abundant. Several countries in the region have been experimenting with this policy. Among the countries that have developed works programs with voluntary labor, though using different types of organizations, the most notable are Ceylon, China (both Mainland and Taiwan), India, South Korea, and South Vietnam.

In South Vietnam the old tradition of requiring every farmer and his family to contribute ten days' labor a year for public works has been replaced by a system of voluntary labor, especially for types of work that yield them direct benefits. A similar program, shown as "Shramdhan" (labor gift) was in operation in Ceylon and India under the sponsorship of the Community Development Block. The experience of these countries has shown that the success of a rural works program based on voluntary labor depends on the enthusiasm of the farmer, dedicated leadership, and a deep sense of ideological or national commitment, which are not easy to inculcate and sustain.

THE TRANSITION FROM VOLUNTARY
TO COMPULSORY SERVICE

In view of the limitations inherent in a voluntary program, some countries have had recourse to a strategy of compulsion. For example, Iran formed its "Literacy Corps" and "Development Corps" as options for young draftees to the military. South Korea has adopted a similar method. Ceylon has adopted a variant of this method by recruiting volunteers into the armed forces and placing them under military discipline in undertaking specific public works. The induction of the educated youth into this program is intended to serve the additional purpose of finding an outlet for the educated unemployed while introducing changes in the traditional rural society. Some countries may naturally have reservations about any method that involves compulsion, though it is not uncommon to mobilize the armed forces for public works during emergencies such as national calamities. The value of the exposure of youth to the realities of life through work experience seems to be gaining increasing recognition even in the Western countries.

WORK PROGRAMS

Another alternative tried by some countries in the region, Bangladesh being a notable example, is a rural works program based on paid labor carried out under the auspices of the village communities. The first five-year plan of Bangladesh lays a special stress on the works program as a means of generating employment and of community development.

Mainland China has an impressive record of mobilizing rural labor to carry out projects in various fields directly related to the development of the rural areas. These projects include water conservation, afforestation, flood control, land reclamation, and road construction.

The success achieved by China in dealing with the problems of mass poverty and unemployment stands in sharp contrast with the deteriorating situation in the other populous countries of the region. There is now a growing opinion that conventional growth techniques, even with high priority assigned to labor-intensive production methods, are by themselves unlikely to produce any noticeable immediate effect on the appalling and widespread poverty in the region. It is argued that the situation is desperate and calls for a remedy as drastic as the malady is grave. Those who are familiar with the Chinese strategy, however, recognize that it forms a whole package and cannot be taken out in parts for application to a different social situation. An alternative model suited to the social situation in South and Southeast Asia, but capable of producing equally effective results, remains to be found.

The studies so far undertaken, however, seem to fall within the classical economic frame and do not appear to indicate a path towards any major breakthrough within a reasonable span of time. The study in India by Dandekar and Rath estimates that a transfer of Rs. 8,000 million (in 1968/69 prices) to the poorest 35 percent through a program of gainful employment should ensure the minimum income necessary for a minimum standard of living. A second study estimates the cost of such a program for India at Rs. 28,321 million (also in 1968/69 prices).[31] The Indian Planning Commission in "Approach to the Fifth Five-Year Plan" expresses the view based on "available estimates" that "at 1960-61 prices, private consumption of Rs. 20 per mensem would be needed to assure a reasonable minimum level. In present day prices, these figures will have to be multiplied by a factor of about 1.86. At present over 220 million people are estimated to be living below this level."[32]

On this basis the amount required annually for assuring a minimum level of living to the people now living below the poverty line works out at Rs. 98,200 million (Rs. 20 × the 1.86 factor × 12 months × 220 million people). In the "approach paper" a total outlay of Rs. 105,000 million to Rs. 115,000 million is envisaged for employment-intensive programs and a national plan for social consumption, which are together contemplated as a two-pronged attack on poverty. Assuming that the higher amount of Rs. 115,000 million is finally made available in the fifth five-year plan, it means an annual allocation of Rs. 23,000 million, which at present prices and population level is less than a quarter of the yearly requirement indicated in the approach paper. It may of course be argued that allowance should be made for the present income of the poorer sections; however, according to the available data nearly 30 percent of the poorest 40 percent population have a mean per capita income as low as Rs. 8.45 to Rs. 12.18 per month, or less than half of what the Planning Commission considers to be the requirement for a reasonable minimum living level. On the other hand, only a part of the proposed outlay depending on the ratio of the labor-capital content of the programs will result in augmented income, again reduced by the rate of growth in population (2.5 percent per year) and the rate of inflation (4 to 5 percent per year if not more). If the intention is to approach the solution to the problem through an incremental process, and if past experiences of short-falls in the implementation of earlier plans with similar goals are a guide to the pace of progress, the time it will take to banish poverty may very well be not much shorter than what the Commission wisely rejects as "neither feasible nor desirable" as a waiting period.[33]

A notable feature of the paper is the realistic recognition that even if the program of employment creation is successfully carried out the poor "will not be able, with their level of earnings, to buy for themselves all the essential goods and services which constitute quality of life."[34] It proposes that this deficiency be met by a supplementary plan "for the provision of social consumption in the form of education, health, nutrition, drinking water, housing, communications and electricity up to a minimum standard."[35] The plan outlay envisaged for "social consumption" is, however, estimated at Rs. 30,000/35,000 million in five years, which is only 10 percent of the total public sector plan outlay, as compared to 17.5 percent in the fourth plan, and works out at Rs. 12 per person per year, as compared to Rs. 10 per person per year set for the fourth plan. The proposed educational program, with its emphasis on formal elementary education, also does not appear to be directly related to the economic and social needs of the vast adult illiterate population. This wide gap between declared goals and the means proposed to accomplish them has characterized the national plans of the developing countries in the past as well.

The conclusion seems to be inescapable that these shortcomings stem from the constraints inherent in the plan structure and the discipline orientation of the plan formulators. As a result, notwithstanding the welcome shift in the growth philosophy the plan-strategy still seems to retain the basic classical macroeconomic frame, making the changes envisaged in the future plans more likely to be lateral than radical or innovative.

NECESSARY CHANGES IN PLAN-STRUCTURE

It is theoretically possible even within a conventional plan-frame to step up employment creation by public sector activity in the form of a public works program and of investment in infrastructures with a predominantly labor content. However, if this policy cannot be backed up by a corresponding increase in the tempo of production of wage goods, then the general well-being of the society as a whole is jeopardized by inflation in prices, which hurts the poor more than the rich. Even if the economic policy is reoriented with the emphasis shifted to agriculture and to industrial growth subserving agricultural growth, as indicated by the plan-provisions in Bangladesh, India, Indonesia, and Malaysia, progress towards the goal of employment creation and elimination of poverty is unlikely to be fast enough because of the constraints on resource mobilization inherent in a conventional macroeconomic plan-structure and accentuated by the current inflationary trend, which is also historically confirmed by the recent reduction in the size of the annual plan in India.

As a logical corollary to the welfare goals that the countries in the region have set before them, they should cast off the straitjacket of a conventional plan-frame in which they have been confined since 1950 and boldly reach forward towards new frontiers in planning and resource mobilization. One such frontier seems to be that of local planning to mobilize local resources, particularly the human resources available in the extensive non-monetized sector but left untapped so far. Through appropriate institutional arrangements the local communities should be directly involved in formulating and implementing plans for their economic and social development, with the needed skills provided through suitably designed educational programs that are not of the conventional formal type. The vast supply of now unutilized human resources would be transformed into valuable productive capital in developing viable and largely selfsustaining programs. This would imply a major change in plan-concept and techniques, the decentralization of the planning apparatus to a large degree, and the creation of autonomous local institutions.

The Comilla Cooperative Model, conducted under the aegis of the Bangladesh Academy for Rural Development, is a well-tested experiment in institution building at the local level, with a network of village cooperatives for a base and the Thana Cooperative at the apex to plan, coordinate, and secure the needed facilities and also the needed skills in achieving agricultural development goals through collective group efforts.

The Comilla project is also notable as an example of integrated planning at the local level and of the interplay of the various sectors of development, including education, in interrelated and mutually supporting roles.[36]

The Comilla model was successfully tried out in Rangunia in the Chittagong district and has now spread to ten thanas in the district of Chittagong, four in Bogra, three in Noakhali, and one in Patuakhali through local community initiative. The Integrated Rural Development Program of the Bangladesh Government expects the extension of this model to cover the entire country within a period of five years.

In .the transfer of the experience of the Comilla project to the rest of the country, the results will naturally depend on the degree to which the conditions accounting for the original success of this model can be reproduced successfully over a large area, and among these conditions the role of leadership and training, provided by the Academy in the case of the Comilla project, seems to stand out as the most crucial. The model itself will have to be suitably modified to make it more effective by removal of the gaps and pitfalls noticed during its experimental stage.[37] For example, (1) structurally, the institutional frame of the village cooperatives needs to be broadened to include minifarmers and landless laborers and to eliminate the domination of the cooperatives and inefficient use of their facilities by large farmers; (2) motivationally, the central emphasis has to be shifted from the supply of credit to an equitable sharing of the manifold economic and social gains flowing from increasing employment and productivity and improvement in the quality of life; and (3) educationally, the program content should be enlarged and considerably enriched by including elements of social education including population education, education in health and hygiene, and civic education. Above all there is a need for continuing research-in-depth on both the institutional framework and on the design of a rural education program most conducive to rural development.

THE NEED FOR CHANGES IN SOCIAL STRUCTURES, VALUES, AND ATTITUDES

Social structures, values, and attitudes appear to be receiving increasing attention from the planners in South and Southeast Asia as motives for productive effort, but not to the extent warranted by their crucial role in development. Although increasing education and communication have doubtlessly broken down social barriers, the social, cultural, and administrative structures in the region still continue to impede the mobility of labor.

All occupations are still largely governed by conditions that are more ascriptive than universalistic, and the achievement criteria, even if legally recognized, are seldom applied in practice. The allocation of human resources to the various sectors of public service is heavily biased in favor of certain traditionally prestigious classes. The situation is aggravated by the rigid hierarchical stratification of this elite, a lack of mobility from one occupation to another, and vast differences in the pay structures.

The Columbo Plan Bureau points out in a report that

> there are wide differences in the pay structures of craftsmen, technicians, technologists, and engineers in nearly all the developing countries of Asia. In advanced industrial countries, a senior craftsman earns more than a junior technician, and a senior technician more than a junior engineer. Such overlapping is rare in Asia, where in some countries a works engineer of no great seniority will earn ten times as much as craftsmen, and where there are also marked gaps between the pay of craftsmen and technicians, and of technicians and engineers.[38]

For example, in Bangladesh, until the recent reorganization of the structure of public services and pay scales into ten grades, there were as many as 2,200 pay scales in the public sector.[39] The wide disparity between the lowest and the highest salary was another characteristic of the structure of services. In Pakistan the salary of a Central Secretary (Rs. 4,000) was over 33 times the lowest salary (Rs. 120), drawn by a qualified primary school teacher in 1970, and over 118 times the country's GDP per capita.

An important caveat is that an expansion of public sector activity, which is the general policy in the region, does not by itself fulfill the requirement for institutional changes that achieve greater justice without retarding growth. The past experiences of the countries in the region indicate that it is possible for an expanding public sector to coexist with economic and social structures conducive to income disparity and conspicuous consumption, to the benefit of a small elitist privileged group managing the public sector, and also of those serving as its agents employed by the public trading corporations. The latter are "none other than the traders these agencies were meant to replace. Public sector enterprises, that are established with the hoary objective of ensuring commanding heights of economy for the state end up working inefficiently and thus ensuring even higher profits for private units in the same industry that manage to work efficiently."[40] It will thus appear that institutional changes must encompass the entire range of the social structures and values in which the problems of inequality are rooted. If fiscal measures that were intended to curb the growth of inequality have turned out to benefit the large industrial houses, the big landowners, and the rich farmers, that was because these groups formed a part of the power structure in the social hierarchy that was not basically affected by these changes. In spite of some erosion in the rigidity of the class structures by the political changes and expansion of educational opportunities, the social stratifications still follow the traditional lines, with the source of power posited in the upper

strata, including among others the landed aristocracy, the large industrial houses, and the elite bureaucracy. The influence on the making
and implementation of state policy that is still exercised by this small
group is abundantly demonstrated by the course that development and
reform efforts took during the 1950s and 1960s, including such instances
of distinct policy bias in favor of the rich as fiscal concessions and tax
holidays for the private industrialists, price supports for wheat, and
the exemption of agricultural income from taxation. The same bias
accounts for the failure of the land reforms, which seem to lie at the
heart both of equalization policies and of agricultural development.
Notwithstanding the series of legislative measures adopted in India to
reform the land system, "the top 5 per cent of the landowning households
held 36 per cent of the land (forming two-thirds of all assets in the
rural area)."[41] Social realities belied the expectation that a few emis-
saries of the government could, through their occasional visits, alter
the essential pattern of village life and of ownership and operation of
land to counter the entrenched paternalistic influence of the landed
aristocracy.

Pakistan provides a striking example of the vise-like grip in
which the landed aristocracy holds the peasantry and the tremendous
political influence wielded by the former as a consequence. According
to a study by a member of Pakistan's elite civil service, the big land-
lords in Punjab, before they surrendered part of their land under the
1958 Martial Law, had owned an average of 11, 280 acres per person.

> This means that the landlords who were politically active
> in the pre-Ayub era were able to control completely at
> least 20 Punjabi villages. . . . His land more often than
> not was scattered over scores (sometimes hundreds) of
> villages. In each of them, he was the headman, the
> lambardar, the moneylender, the most prominent person.
> Therefore, the political and economic constituency of
> the big landlord was not the 11, 280 acres that he owned,
> but the fifty to one hundred thousand acres of cultivable
> land in the villages in which he was the paramount power.[42]

This finding is confirmed by the fact that the big landowning families
captured 80 percent of the seats in the Punjab legislature in 1951,
90 percent in the Sind legislature in 1953, and also the majority of the
seats in the Northwest Frontier Legislature.

Though it is only in recent years that the flagrant inequalities in
wealth and income have been brought into the focus of public attention,
the roots of the problem are imbedded in history. The existence of a
small oligarchical group as the repository of economic and political
power has been a feature of the highly stratified society in the subcontinent for thousands of years. Even during its heyday before the
advent of the British rule, when the subcontinent enjoyed a favorable

balance of trade mainly by her industrial-sector production of luxury goods, an example of the social inequalities was that these luxury goods were primarily produced for the consumption of the small upper class while many people lived in poverty. Clive is quoted by Jawaharlal Nehru as describing "the city of Murshidabad in Bengal in 1757, as a city extensive, populous, and rich as the city of London, with this difference, that there are individuals in the first possessing infinitely greater poverty than in the last."[43]

For lack of adequate data it is not possible to compare the levels of poverty and inequality during the precolonial and post-independence periods. However, it can be seen that in two important respects they bore the imprint of contrasting value systems. First, during the former period, though inequality and poverty were social realities, conspicuous consumption was not valued as worthy of emulation. On the contrary, many in the upper social strata not only valued but publicly lived an austere life. This self-imposed austerity certainly did not solve the problem of poverty, though it perhaps made poverty more tolerable by making austerity a value worthy of emulation. Secondly, in spite of the economic inequalities existing in precolonial society, the stress was not on the acquisition of wealth as a goal in itself. Those among the wealthy who used their wealth for education, charity, or art enjoyed greater prestige in the society than those who squandered or dissipated it.

This region went through significant changes during the colonial era, not only in its economic status but also in its social structures and values and saw the emergence of a new elite emulating western life styles that depended on imported consumer goods. The traditional value system also underwent a major change, with many new values implanted in the society. Acquisition of wealth and pursuit of profits were accepted as basic incentives to economic and social progress. In the absence of representative political institutions, a well-developed press, and an educated citizenry, which serve as watchdogs in the Western countries, these values soon became corrupted. Profiteering, graft, increasing exploitation of the poor, and widening disparity in income and life styles corroded the entire social fabric. Despite these terrible social consequences, the same values formed the keystones of planning strategy during the post-independence period. As a result, corruption in various forms assumed a horrendous magnitude and operated as the most serious disincentive to work and productivity. The task of combating this growing menace presents a challenge not only to education but also to the political leadership of each country and its society as a whole.

It will thus appear that the goal of distributive justice with growth cannot be realized by fiscal measures and economic controls alone. The strategy will have to include effective measures for changing social structures and values, including the structures of income, wages, and incentives. Soon after its emergence the government of

Bangladesh moved to rationalize salary levels and fixed a ceiling of
33 acres on land owned by a single individual. These are doubtless
measures that are likely to alleviate the existing inequalities; yet in a
country where the vast majority live at a bare subsistence level and the
per capita landholding works out at a mere 2.5 acres, the income and
wages structures and also the size of the land ceiling need to be further
rationalized so as to bring them more in line with the economic realities
and the needs of social justice.

The social realities of the region also seem to indicate the valuable role that some of the traditional values, with proper reorientation
to the ends of both justice and growth, can play in reinforcing the
institutional changes. For example, if the value of austerity can be
reestablished in the life of the people in all ranks of the society, it
will help them to abandon pretentious life styles that the present economy is unable to sustain and to evolve a rational pattern of life that is
capable of realization for the nation as a whole. The "austerity ethic,"
if emulated by the whole society, can also become a more effective
and less inequitous source of motivation to growth than "profit based
income-inequality" has proven to be. In this context it is worthwhile
to underline the view held by Max Weber that Protestant asceticism
boosted productivity in England during 1700-50 because the people
spent less and thus were left with more to save and invest.[44]

It will thus appear from the experiences of the countries in South
and Southeast Asia that the economic and social problems afflicting
them indicate the need for widening the employment base and income
distribution through more extensive and innovative use of labor-intensive
techniques, larger investment in agriculture and allied industries, population control, reform of the system of wages and incentives, adoption
of realistic life styles accompanied by the ethic of shared austerity,
and other changes in social structures and values to make them more
conducive to productivity, decentralization of planning, and institution-
building at the local level to involve the whole community in the development effort. Such a design of growth strategy renders the development
and utilization of the vast human resource potential economically viable
and also creates the precondition for education to change and play a
worthwhile role in contributing the knowledge, skills, attitudes, and
values relevant to the tasks that the people are called upon to perform
within the overall national development.

NOTES

1. A. Maddison, Class Structure and Economic Growth: India
and Pakistan since the Moghuls (New York: W.W. Norton and Co.,
1971), pp. 15-16.
2. Asa Briggs, "Technology and Economic Development" in The
Scientific American 204, no. 3 (1963), p. 55.

3. Muhammad S. Huq, Education and Development Strategy in South and Southeast Asia (Honolulu: East-West Center Press, 1965), p. 5.

4. Five-Year Plan of Ceylon (1972-76), November 1971, p. 121.

5. Fourth Five-Year Plan of India (1969-74), p. 31.

6. Fourth Five-Year Plan of Pakistan (1970-75).

7. Five-Year Development Plan of Indonesia (1969/70-1973/74), Vol. 2c, p. 70.

8. Second Five-Year Plan of Malaysia (1971-75), pp. 253-54.

9. Four-Year Development Plan of the Philippines (1971-74), pp. 66-67.

10. Five-Year Plan of Ceylon, op. cit., pp. 1-2.

11. Mahfooz Ahmed and N. Bhattacharya, "Size Distribution of per Capita Income in India" in Economic and Political Weekly (Bombay, Sameeksha Trust) 7, nos. 31-33.

12. V. M. Dandekar and N. Rath, "Poverty in India" in Economic and Political Weekly (January 2 and 9, 1971), pp. 25-48, 106-66.

13. Indian Planning Commission, Approach to the Fifth Five-Year Plan (1972), p. 3.

14. K. B. Sayeed, "The Breakdown of Pakistan's Political System," International Journal (Ottawa) 27, no. 3 (Summer 1972), p. 403.

15. Fourth Five-Year Plan of Pakistan, op. cit., p. 13.

16. Ibid., p. 1.

17. "The Socio-Economic Survey (1969-70) Government of Ceylon" cited in Dudley Seers, Matching Employment Opportunities and Expectations (International Labour Organization, Geneva, 1971).

18. T. S. Papola, "Employment by Spending" in Economic and Political Weekly (May 6, 1972), p. 925.

19. Ibid., p. 925.

20. The Times of India, December 11, 1972.

21. Fourth Five-Year Plan of Pakistan, op. cit., p. 13.

22. Ranjit K. Sau, "Indian Economic Growth—Constraints and Prospects" in Economic and Political Weekly, annual number (February 1972), pp. 364-65.

23. The New York Times, November 20, 1971.

24. Kenneth W. Thompson, "The Green Revolution: Leadership and Partnership in Agriculture" in The Review of Politics 34, no. 2 (April 1972), pp. 188-89.

25. Economic Development and Human Resources, ECAFE, p. 60.

26. Ibid., p. 49.

27. Gustav Ranis, "Technology, Employment and Growth: Lessons from the Experience of Japan" in Automation in Developing Countries (Geneva: ILO, 1972), p. 49.

28. Ibid., pp. 49-50.

29. Ibid., p. 50.

30. James Grant, "Accelerating Progress through Justice" in International Development Review 14, no. 3 (1972/73), p. 5.

31. Sau, op. cit., p. 369.

32. Indian Planning Commission, op. cit., p. 4.

33. Ibid., p. 1.

34. Ibid., p. 8.

35. Ibid.

36. See Arthur Raper, Rural Development in Action (Ithaca, N.Y.: Cornell University Press, 1970); and Abdul Muyeed, "Strategies Evolved in a Developing System" (unpublished Ph. D. thesis, Michigan State University, 1969).

37. A.H. Khan, Tour of Twenty Thanas (Comilla, BARD, 1971); Anisur Rahman, "Reflections on the Comilla Experiment" (Dacca, January 30, 1973); Rene Dumont, "A Self-reliant Rural Development Policy for Peasantry of Sonar Bangladesh—a Tentative Report" (Dacca: The Ford Foundation, 1973) and "Problems and Prospects for Development in Bangladesh—Second Tentative Report" (Dacca: Ford Foundation, 1973); and M. Nurul Haq, Village Development in Bangladesh (Comilla, BARD, 1973).

38. United Nations, "Economic Development and Human Resources," ECAFE Growth Studies Series No. 3 (Bangkok: ECAFE, 1966), p. 111.

39. Government of Bangladesh, Report of the National Pay Commission (May 1973), pp. 68, 76-77.

40. Arun Shourie, "Growth, Povery and Inequalities" in Foreign Affairs (January 1973), p. 345.

41. S.M. Sundaram, "Studies in Planning Techniques" in Economic and Political Weekly (May 1972), pp. 1061-62.

42. S.J. Burki, "Development of West Pakistan's Agriculture: Interdisciplinary Explanation," paper read at the Workshop on Rural Development in Pakistan, Michigan State University, July 1971, pp. 17-18.

43. J. Nehru, Glimpses of World History (London: Lindsay Drummond, 1945), p. 417.

44. Max Weber, The Protestant Ethic and the Spirit of Capitalism (New York: Charles Scribner's Sons, 1930).

7

**EDUCATIONAL SYSTEMS
IN SOUTH AND
SOUTHEAST ASIA**

The educational systems in the Asian region vary widely in their structure and characteristics of production function. They bear the imprint of the historical forces that shaped them during the three phases of their evolution noted in Chapters 1 and 6. The indigenous system of education, which centered around the prevalent religions during the earliest period, shrank greatly in size but did not altogether die out when the Western system of education was established during the colonial period. The latter gradually became the main form of education, but its number of schools did not grow fast enough to meet the rising demand. The vacuum thus created was filled by private schools, some of which were run on commercial lines and charged high fees.

As a result, as many as three subsystems of education will be found in many countries in the region, representing (1) the state schools, which are government managed and financed; (2) the private schools, which are independent or government aided; and (3) the indigenous schools. The first and second subsystems are the prevalent forms of education and are structured alike academically, though the first by its rapid growth is increasingly overshadowing the second in size.

STRUCTURAL CHARACTERISTICS

Table 7.1 summarizes the structural characteristics of the main types of education, including both public and private schools, in the Asian region. Entry into the system is ordinarily through Grade 1 of the first level or through preprimary classes where they exist. Therefore the pressure applied by the growth of population, combined with the goal of universal primary education, is felt first at the grade that is the point of entry into the system and then gradually carried forward to the higher grades one year at a time.

TABLE 7.1

Structure of Educational Systems in Selected Asian Countries

Country	First Level			Second Level (General)			Third Level
	Entrance Age	Total	Duration (in years) In Subdivisions	Entrance Age	Total	Duration (in years) In Subdivisions	Entrance Age
Bangladesh[a]	6	5	–	11	7	5-2	18
Burma[b]	6	4	–	10	3/5	3-2	15
Cambodia	6	6	3-3	12	7	4-3	18
Ceylon	5	5	–	10	7	4-3	17
China (Taiwan)	6	6	–	12	6	3-3	18
India[c]	6	5/7/8	5-3	13/14	4/5	2-2, 3-2	17/18
Indonesia	6	6	–	12	6	3-3	18
Japan	6	6	–	12	6	3-3	18
Korea, Republic of	6	6	–	12	6	3-3	18
Laos	6	6	–	12	7	4-3	19
Malaysia	6	6	–	12	7	3-2-2	19
Nepal[d]	6	5	–	11	5	3-2	16
Pakistan	5/6	5	–	10/11	7	5-2	17/18
Philippines[e]	7	6	4-2	13	4	2-2	17
Singapore	6	6	–	12	6	4-2	18
Thailand[f]	7	7	4-3	14	5	3-2	19
Vietnam, Republic of (South)	6	5	3-2	11	7	4-3	18

[a]Major educational reforms are now underway in Bangladesh.

[b]In the current reorganization in Burma the primary level is to be five years, followed by four years of lower secondary and two years of secondary, the total duration of school-level education being eleven years.

[c]The patterns in India differ from state to state, but the most common are five years, eight years divided into 5-3, or seven years for first level. The duration of second level changes accordingly to make either eleven or twelve years of school-level education.

[d]In Nepal, grades 11 and 12 form intermediate classes and are part of colleges.

[e]The presidential commission to survey Philippine education has since recommended the reorganization of school education into two stages, elementary (first level) for six years, and secondary (second level) for five years.

[f]Until 1962 first-level education in Thailand was four years; in 1962 it was extended to seven years. The data refer to seven-year first-level education

Sources: First Five-Year Plan of Bangladesh (1973-78); Five-Year Plan of Ceylon (1972-76); Fourth Five-Year Plan of India (1969-74); First Five-Year Plan of Indonesia (1969/70-1973/74); Second Five-Year Plan of Malaysia (1971-75); Fourth Five-Year Plan of Pakistan (1970-75); Four-Year Development Plan of the Philippines (1971-74); and UNESCO, Progress of Education in the Asian Region (Bangkok: the United Nations, 1969).

TABLE 7.2

Distribution of Enrollment by Levels of Education,
Asian Region, 1968

Level	Enrollment	Percent of Total Enrollment
First level	109, 078, 000	74.9
Second level	32, 275, 000	22.1
General	30, 221, 000	20.7
Vocational	1, 722, 000	1.2
Teacher training	332, 000	0.2
Third level	4, 361, 000	3.0
Total	145, 714, 000	100.0

Source: UNESCO, Development of Education in Asia: Third Asian Ministers' Conference (Singapore: UNESCO, 1971).

The distribution of the total enrollment by level of education in the Asian region in 1968 is shown in Table 7.2. The educational pyramid statistically represented in the above table typifies the structure of the educational systems in the developing countries of the region, the enrollment being the largest in the first level, declining sharply to less than a third at the second level, and then tapering off altogether in the third level. The structural skewness thus emerges as a major characteristic of the educational systems and is a serious problem in most of the countries in the region. Notable exceptions are Japan and the Philippines.

TRENDS IN ENROLLMENT GROWTH

The growth phenomenon in education is common to all countries of the developing world, but the Asian region has experienced the growth in education at a much faster rate, and its quantitative dimension dominated the development scene for the sheer size of it, the total enrollment having practically trebled itself, from 49.9 million in 1950 to 145.7 million in 1968.

Several forces have operated to produce this rapid growth. As earlier mentioned, education was sought in this region because of the cultural value traditionally attached to it, because of the social status that came to be associated with it, and because of the economic

advantages that it was supposed to confer. More importantly, following
independence the people also came to look upon education as a birth-
right, as an instrument of national development, and as a means of
access to the benefits of development.

Under the combined action of all these factors, the educational
systems received a much larger input, to which the rapid growth of population and the changing age-structure added a special thrust, as shown
in Table 7.3. It will appear from this table that the structure of the
Asian population has a large and growing component that is under 25
years old, having risen from 60.7 percent of the total population in
1960 to 62 percent in 1970, and likely to rise further during the 1970s,
with a corresponding increase in the school-age population and larger
pressure on the educational systems of the region than on those of the
more developed regions, as shown in Table 7.4, which shows that of
the estimated addition of 185.4 million the school-age group only 2.9
million are likely to be in the more developed regions, while 182.3
million will be in the less developed regions. Of the latter, 101.5
million will be in the Asian region. According to one estimate, "it will
require an increase of over 50 percent in schooling facilities in about
15 years just to maintain the enrollment ratios at the existing level."[1]

The Asian region, which has experienced a faster growth rate in
education since 1950 than the rest of the world, has also a vastly
greater educational challenge to meet in the future. If all three levels
of education are taken into consideration, this challenge becomes
still more formidable. The wide educational gap between the Asian
region and the developed regions is demonstrated by the enrollment
ratios, as summarized in Table 7.5.

If the rate of increase in the enrollment ratio, making allowance
for increasing population in the 5- to 24-year age group, remains at
about one percent per year, as it did during the 1950s and 1960s, it
will take the Asian region 27 years to attain the level of enrollment of
Europe in 1965 and 44 years to attain that of North America.

Another interesting trend in the growth of enrollment has been
that although the rate of growth showed considerable variations within
the same level from period to period, during a given period it varied
directly with the level of education; that is, the higher the level of
education, the greater the rate of growth, as shown in Table 7.6.

The higher rate of growth in the second and third levels seems
to be caused primarily by the pressure applied by the rapidly increasing
enrollment in the first level on the higher levels, which started from a
comparatively narrower base, as indicated by a historical study of the
distribution of enrollment by levels, which is summarized in Table 7.7.
The plan-strategy of many of the countries that stressed second- and
third-level education in order to step up the supply of critical manpower was also an important contributory factor. In any case this is
clearly a trend in the direction of a better interlevel balance in the
educational systems of the region. It represents an important aspect

TABLE 7.3

Age Structure of the Asian Population, 1960-80

Age	Population in Millions			Population in Percent		
	1960	1970	1980	1960	1970	1980
Up to 24 years	501	665	879	60.7	62.0	62.2
25 years and over	324	407	533	39.3	38.0	37.8
All ages	825	1,072	1,412	100.0	100.0	100.0

Source: UNESCO, Development of Education in Asia: Third Asian Ministers' Conference (Singapore: UNESCO, 1971).

TABLE 7.4

School-Age (First Level) Population (5-14 Years), 1970-80

Region	Population, Five to Fourteen Years (in millions)		Increase	
	1970	1980	(in millions)	(in percent)
World	836.2	1,021.6	185.4	22.2
More developed regions	196.5	199.4	2.9	1.5
Less developed regions	639.6	821.9	182.3	28.5
Asian region	277.1	378.6	101.5	36.6

Source: UNESCO, Development of Education in Asia: Third Asian Ministers' Conference (Singapore: UNESCO, 1971).

TABLE 7.5

Enrollments as Percentage of Population in the Five- to Twenty-four Year Age Group

	1950	1960	1965
Europe	46.5	53.7	58.7
North America	59.3	73.0	74.1
Asian Region	17.3	25.2	30.6 (31.9 in 1967)

Source: UNESCO, Progress of Education in the Asian Region: A Statistical Review (Bangkok: UNESCO, 1969).

TABLE 7.6

Growth of Asian Enrollment by Levels of Education, 1950-68

	First Level	Second Level	Third Level
1950-55	4.8	7.7	10.4
1955-60	5.9	9.1	9.7
1960-65	6.4	9.2	11.1
1965-68	3.7	7.5	11.6

Source: UNESCO, Development of Education in Asia: Third Asian
Ministers' Conference (Singapore: UNESCO, 1971).

TABLE 7.7

Distribution of Enrollment in Asia by Levels of Education
as a Percentage of Total Enrollment, 1950-68

Year	First Level	Second Level	Third Level
1950	83	15	1.4
1955	81	17	1.9
1960	79	19	2.2
1965	77	21	2.3
1968	74.9	22.1	3.0

Source: UNESCO, Development of Education in Asia: Third Asian
Ministers' Conference (Singapore: UNESCO, 1971).

TABLE 7.8

Female Enrollment as a Percentage of Total Enrollment in Asia

Year	All Levels	First Level	Second Level	Third Level
1950	30	32	19	15
1955	33	35	22	21
1960	35	37	26	21
1965	37	39	29	24
1967	38	40	30	27

Source: UNESCO, Progress of Education in the Asian Region: A
Statistical Review (Bangkok: UNESCO, 1969).

of the production function of the educational systems that cannot be
overlooked by the countries of South and Southeast Asia in planning
future development of education.

FEMALE ENROLLMENT

In aggregation for the region as a whole, the growth pattern
showed a slight improvement in the ratio of female enrollment to total
enrollment. Here also the degree of improvement varied with the levels
of education, being greater in the upper levels, as shown in Table 7.8.
There are, however, wide variations within the region, since the ratio
of total female enrollment is still very low in some of the countries
with very large populations. In 1965, for example, it ranged from 36
percent in the first level to 19 percent in the third level in India and
from 28 percent in the first level to 17 percent in the third level in
Pakistan.

TEACHER INPUT

The teacher input increased from 1.43 million in 1950 to 4.6 million in 1967; that is, by 184 percent, compared to an increase of about
200 percent in student input. The increase in the number of teachers
by levels of education is shown in Table 7.9.

The rate of increase in teacher input in the first level was slower
than the rate of growth in student input, with the result that the pupil-
teacher ratio rose from 38 in 1955 to 45 in 1967. This ratio was much
higher in some countries; for example, it was 50 in Cambodia (1967),
52 in India (1967), and 55 in Burma (1967). The pupil-teacher ratio in
the second level of education gained slightly, however, from 22 to 20,
and remained unchanged at 19 in the third level.

QUALIFICATION OF TEACHERS

There is a considerable information gap in regard to the qualifications of teachers in the region. One welcome trend, however, is
the movement in the direction of raising the qualifications of teachers
with the development of second and third levels of education.

For example, in Bangladesh the number of trained teachers in
the primary stage (Grades 1 through 5) rose from 43 percent in 1947-48
to 65 percent in 1969-70, and of the total number of teachers, trained
and untrained, 73 percent were graduates of high school or possessed

TABLE 7.9

Total Numbers of Teachers and Increase by Level of Education, in Asia, 1950-67

Year	All Levels Number (in thousands)	Index	First Level Number (in thousands)	Index	Second Level Number (in thousands)	Index	Third Level Number (in thousands)	Index
1950	1,427	100	1,047	100	342	100	38	100
1955	1,976	138	1,373	132	542	158	62	162
1960	2,724	191	1,691	163	932	272	102	265
1965	3,670	257	2,228	215	1,289	376	153	400
1967	4,057	284	2,336	225	1,534	448	187	486

Source: UNESCO, Progress of Education in the Asian Region: A Statistical Review (Bangkok: UNESCO, 1969).

a higher qualification in 1969-70. In India the number of qualified teachers, that is, graduates of high school and above, in primary schools increased from 10.3 percent in 1950-51 to 51 percent in 1965-66, and in the higher primary stage the ratio of qualified teachers rose from 47.2 percent to 60 percent during the same period. The Indian Education Commission, in its 1964-66 report, estimated that at this rate of growth it might take as long as 20 to 25 years to ensure that every primary school teacher had at least completed 10 years of general education.

In Thailand the ratio of qualified teachers increased from 24.1 percent to 49.1 percent in the elementary schools (Grades 1 through 6) and from 83.1 percent to 85.2 percent in the secondary schools (Grades 7 through 12) during 1961-67. In South Korea the number of teachers who had nine years of basic schooling or less was reduced to 10.6 percent of the teaching force by 1967. The problems that faced most countries in the region were those of upgrading the qualifications of the teachers already in service; attracting persons with higher basic education, such as specialists in the new scientific and technical subjects, to the teaching profession; and expanding the capacity of the teacher training institutions. What is disturbing in this connection is that the salary structure in most countries operates against the teaching profession. In some countries the teachers' salary scales have been raised, but the increases have often been neutralized by the rise in prices.

THE CONVERSION MECHANISM OF EDUCATIONAL SYSTEMS

Educational systems in the region have been developed on a lock-step pattern, and entry for students is through a single point that is the bottom grade of the system, as noted earlier. The "output" of one grade becomes the "input" of the next higher grade.

An important indicator of the efficiency of the conversion mechanism is the output-input ratio from grade to grade and from level to level, subject, of course, to the goals and policies of education. The present trend is one of huge wastage at the first level, as discussed later in this chapter, the rate of wastage declining with the upward movement of students. The dropout rate, however, rises sharply between levels of education, as shown in Table 7.10, the dropout rate and the large percentage of failure at final examinations indicating the "selective" character of education beyond the first level.

TABLE 7.10

Asian Enrollments in the Terminal Grade of First Level
and Commencing Grades of Second Level

Country	Year	Last Grade of First Level		First Grade of Second Level, Cycle 1		First Grade of Second Level, Cycle 2	
		Number of Grade	Enroll-ment	Number of Grade	Enroll-ment	Number of Grade	Enroll-ment
Bangladesh	1967/68	5	529,731	6	288,242	9	163,441
Ceylon	1964	6	179,833	7	149,544	11	22,644
India	1963	5	4,572,843	6	2,593,472	9	1,816,989
Indonesia	1960	5	707,445	—		—	
Malaysia	1967	6	180,907	7	176,704	10	46,508
Philippines	1964	6	540,911	7	300,915	9	185,346

Source: UNESCO, Development of Education in Asia: Third Asian
Ministers' Conference (Singapore: UNESCO, 1971); and UNESCO,
Education in Pakistan (Paris: UNESCO, 1970).

MAJOR OBJECTIVES AND PROBLEMS

All the developing countries in the region are committed to the
objective of universal primary education. Universal basic education
is, of course, an essential tool in the development of human resources,
which in this study is viewed as central to both economic and social
development. The developing countries in this region have usually
approached this task by expanding the facilities of primary education
for the school-age population within the formal school system, hoping
thereby to reach the future generations of the adult population. Towards
this goal they have been making heroic efforts since 1950, with considerable inspiration and assistance from UNESCO, through conferences,
seminars, studies, and advisory services. The progress made by the
countries in the region in realizing the goal of universal primary education is indicated in Table 7.11.

It will thus appear that a number of the developing countries in
the region, such as Burma, Ceylon, the Republic of China (Taiwan),
South Korea, Malaysia, and the Philippines have either actually
achieved or are very near achieving the goal of universal enrollment
in primary education. Except Burma, all of these countries already
had 60 percent or more of the age group in school at the beginning of
the 1950s. Countries with large population, such as India, Indonesia,

TABLE 7. 11

Ratio of Enrollment to School-Age Population in the First Level
for Selected Asian Countries, 1950-67
(in percent)

Country	1950	1955	1960	1965	1967	Grades
Bangladesh	–	40	–	47	55	1-5
					(1969/70)	(ages 6-11)
Burma	20	56	71	77	106	1-4
				(1964)		(ages 6-9)
Cambodia	27	48	59	72	74	1-4
					(1966)	(ages 6-11)
Ceylon	89	89	93	93	–	1A-5
				(1964)		(ages 5-10)
China, Republic	63	80	100	104	105	1-4
of (Taiwan)						(ages 6-11)
India	42	50	62	76	76	1-5
						(ages 6-11)
Indonesia	39	53	59	80	63	1-6
			(1961)			(ages 6-11)
Korea, Republic	83	86	94	98	102	1-6
of (South)						(ages 6-11)
Malaysia	61	74	86	90	94	1-6
						(ages 6-11)
Pakistan	–	30	–	–	47	1-5
					(1969/70)	(ages 6-10)
Philippines	124	89	92	104	107	1-6
				(1964)		(ages 6-12)
Thailand	80	80	81	77	77	1-6
						(ages 7-13)

Sources: UNESCO, Progress of Education in the Asian Region: A
Statistical Review (Bangkok: UNESCO, 1969); and Fourth Five-Year
Plan of Pakistan (1970-75).

Bangladesh, and Pakistan, are among those lagging behind. India,
Thailand, and Cambodia, which have reached the level of about 75 percent, may be able to attain the goal by 1980. Some of the other countries may also find this possible if a vigorous program can be mounted
to eliminate the interferences with the conversion mechanism of the
education systems, both internal and external. These interferences
tend to retard the faster enrollment of the school-age female population
and hold back improvements in the retention rate.

Both of these problems are intimately bound up with several
factors, some lying within the educational system, such as physical

facilities, motivation, and the contents and methods of education, and some outside the system, such as social attitudes towards female education, home environment, and the economic dependence of some families on the employment of school-age children.

THE PROBLEM OF RETENTION

By far the most intractable problem before most of the countries, including some that have achieved universal enrollment, is that of the low rate of retention resulting in a high rate of wastage, which has accompanied expansion of education in this region, the rate of wastage being most pronounced in the first level.

Though wastage is commonly regarded to have two components, namely "the drop-out" and "the repeater," it also has a third, which is qualitative in character, and not so tangible as the other two components. This third component is represented by the degree of retardation in intellectual and educational development due to an unfavorable environment within or outside the school, or in other words by the difference between the potential for educational development and the actual development. Though difficult to measure, this qualitative wastage can be enormous even where the retention rates and the output are high quantitatively, if the school curricula, technology, and tools of evaluation are not adequate for the development of each individual's full potential.

Even if wastage is considered only in terms of "drop-out" and "repeater," which lend themselves to quantitative measurement, its magnitude is staggering. It is estimated on the basis of regional aggregation that out of an enrollment of 24.5 million pupils in Grade 1 in 1960, approximately 11.5 million, or 47 percent, only reached Grade 4, while the remainder, or 53 percent, dropped out. The retention ratios in Table 7.12 show that the rate of wastage is the highest between grades 1 and 2.

TABLE 7.12

Retention Ratios in the First Four Grades of
Primary Education, Asian Region

Grade	Year	Enrollment (in thousands)	Retention Ratios from Grade One (in percentage)
1	1960	24,520	100.0
2	1961	15,735	64.2
3	1962	13,366	54.5
4	1963	11,530	47.0

Source: UNESCO, Progress of Education in the Asian Region: A Statistical Review (Bangkok: UNESCO, 1969).

TABLE 7.13

Indices of Educational Wastage at the First Level in Some Asian Countries

Country	Normal Duration (in years)	Unit-cost (in pupil-years invested)	Input-Output Ratio[a]	Overall Drop-out[b]	Output by Number of Years Repeated[b]					
					Total	0	1	2	3	4 or more
Cambodia	6	14.9	2.48	640	360	88	109	83	48	32
China, Republic of (Taiwan)	6	6.21	1.04	88	912	912	–	–	–	–
India	5	8.91	1.78	549	451	155	153	92	51	–
Iran	6	7.55	1.26	221	779	390	268	121	–	–
Korea, Republic of (South)	6	6.38	1.06	132	868	868	–	–	–	–
Malaysia (West)	6	6.65	1.11	155	845	845	–	–	–	–
Thailand										
Lower stage	4	5.25	1.31	179	821	393	270	114	44	–
Upper stage	3	3.42	1.14	137	863	723	119	21	–	–

[a]Ratio of two columns preceding

[b]Based on an initial intake of 1,000 pupils in Grade 1.

Source: UNESCO, Development of Education in Asia: Third Asian Ministers' Conference (Singapore: UNESCO, 1971).

Table 7.12 is based on the "cohort method," wherein enrollment in Grade 1 is followed up from year to year. It does not, however, reveal the number of repeaters, and therefore it cannot be regarded as a full measure of the wastage, although adequate information on the repeaters is not available. Different aspects of wastage and the social and economic factors with which they are bound up call for more research on this problem than has hitherto been made.

A 1971 survey conducted by UNESCO on the basis of repetition data provided by seven countries gives a more accurate picture of the wastage.

In this survey, "the unit cost of wastage for a cohort is the total number of pupil-years absorbed by a cohort before completing or leaving a stage, divided by the number of pupils successfully completing the stage. The input-output ratio is the total number of pupil-years invested in a cohort expressed as a ratio of the minimum number of pupil years required by those pupils who completed the stage."[2] The survey yielded some interesting results in the form of the indices of wastage given in Table 7.13.

It will appear from the table that the "costs" of effective output as indicated by the input-output ratio vary widely. For example, these "costs" in the Cambodian system (2.48) are nearly two and a half times as much in terms of pupil years invested as would have been minimally required, compared to 1.78 in India, 1.26 in Iran, and 1.31 in Thailand. On the other hand, in the Republic of China (Taiwan), South Korea, and Malaysia, with automatic promotion systems, the input-output ratio is near the optimum.

Even if there were no repeaters, it would appear from Table 7.12 that the educational systems of the region lost as much as 53 percent of their student input of 1960, spread over the period of 1961-63 as follows: (1) 35.8 percent at the end of the first year; (2) 9.7 percent at the end of the second year; and (3) 7.5 percent at the end of the third year, indicating that 67 percent of the wastage occurred at the end of the first year. Two conclusions seem to follow from the available data: that the first year of schooling was most crucial to the final output and that in the present state of the conversion mechanism the waste product at the first level added more to the school-age population remaining outside school than did the population growth.

There is, however, another disturbing dimension to the problem. Viewed in terms of development of human resources, the ratio of the school-age population outside the school system does not convey a complete idea of the magnitude of the educational task before the Asian countries; to this number must be added the vast part of the labor force that is illiterate or lacking the basic education needed for learning occupational skills.

It is difficult to determine correctly the extent of illiteracy in the Asian region, since the available data on the subject are inadequate and out of date. Considerable confusion in the interpretation of data

TABLE 7.14

Growth in the Number of Illiterates
in the Asian Region, 1950-70

Year	Number of Illiterates	Percentage of the Population Fifteen Years and Over
1950	307 million	76
1960	322 million	66
1970	355 million	58

Source: UNESCO, Development of Education in Asia: Third Asian Ministers' Conference (Singapore: UNESCO, 1971).

is also caused by the existing differences in definitions, classifications, and reference periods.

By the results of the census of 1960 and by enrollment ratios for the subsequent years, the number of illiterates among the adult population (15 years and over) in the region is estimated in Table 7.14. It will appear that, while the ratio of illiteracy was reduced by about 18 percent between 1950 and 1970, still over half of the adult population remains illiterate, and the total number of illiterates has actually increased by nearly 50 million. The volume of existing illiteracy and its growing trend underline not only a major deficiency in the educational systems of the region but also the fact that at this rate of growth of literacy, half of the labor force will remain illiterate at the end of the 1970s, with its inevitable adverse effect on labor productivity and the pace of modernization. The need is therefore indicated for programs of adult education outside the formal system to deal with this problem. However, the situation varies considerably from country to country within the region, as Table 7.15 will show.

There is a close link between wastage and illiteracy: in the Asian region much of the wastage in the early stages of the first level of education directly adds to the number of illiterates, in the absence of significant arrangements for education outside the formal system. The situation in regard to wastage and illiteracy also varies widely from country to country. At the same time, so far as growth in per capita income, enrollment, ratio of retention, and ratio of literacy are concerned, some interesting trends and relationships are observable.

It will appear from Table 7.15 that the countries that have achieved the highest retention ratios in the first level of education are also the countries with the highest rates of growth in overall school enrollment as a ratio of total population and the highest GDP per capita. This seems to suggest that wastage is a factor of the overall state of education and the economy, although bearing an

TABLE 7.15

Growth in Population, Economy, and First Level Education, with Rates
of Retention and Literacy, in Selected Asian Countries

Country	Density per Km²	Rate of Growth (in percentage)	GDP per Capita (in U.S. dollars)	Ratio of Enrollment to Total Population (in percentage)	Ratio of First Level Enrollment to Age Group (in percentage)	Percentage of First Grade Retained	Number of Pupils per Teacher, First Level	Literacy (in percentage)
Bangladesh	530	3.3	60 (1969)	10.8 (1972)	55	30 (5)	48	22.0
Burma	39	2.1	59 (1968)	13.2 (1967)	106	18 (4)	55	67.7
Ceylon	182	2.6	155 (1968)	24.0 (1964)	93	53 (6)	29	75.1
China, Republic of (Taiwan)	374	3.2	257 (1969)	24.9 (1967)	105	91 (6)	42	53.9
India	160	2.5	90 (1968)	14.1 (1967)	76	36 (5)	52	27.8
Indonesia	59	2.9	95 (1969)	13.8 (1967)	63	38.6 (6)	45	42.9
Korea, Republic of (South)	441	2.8	180 (1969)	23.3 (1967)	102	87 (6)	60	70.6
Malaysia	31	2.7	309 (1969)	21.0 (1967)	94	84 (6)	28	23.5
Pakistan	74	2.5	91 (1969)	9.5 (1966)	47	48 (5)	41	18.8
Philippines	120	3.5	164 (1969)	21.8 (1963)	107	53 (6)	34	71.9
Singapore	581	2.7	681 (1969)	27.8 (1967)	101	108 (6)	30	49.8
Thailand	66	3.1	140 (1969)	16.8 (1967)	77	15 (5); 12 (7)	34	67.7
Japan	273	1.1	1218 (1969)	21.7 (1966)	100	99 (6)	27	97.8

Sources: First Five-Year Plan of Bangladesh (1973-78); Five-Year Plan of Ceylon (1971-76); Fourth Five-Year Plan of India (1969-74); Second Five-Year Plan of Malaysia (1971-78); First Five-Year Plan of Indonesia (1969/70-1973/74); Fourth Five-Year Plan of Pakistan (1970-75); Four-Year Plan of the Philippines (1971-74); UNESCO Statistical Year Book (New York: the United Nations, 1969); IBRD, World Tables (1971), Table 3; UNESCO, Asian Region Statistical Review (Bangkok: the United Nations, 1969).

inverse relationship to them. Apart from the well-recognized adverse
effect of economic backwardness and consequent poor home environment on education, a more direct evidence of this influence on the
dropout rate is child labor between 10 and 14 years, which runs as
high as 39.2 percent among male children in India, 22.6 percent in
Indonesia, 49.3 percent in Pakistan, and 40.5 percent in Thailand.
In all of these countries the retention rate is among the lowest.

The relationship observed between enrollment and the retention
rate seems to indicate that the social and economic conditions favorable to the overall growth of education, all levels taken together, also
favor retention and that wastage does not necessarily increase with
the expansion of an education system. However, the same cannot be
said about the relationship between the retention ratio and the enrollment ratio in the first level only. For example, Burma has a first-level
enrollment ratio of 106 percent, but a retention in Grade 4 of 18 percent only. Thailand has a first-level enrollment ratio of 77 percent,
but a retention ratio in Grade 5 of only 15 percent and in Grade 6 only
12 percent.

It is also interesting to note that the same degree of correlation
does not seem to exist between growth in enrollment and growth in
literacy. Malaysia and Singapore, each with a high enrollment ratio
and also a high retention ratio, have a rather high illiteracy rate, indicating the slow impact of formal schooling over the backlog of adult
illiteracy.

The history of educational growth in the region seems to suggest
that restriction of education is not necessarily the direction along
which the solution to the problem of wastage should be sought. The
same inference is also suggested by the historical data on the growth
of education in the United States, which has among the industrial
countries the highest overall enrollment as a ratio of the total population. Expansion of education and increase in the retention rate in the
United States have moved together, along with economic growth. For
example, while the enrollment of the population 5 to 17 years of age
in the United States rose from 57 percent in 1869-70 to 78.3 percent
in 1919-20, the retention rate was no more than 47 percent in grade 10
and 34.4 percent in grade 12, even in 1924-25. However, both the
enrollment rate and retention ratio continued to rise; in 1949/50 the
retention ratio reached 80 percent in grade 10. It was 63.2 percent in
grade 12 in 1950/51. This time-lag between growth in enrollment and
reduction of the retention rate, viewed in its historical perspective,
underscores an important characteristic of the growth process that the
planner cannot altogether overlook in charting out a strategy to deal
with the problem.

All of the countries in the Asian region that have reached a
retention ratio of 50 percent or more have achieved an enrollment of
over 20 as a percentage of total population. Although it is not correct
to generalize, this strong correlation points in the direction of a

possible critical level in enrollment growth, an interesting problem for
research.

If over 50 percent of the children enrolled in Grade 1 drop out
within the first four years, thus involving the wastage of a proportionate amount of scarce resources, an obvious strategy would appear to
be to halt the expansionary trend in enrollment and concentrate on
measures likely to reduce and if possible eliminate the wastage.

What are the choices available in this regard? Hypothetically
it may be argued that the number of students in the last grade of the
primary stage is a guide to the maximum enrollment that the educational
system in its present stage of development can effectively absorb. If
the future entry to the first grade were limited to a number not far in
excess of this number, the output-input ratio and also the benefit-cost
ratio would be likely to be maximized, and the resources now wasted
would be available for application to the much-needed qualitative
improvement of education and for meeting educational needs in other
critical areas. This model, irrespective of any consideration of the
many questionable assumptions underlying it, can be ruled out as
altogether unrealistic, since any cut-down in the enrollment in Grade 1
is totally impracticable.

A second option that suggests itself is that the enrollment in
Grade 1 need not be reduced but stabilized at the current limit and that
the additional resources available be applied to intensive efforts to
retain the number already enrolled through the enrichment and strengthening of the curricula and of the teacher and technology inputs.

There is, however, a lack of evidence based on reliable empirical
studies that would show the precise relationship between the rate of
retention and the rate of investment in teacher and technology inputs
in a mass-education system if the expansionary tendency is held under
check. There is no way to find this out from historical data either, because throughout the 1950s and 1960s the trend of enrollment has been
one of unchecked expansion at all levels and in all types of education
including teacher education.

As shown in Table 7.16, the growth trends in two countries that
are among those with the lowest retention rates show that the enrollment in the last grade of the primary stage increased at a rate greater
than the rate of growth in total primary enrollment and that the ratio
of enrollment in the final grade to the total primary enrollment also
showed a substantial increase. Another remarkable trend was the
significant increase in the number of qualified teachers during the
same period.

While the positive correlation between the increase in the quality
of teacher input and the rising ratio of the final-grade enrollment in
the primary stage is quite evident, it is not, however, possible to
determine from the data in Table 7.16 the precise correlation between
the two. In like manner, while the historical data indicate the wisdom
of increasing investment in teacher input, no conclusion can be drawn

TABLE 7.16

Trends of Growth in Total Enrollment in Primary Classes
and in Class 5, and Number of Trained Teachers

Country	Years		Percentage Increase
Bangladesh	1947-48	1967-68	
Total enrollment			
1. 1-4	2, 756, 719	5, 196, 342	88
2. Grade 5 only	95, 172	529, 731	456
3. Ratio of 2. to 1.	3. 5 percent	10 percent	
Trained teachers	43 percent	65 percent	Proportion of matriculate teachers rose to 73
India	1950-51	1965-66	
Total enrollment			
1. Grades 1-4	18. 2 million	40. 6 million	117
2. Grade 4 only	2. 6 million	6. 9 million	165
3. Ratio of 2. to 1.	14 percent	17 percent	
Trained teachers	56. 9 percent	67. 9 percent	

Note: Number of matriculates or above rose from 10% to 51%.

Source: Indian Education Commission Report (1964-66); Pakistan
Education Index, Ministry of Education, Government of Pakistan, 1970.

from the given sets of data about the degree to which the rates of retention improve if entry into Grade 1 can be stabilized at the current level,
nor about the degree of influence exercised on the situation by changes
in variables outside the education system.

Assuming, however, that the second model for checking wastage
may reasonably be expected to succeed, certain other related factors
need to be taken into account in examining its soundness and suita-
bility. First, if this approach were successful in eliminating wastage
it would also create the necessity of increasing the teaching staff by
at least 50 percent to cope with the additional number of students,
which had hitherto been wasted but now would be retained in the system. This would also require a 50 percent increase in the current outlay for teachers' salaries, as well as capital outlay to provide
accommodation, furniture, and equipmtnt. It is open to question
whether many of the developing countries would be able to mobilize
the necessary human and material resources on such a scale within a

short period of four or five years or will be willing to do so. This is
even more unlikely when no definite assurance can be given on the
basis of the evidence available about the precise result of the educational investment.

Second, and more important, the proposed model will have no
positive effect on the educational level of the existing labor force. As
observed in Chapter 4, the vast majority of the labor force, including
over 72 percent in India, 75 percent in Indonesia, 71 percent in
Malaysia, 87 percent in Pakistan, and 50 percent in the Philippines is
either illiterate or nearly illiterate, and this particular model would
fail to meet the immediate need to develop human capital to be used
in expanding the economic sector.

Third, the thrust of growth in the school-age population will
make it, for all practical purposes, politically impossible for the
developing countries to accept or enforce a stationary state of enrollment. If the past growth trends are any guide it can reasonably be
predicted that total enrollment and also the ratio of retention will both
grow in size. Growth curves, however, indicate that in most countries
of the region the rate of increase in enrollment at the first level is
likely to remain steady, and it may even slightly diminish in countries
where the enrollment ratio has already reached 70 percent or more. A
strategy will, therefore, have to be evolved that is consistent with
these trends, with the political realities and aspirations of the people
in the region, and with the need of the present adult illiterate population for the knowledge and skill necessary for more productive work.

A STRATEGY OF DEALING WITH WASTAGE

Such a strategy seems to lie in changing the traditional concept
of education, which has a rigid and formal structure and offers no educational opportunities for those who are barred from the system by age
or thrown out of it as waste-product. The economic and social situation
in the region and the historical trends seem to warrant that the educational system be restructured to include an adequate and flexible mechanism for processing the waste-product and also for reaching those of
the adult population who have never had the opportunity of attending
school or who have relapsed into illiteracy after leaving school. The
strategy implies a three-dimensional move.

1. The system of education should be restructured to meet the
total educational needs of the community, thus involving all age groups
according to their needs, through formal as well as nonformal courses
within the framework of development goals set at local and national
levels and taking into account the total community resources. Such an
objective also requires considerable flexibility in the structure of the
courses, both in duration and in content, to allow for the mobility now

lacking between school and work. We shall return to this aspect in Chapter 8.

2. In coping with the additional enrollments of children of school age and also of those beyond it, all possible devices should be adopted to maximize the use of the existing school plants. One such device is the use of schools in shifts, thereby separating the preschool children who in many countries crowd Grade 1 and arranging a shorter session for them outside the normal school hours, using any other available accommodation within the community including other educational buildings. Additional schoolhouses should be built that follow functional, economical, and simple designs that can be executed through local efforts.

3. Proportionately more of the additional resources should be invested in teachers, both in recruiting qualified teachers and in upgrading the qualifications of existing teachers. For reasons of economy and effectiveness, the teaching technology should be reinforced by the use of such media as films, radio, and television where such resources are available. Teacher education programs should be oriented to the new role, as distinct from the traditional, that the teacher will be called upon to play within the community, as implied in the broader, more comprehensive, and more flexible concept of education centering around the total needs and resources of the community. The necessary institutional changes are discussed later in Chapter 8.

VERTICAL AND HORIZONTAL IMBALANCE

It was observed in the opening section of this chapter that in spite of the higher rates of growth in second- and third-level enrollment during the 1950s and 1960s, the educational systems of the region considered as a whole still remained highly imbalanced in their vertical growth. Here also there is considerable variation in the degree of imbalance, as shown in Table 7.17.

It will appear that, except in the cases of the Philippines, Taiwan, and Korea, second- and third-level education continues to remain proportionately much less developed than first-level education. It is also striking that except in the case of Ceylon the historical data of enrollment growth show a strong positive correlation (as expected) between the rates of growth in first-, second-, and third-level enrollments. This has an important implication for the planning of future educational development, in that second- and third-level education is bound to claim a proportionately larger investment to meet the increasingly greater future demand caused by the expansion of first-level education and also to correct the present interlevel imbalance.

Since the supply of high-level critical manpower depends on second- and third-level education, most national plans have underlined

a strategy of greater attention to these levels, particularly the second level. The systemic weakness, which is a matter of the deepest concern to all the developing nations in the region and which is directly associated with the mismatch between educational supply and demand at various levels, is the horizontal imbalance between various types of education within the same level.

This imbalance is regarded as a major cause of unemployment among the graduates of high schools and colleges, even in countries where second- and third-level education is noticeably underdeveloped in terms of enrollment, such as Ceylon, India, Indonesia, Malaysia, and Pakistan. Though data on the distribution of enrollment by fields of special study at the second level are not available for all countries, those shown in Table 7.18 for the third level serve as an index of the composition of the present output of the educational systems in the field of high-level manpower.

Among the developing countries of the region the Philippines has achieved the highest growth in the third level of education. Unfortunately, however, the Philippines also stands out as the most glaring example of imbalance in the growth of the various fields of study within that level. It can be seen in Table 7.18 that out of a total output of 66,170 graduates in the Philippines in 1964, as many as 54,130, or over 82 percent, were in fields other than the sciences and the applied sciences (the applied sciences include engineering, medicine, and agriculture). This imbalance accounts at least partially for the mismatch between educational output and demand that is causing a rising number of educated unemployed, although, as observed in earlier chapters, the central cause of unemployment among the educated as well as among the uneducated is the failure of the strategy of economic growth during the 1950s and 1960s to generate the required employment opportunities even for those trained in the fields of science and technology. It is of course true that if jobs were available many of the educated unemployed could be retrained to fit the job requirements.

The experience of the Philippines underlines the important fact that the problems of structural balance within a system of education are much more complex than generally realized. If interlevel balance is made by merely stepping up the second- and third-level enrollment in education without reference to manpower needs, the system may appear to be better balanced but in fact will have more problems than before. The problems of vertical balance are so intimately bound up with those of horizontal balance that unplanned growth in either direction, far from correcting the imbalance, is likely to aggravate it.

The second characteristic of the growth pattern is the high rate of wastage in both the second and third levels, as indicated by the high percentage of failure at the terminal level of high school and college courses.

If is of course beyond question, as well as evident from Table 7.18, that science and technology represent the weakest and least

TABLE 7.19

Percentage of Distribution of Enrollment in the Second Level
by Types of Education in the Asian Region, 1950-67

Type of Enrollment	Ratio of Total Enrollment		
	1950	1960	1967
Second level	15.3	19.1	22.2
General	14.2	17.8	20.7
Vocational-technical	0.7	1.2	1.2
Teacher training	0.4	0.1	0.3

Source: UNESCO, Development of Education in Asia: Third Asian
Ministers' Conference (Singapore: UNESCO, 1971).

TABLE 7.20

Enrollment in the Second Level by Types of Education in
Selected Asian Countries, 1967

	Total	General	Vocational-Technical	Teacher Training
Bangladesh (1967/68)	1,193,371	1,170,129	23,343	–
Burma (1967)	593,563	586,306	4,027	3,230
Ceylon (1965)	828,725	823,600[a]	–	5,125
China, Republic of (Taiwan) (1967)	785,313	640,447	143,296	1,570
India (1965)	16,359,000	15,658,000	701,000[b]	–
Indonesia (1967)	2,119,832	1,690,012	323,245	106,575
Korea, Republic of (South) (1967)	1,375,232	1,171,022	204,210	–
Malaysia (1965)	402,795	382,963	10,287	9,545
Pakistan (1965/66)	1,032,700	1,012,019	20,681	–
Philippines (1965)	1,037,256	949,434	87,822	–
Thailand (1967)	483,995	358,221	106,378	19,396

[a]Includes technical-vocational.

[b]Includes teacher training.

Sources: UNESCO, Progress of Education in the Asian Region: A
Statistical Review (Bangkok: UNESCO, 1969); UNESCO, Education in
Pakistan (Paris: UNESCO, 1970).

developed areas of education and that their share in educational growth during the 1950s and 1960s has lagged far behind general education. However, this lag is much more pronounced in the case of technical-vocational education at the second level, as shown in Table 7.19. This is demonstrated country by country in Table 7.20.

The high value attached to scientific and technological education as the key to national development and progress is a dominant strain that runs through the national plans and policy-documents of all the developing countries in the region, as noted in Chapter 1. "The basic approach and philosophy underlying the reconstruction of education . . . rests on one deep conviction that progress, welfare and security of the nation depend critically on a rapid, planned growth in quality and extent of education and research in science and technology."[3]

Under the circumstances it is only natural that the national objectives of improved scientific and technological education should receive a high priority in the allocation of resources. The task involved is not one that can be achieved merely by raising the level of investment and the number of physical facilities, though both are important, but has a whole set of other implications and faces numerous difficulties.

SCIENCE EDUCATION

If science education is viewed as "the principal means . . . for transmitting scientific literacy to a broadening stream of population as well as for creating the scientific and technological manpower necessary and indispensable for economic and social advance,"[4] it must be viewed as a strategic component of all education at all levels, thus implying a major change in the concept, structure, and technology of education.

Science is more than a body of knowledge; it is a way of thinking and doing. Doubting, questioning, inquiring, analyzing, solving problems, and coping with the environment are ingredients of science education as important as the knowledge of scientific facts. Science education is thus a cultural and educational discipline through which the pupils cultivate an understanding of the objective phenomena and the scientific way of comprehending them. In this sense it becomes a part of general education and the foundation of learning other skills. At a higher and more specialized level, science education involves the training of future scientists: scientific and technical workers in depth in various branches of science and technology.

The development of science education in the countries of the Asian region poses the following questions:

1. Science education is incompatible with the tradition-bound, rigid, and authoritarian systems of education now existing in these

countries. Will these systems be amenable to the radical transformation in concept, content, and methods of education that is necessary to a fruitful program of science education?

2. The social environment offers little of the experience in the application of science that is found in abundance in the industrial countries. How can the children be motivated to be curious and acquire an inquiring attitude, which is basic to a successful program in science education, in such a climate?

3. The program of science education must be built up from the earliest stages of education if it is to be effective. The level of scientific literacy of the future adult population will largely depend on the nature of education of the present generation of school children. Considering the difficulties mentioned earlier and also the much greater requirement of books and equipment for science education, what is the prospect for developing a sound program of science education to cover the entire network of schools?

4. Science is a rapidly changing field of knowledge. As observed in Chapter 1, scientific knowledge doubles itself every 10 to 15 years. In systems of education already burdened with outdated curricula in the existing fields of study, how can science education hope to remain abreast of the changes?

So far the efforts made by the Asian countries in grappling with these problems are most noticeable in the reconstruction of their curricula to include science at all levels and in the shift to science education through creation of additional facilities in the second and third levels, in the revision of the science and mathematics syllabuses, and in teacher training in the second level. The time allotted to "science" in the first level varies from 5 to 15 percent of the curriculum time, and in the second level it rises to well above 25 percent in many countries. This compares favorably with the time assigned to science and mathematics in industrial countries, such as the USSR, where science education is an integral part of the curriculum. However, the teaching facilities, including the supply of qualified teachers, falls far short of the vast needs implicit in this desirable but ambitious objective.

> It was estimated for one of the larger countries in the region that nearly 60 percent of the pupils at the second level had no access to science education in any adequate form. It is not possible that the picture for the region as a whole may not be substantially different.[5]

Most of those problems of science education briefly mentioned earlier that are related to needed changes in the concept and methods of education depend for their solution not only on the degree of leadership and professional competence of the teachers, and in particular those directly concerned with science education, but also on the availability of an adequate supply of science graduates to work as teachers. The present position is discouraging, however.

From surveys carried out in some countries of the region,
it would appear that nearly 60 percent of the teachers in
primary schools had little or no background of science.
At the second level also there is an acute shortage of
science teachers (in one country, the authorized strength
is reported to be short by 40 percent). Besides, most of
those teaching science are inadequately prepared.[6]

The first imperative in the development of science education is
an increase in the supply of science teachers through such incentives
as the conditions of a country may warrant and an adequate program of
in-service training of teachers as well as supervisors for both the first
and second levels of education. Summer institutes developed in some
countries have yielded encouraging results and can be expanded. Inclusion of some elements of pedagogy in the science courses in the
third level may also prove useful in easing present difficulties. The
following short-term measures also merit consideration in narrowing
the vast existing gap in the supply of science teachers: (1) raising the
retirement age; (2) recalling those who have retired; (3) inducing qualified married women to return to teaching; and (4) part-time employment
of persons in other professions who are qualified to teach science.
The teacher training program may be strengthened by radio and television, by the services of science advisors, and by special study
guides developed by specialists.
    Next to the teacher, the most important component of science
education is the equipment for science teaching. The laboratory is the
vital tool in science education in which the emphasis is on the experimental method, and laboratory learning is an exciting experience in
inquiry and discovery. Laboratory facilities need not be lavish, but
must be functionally adequate. Often a study may find simple and
inexpensive equipment more helpful to his comprehension of important
concepts than equipment that is elaborate and expensive, and the
resourcefulness and creative effort of teachers and students can also
be fruitfully channeled into the making of some of this equipment
locally. To say this, however, is not to underestimate the much higher
cost of science education, compared to education in the humanities
and social sciences. According to one of the estimates, the per pupil
cost in U.S. dollars of scientific and technological education is as
follows:[7]

	Capital		Recurring	
	Third Level	Second Level	Third Level	Second Level
Science, science-based, and technological	2,080	346[*]	427	149.50
Arts, humanities, and social sciences	660	186	183	60.45

[*]Including technical education in Grades 11 through 12.

Some of the countries in the region have successfully experimented with designing, developing, and producing science apparatus, simple kits and other materials, and central science equipment workshops. Efforts in this direction will have to be continued on an increasing scale to cope with the needs that are nationwide up to the second level. This is an area where regional cooperation and exchange of experiences can prove extremely valuable in making the programs economically viable and educationally fruitful.

TECHNICAL-VOCATIONAL EDUCATION

Like science education, technical education remains high in the order of priorities in the national plans, as shown in Table 7.21.

Technical education has in the past taken the form of courses offered in industrial technology in separate institutions at the second and third levels. The efforts made to develop technical education were a new experience for the developing countries in the Asian region, where facilities for technical education were previously either nonexistent or extremely meager. It is against this background that the rate of growth achieved in technical education, which is shown in Table 7.22, should be viewed.

The sharp rise in the rate of growth in enrollment in the initial years is explained primarily by the low starting base of technical education, and the subsequent decline in the growth rate in most countries

TABLE 7.21

Share of Technical-Vocational Education in the Allocation of
Financial Resources for Education in the National
Development Plans of Selected Asian Countries

Country	Percentage of Allocation
Bangladesh	15.5
Ceylon	9.3
India	15.0
Indonesia	21.0
Malaysia	8.0
Pakistan	25.2

Sources: First Five-Year Plan of Bangladesh (1973-78); Five-Year Plan of Ceylon (1972-76); Fourth Five-Year Plan of India (1969-74); First Five-Year Plan of Indonesia (1969/70-1973/74); Second Five-Year Plan of Malaysia (1971-75); Fourth Five-Year Plan of Pakistan (1970-75).

TABLE 7.22

Annual Rate of Increase in Enrollment in Second Level
Technical Education in Selected Asian Countries

Country	1950-55	1955-60	1960-65
Burma	—	18.9	15.5
Cambodia	10.4	35.0	17.7
Ceylon	8.3	10.2	6.9
China, Republic of (Taiwan)	11.9	6.9	16.1
India	9.4	9.0	10.5*
Indonesia	24.3	15.5	6.0
Malaysia	30.2	—	4.2
Pakistan	4.8	3.2	7.4
Philippines	6.9	7.8	9.0
Thailand	19.3	12.0	1.9

*Includes teacher training.

Source: UNESCO, Progress of Education in the Asian Region: A
Statistical Review (Bangkok: UNESCO, 1969).

indicates a slackening demand for technical education for several
reasons: (1) As observed earlier in the case of Indonesia and on a
smaller scale in India and Pakistan, the economy did not grow fast
enough to be able to absorb the increasing output of technical-
vocational education; (2) the type and quality of technical training
provided in some of the technical-vocational institutions was not
considered suitable by the employers; (3) the lack of linkage between
the institutions of technical-vocational education and industry and the
imperfect labor market also contributed to the mismatch. In the case of
Indonesia the location of many of the institutions of technical education far away from industries is also stated as the cause of about
70 percent of technically trained persons remaining unemployed. In
the Philippines, also, "Vocational programs have been instituted
without due consideration of the manpower needs in the area where
the school is located."[8]
        While all of these factors are important, the basic cause of the
mismatch between the supply of and demand for technically-trained
manpower seems to lie in the conception and design of the programs
of technical-vocational education. Technical education has represented the "modern sector" of the educational model, as narrowly
designed as the "modern industries sector" of the economic growth
model and intended chiefly to serve the latter. It has been isolated
from the mainstream of economic life because it has not been concerned

with agricultural technologies, for which a separate and inadequate system of education was created. Like the "modern sector" in the economic model, it was viewed as the panacea for all economic ills, and its expansion within this narrower conceptual framework was vigorously encouraged even though there were hardly any national statistics to identify and forecast the specific skills required by industry.

The following evaluation by a team of experts on the situation in technical education in Bangladesh is applicable to many other countries in the region:

> Sufficient attention was not given to the low rate of utili-
> zation of existing institutions . . . in relation to their
> total capacity, heavy drop-outs, single shift operations
> and limited evening courses. . . . Present institutions
> such as Technical Teacher Training College and instructor
> training centers are understaffed and underenrolled. . . .
> In many instances, valuable equipment is idle for lack
> of simple inexpensive parts.[9]

The President's Commission to survey education in the Philippines observed:

> Specialized vocational training depends on a sound base
> of general education. . . . The existence of separate
> vocational and separate academic institutions has not
> improved the quality nor increased the attractiveness of
> both technical and vocational work.[10]

The frustrating experience in the field of technical-vocational education shows the need for a reexamination of some of the basic concepts regarding the functions of general and technical education and their mutual relationship.

One of the aims of establishing more expensive, better housed, and better equipped technical institutions that were separated from the academic mainstream was to attract young people of superior ability to technical education and to develop in them not only the needed technological skills but also a sense of the dignity of manual labor and an urge for creative and innovative efforts, which were admittedly suppressed in the traditional academic system. This aim was not realized.

General education has continued to be more prestigious because the more prestigious positions in the economic, political, and administrative heirarchy have continued to be filled by persons drawn from this system, though their number was no more than an insignificant fraction of the systems' total output. Aversion to manual labor is as conspicuous among the products of the new institutions as among those of the traditional system. As observed in Chapter 1, the new modern sector of education, instead of being able to produce an impact on the traditional system, was gradually drawn into the latter's gravitational orbit and soon began to imbibe many of the latter's characteristics, including the examination system. The moral of this is significant: Piecemeal reforms that are limited to a segment of the total system of education tend to succumb to the influences of the larger system if the reformed system is not large enough to have the effect of a "critical mass."

In like manner, the prestige of technical-vocational education, recognition of the dignity of labor, and similar other desirable changes in the value system cannot be achieved by education alone. As the Ceylon plan rightly stresses, such efforts must be supported by "reforms in the wage structure to narrow the differential between occupations,"[11] with a positive advantage to occupations contributing to the creation of wealth and to improvement in the conditions of work.

Since some of the basic notions underlying the program of technical-vocational education have turned out to be wrong, the entire system has been exposed to a fresh scrutiny in light of the educational needs of the countries in the Asian region. Though phrased differently, all the nations in the region stress in their plans the humanistic, moral, scientific, and skill contents of education that are necessary to enable every individual to contribute to the social and economic development of the nation. These aims of education evidently cannot be realized for the vast majority of the people if technical-vocational education remains expensive and limited to a small number of people beyond the first level, as at present. To say this, however, is not to underemphasize the value of general education or to advocate premature specialization.

As a matter of fact, to the extent that general education, articulated by elements of science, develops the power to observe, to analyze, and to solve problems and in general to cope with the environment, it produces qualities and skills that individuals need for improving their productive efficiency as well as their technical knowhow. Though not often realized, technical skill can be as inert and uncreative as book learning if it is not enlivened and informed by the personal qualities and habits of intellectual discipline that are developed by a sound general education. Studies in the USSR that covered a wide sample of industries, which were discussed in Chapter 4, indicated that the production norms for workers with a higher level of general education were appreciably higher than those of workers with a lower level. It is thus evident that general and technical-vocational education are not only complementary but hardly admit of any clear-cut division into separate categories.

The problem that faces the developing countries is therefore one of reconciling the claims of general education with those of occupational skill in a manner compatible with the needs and resources of a country. Some of the basic facts observed in this connection are:

1. Since agriculture and its allied occupations are the chief source of employment, technologies relevant to them should form the main thrust of the program in technical-vocational education. The level of technological skill required will naturally depend on the degree of differentiation and specialization of the tasks to be performed within an occupation. In today's situation, however, these tasks often involve simple skills and simple tools without requiring any high degree of specialization, though changes in technology involving an increasing degree of specialization are implicit in the process of development. This will be a continuing process, however, involving a series of adjustments in the labor-capital ratio and corresponding changes in the design of education to produce the required specialized skills.

2. As already noted, 50 percent of the school-age children at the first level drop out of school before reaching the terminal grade, and under 30 percent of the school-age population at the second level attend school. Thus the bulk of the young population that drops out of the school system at various stages and is drawn into the labor market will go without technical skills if technical-vocational eduction is postponed beyond the second level or even beyond the first level.

3. The present limitations of both human and material resources clearly rule out the possibility of introducing on a nationwide scale technologies involving the use of sophisticated equipment and highly trained specialized instructors. Instruction in such specialized technologies will have to be confined to selected centers, the number of which must depend on the developing needs.

The present stage of development of the countries in the region indicates a need for caution against overspecialized courses of training and their indiscriminate expansion, which have proved to be one of the major causes of the mismatch between the supply of and demand for trained manpower, even in the industrially advanced countries. A study in the USSR, the country with the longest experience in manpower planning, reports that

> according to data from sample surveys in Moscow, Kiev, Lugansk, and Sverdlovsk only 11 to 12 percent of graduates from schools with production training entered work in production. Moreover, only a quarter of them were employed in those specializations for which they had been trained in school. Plans to train students for specific trades did not correspond with needs for those types of personnel in the national economy.[12]

This problem of mismatch between the supply of and demand for the small output of technical-vocational education trained in industrial technologies could largely have been avoided if the industries themselves had participated in providing the training facilities, as did those of Japan in the initial period of development of her technical-vocational education.

The conclusions emerging from the above analysis of the needs and resources of the countries in the region seem to be in favor of expanding the scope of technical-vocational education to include agriculture and its allied occupations and of introducing elements of technical-vocational education involving simple skills and tools in both the first and second levels of general education. The plans of a number of countries, including Ceylon, India, Indonesia, Pakistan, and the Philippines, envisage the integration of technical-vocational courses with those of general education, starting at the junior secondary level within the general school system. This does not imply any reduction in academic content, but the materials taught and the whole idiom of teaching must have meaning for the student and stand him in good stead when he leaves the system. The skills and tools of vocational education should be selected in such a manner that the programs in science education and technical-vocational education will reinforce each other.

Since a nationwide science education program should call for a considerable amount of creative and innovative effort in developing laboratory materials and making simple equipment, it can be linked meaningfully with the program in technical-vocational education. In like manner, the two programs can move in harmony in the study of soil characteristics, plants, seed varieties, fertilizers, pesticides, natural and irrigated waters, marketing, storage, forestry, farm mechanics, farm accounts, credit, and the like. To develop an effective program of technical-vocational eduction it will be necessary for the school and the community to pool their resources and form common centers of work and training where specialist instructors are available to help both students and workers. Such centers might be ordinary farms, demonstration farms, rural or urban workshops, or school laboratories.

The major part of the technical-vocational program will, however, have to be directed to the vast population outside the formal education system and be built around the specific tasks that have to be performed in agriculture, industry, and related activities to meet the economic and social needs of a community. By thus linking the world of knowledge with the world of work, education can relate itself meaningfully and fruitfully to the goals of national development.

Such an approach to education, whether general or technical-vocational, implies a strong orientation of teacher education to this new plan-concept and also the creation of suitable institutional arrangements to support it. These institutional arrangements will be described in Chapter 8.

HIGHER EDUCATION

As noted earlier, higher education in the Asian region experienced its fastest growth during the 1950s and 1960s, its annual rate of growth being 11.6 percent during 1965-68 and its ratio of enrollment to total enrollment having risen from 1.4 percent in 1950 to 3 percent in 1968. The rising enrollments in the second level and proportionally larger investments in higher education expected by the plans current in 1974, as indicated in Table 7.23, practically assure higher education a similar growth rate during the 1970s.

The problem in higher education that faces the Asian countries is not, therefore, one of achieving fast enough quantitative growth to balance the growth in the lower levels of education, but one of ensuring that the growth is relevant to the goals of national development and conducive to the efficiency of the educational system as a whole.

As noted earlier, the past pattern of growth has shown a serious interdisciplinary imbalance in favor of the humanities, arts, and social sciences, whereas agricultural sciences, which relate to an area of critical economic importance, were among the least developed and had one of the smallest numbers of graduates. One consequence of this imbalance, of course, is the high incidence of unemployment among college graduates.

This imbalance seems to be far from easy to correct within a short period, however. In the first place, there is the matter of "lead-time" in education: the desired shift to sciences and technology will have to be built on a similar shift in the second level. In the second place, in many countries the private colleges have a substantial share in higher education. For example, in the Philippines 90 percent of the total enrollment is in private institutions of higher education. The success of the planning efforts will thus depend correspondingly on the extent to which the private institutions respond to such efforts. In the third place, each student in higher education in sciences and technology costs three to four times as much as one in the arts, humanities, or social sciences; therefore the pace of progress towards a better balance will also be dependent on the availability of the required financial resources. It is important to remember that unless the growth in science and technology is planned cautiously and related more closely to national needs than has been the case in the past, the surplus output in these areas will prove much more costly in terms of financial resources than a comparable surplus in the arts, humanities, or social sciences, which in the past have served as a comparatively inexpensive means of absorbing the growth pressure within the educational system. However, even here the social cost has been devastatingly high. The institutions of higher education that mushroomed in response to the rapidly growing demand (see Table 7.24) eroded the already shaky frame of accreditation and examination so

TABLE 7.23

Share of Higher Education in the Allocation of Resources
in Selected Asian Countries

Country	Amount	Percent of Public Investment
Bangladesh	TK. 560. 0 million	17. 5
India	Rs. 1, 835. 2 million	22. 3
Indonesia	Rp. 15, 500. 0 million	16. 3
Malaysia	M.s. 87.05 million	16. 2
Pakistan	Rs. 225. 0 million	19. 5

Sources: First Five-Year Plan of Bangladesh (1973-78); Fourth
Five-Year Plan of India (1969-74); First Five-Year Plan of Indonesia
(1969/70-1973/74); Second Five-Year Plan of Malaysia (1971-75);
Fourth Five-Year Plan of Pakistan (1970-75).

much that in some countries the holding of the examinations has assumed
the form of a major law-and-order problem.

Many of these institutions of higher education, though accredited,
are so ill-housed, ill-staffed, and ill-equipped that they totally lack
the climate for the serious business of academic pursuits. An inevitable and heartbreaking consequence is mass failure at the examinations, notwithstanding the struggle of some of the academically
ill-prepared young people to avoid failure through nonacademic and
questionable means. The pain of failure, the shame of humiliation,
the sense of frustration, and the resulting disillusionment, cynicism,
and alienation are part of the high social cost that the developing
societies in the region are now paying for a thoroughly unsuitable
system of education.

The few institutions of higher education that are of better
quality are also tragically hampered by the same traditionalism in
values and attitudes. Whether in the fields of arts or sciences, the
scholarship that they produce is by and large characterized by ivory-
towerism, without any significant relevance to national needs and
problems. The vast and yet unrealized potential of the institutions of
higher education, particularly the universities, in intellectual creativity and development-oriented research was dramatically demonstrated by the fact that the piece of research which has had the
greatest impact on the economic life of the people of the region by
sparking off the "Green Revolution" was not the outcome, though it
could have been, of their own efforts. The problem in higher education
is thus much more fundamental than that of correcting the interdisci-
linary and interlevel mismatch: it will be necessary to orient higher
education towards the advancement of knowledge and towards applying

TABLE 7.24

Growth in the Number of Institutions of Higher Education
in Selected Asian Countries

	Number of Universities	Number of Colleges	Total Enrollment
Bangladesh			
1950	1	63[a]	18,000
1960	2	81[a]	47,800
1972	6	200[b]	121,726
China, Republic of (Taiwan)			
1950	4[c]	12[c]	18,174
1960	7	22	35,064
1967	9	70	138,613
India			
1950	27	706	371,800[d]
1960	45	1,491	1,028,660
1967	70	2,684	1,690,000[e]
Indonesia			
1950	2		10,041[f]
1960	14	150	NA
1967	31	250	110,677
Malaysia			
1950	–	–	–
1960	1	2[g]	779
1967	3	4[a]	4,651
Pakistan			
1950	3	50[a]	24,300
1960	4	131[a]	71,000
1967	7	345[a]	218,500
Philippines			
1955	358[h]	*	NA
1960	347[h]	*	NA
1967	408[j]	*	795,310[j]

NA = Not available.   *Included under universities.
[a]Includes intermediate colleges.   [b]Degree colleges only.
[c]1955.   [d]1949.   [e]1968/69.   [f]1952.
[g]Includes colleges and technical colleges but not teachers'
colleges.
[h]Includes state and private colleges.
[i]1962.   [j]1970/71 (estimated).

Sources: UNESCO, Progress of Education in the Asian Region: A
Statistical Review (Bangkok: UNESCO, 1969); Pakistan Education Index
(1970); Education in Malaysia (1970); First Five-Year Plan of Bangladesh
(1973-78); Report of the Presidential Commission to Survey Education
in the Philippines (1970).

the fruits of knowledge to economic and social problems. The university should be the wellspring of inspiration, idealism, and leadership and the spearhead of reform and progress.

Whether viewed in terms of short-term or long-term goals of development, higher education represents the most critical area of education, since it sets the pace and tone of education throughout the system, through its products who staff all the educational institutions as teachers, supervisors, and administrators. Developments in higher education therefore have a multiplier effect, whether for good or evil.

In the reconstruction of the system of higher education, a new dimension has been added to the task by the emerging concepts of "life-long education" and "exciting and useful education for every student at every step." Even in industrial countries, where higher education has contributed significantly to industrial and technological progress in the past, there is growing criticism of higher education, with its emphasis on academic credentials, as rigid, stereotyped, and unresponsive to individual and community needs, with faculties and students isolated from the world of life. A recent appraisal of higher education in the United States stressed that "means must be found to create a diverse and responsive system. We must enlarge our concepts of who can be a student, and when, and what a college is. We need many alternate paths to education."[13]

The need for diversity and alternative choices in higher education seems to be even greater in the developing countries. The rising urge for higher education must be satisfied in a manner that is meaningful to the individual and also to national development, through a variety of courses at various levels according to choice and need.

FINANCING OF EDUCATION

Education's need for financial resources has proved to be insatiable in all countries, whether less developed or more developed. The trend throughout the world is for educational systems to receive an increasingly larger financial input. The most striking point of contrast between the industrial countries and the developing countries in the Asian region is that the former spend a larger proportion of their much larger national income on education, between 4 and 7 percent of gross national product. On the one hand this reflects the distortion in the growth pattern of the developing countries that is discussed in Chapter 2; on the other hand it reflects the constraint of resources that confronts all sectors of development in these countries.

The available data on the financing of education in the Asian region are adequate neither in quality nor in coverage or classification. Information on public and private expenditure on education by ministries other than that of education is either lacking or very meager. These

TABLE 7.25

Enrollment at All Levels as Percentage of Total Population
and Public Expenditure on Education as Percentage of
National Income in Selected Asian Countries, 1950-67

Country	Year	Percentage of Total Population Enrolled	Public Expenditure on Education as Percentage of National Income	Ratio of Percentage Enrolled to Percentage of Expenditure
Ceylon	1950	17.7	3.0	5.9
	1955	19.0	2.8	6.8
	1960	22.7	5.2	4.4
China,	1950	13.6	2.6	5.2
Republic	1954	15.9	3.1	5.1
of	1960	21.5	2.5	8.6
(Taiwan)	1965	24.1	3.4	7.1
	1966	24.5	3.5	7.0
	1967	24.9	3.9	6.4
India	1950	6.7	0.8	8.4
	1955	8.3	1.3	6.7
	1960	10.9	1.9	5.7
	1965	13.9	2.1	6.2
Japan	1950	22.5	4.8	4.7
	1955	24.0	6.1	3.9
	1960	24.1	5.1	4.7
	1965	22.4	5.8	3.9
	1966	21.7	5.7	3.8
Korea,	1959	18.1	5.6[a]	3.2
Republic	1965	22.1	3.3[a]	6.7
of	1966	22.8	2.8	8.1
(South)	1967	23.3	2.9	8.0
Pakistan	1950	5.7	0.4	14.3
	1955	6.5	0.5	13.0
	1960	7.2	1.0	7.2
	1965	9.3	1.7	5.5
	1966	9.5	1.4	6.8
Singapore	1960	24.7	2.9[b]	8.5
	1965	26.5	4.5	6.5
	1966	27.2	4.6	5.9

[a]Including private expenditure relating to private education.
[b]As percentage of gross domestic product at market prices.

Source: UNESCO, Progress of Education in the Asian Region: A Statistical Review (Bangkok: UNESCO, 1969).

are important limitations that substantially impinge on the interpretation
of the available data.

During 1960-68 public expenditure on education in the region
rose by 70 percent, from U.S. \$1.55 billion to U.S. \$2.7 billion, at
an average annual rate of 7.2 percent. The cost per head of total population rose from \$1.84 to \$2.60, and the cost per head of population
in the 5- to 24-year age group rose from \$4.28 to \$6.03.

Public expenditure on education as a percentage of national income
also showed a steady increase, though in some countries this increase
was not commensurate with the increase in the percentage of total population enrolled, as shown in Table 7.25.

The relative change between the ratio of population enrolled and
that of national income spent on education is underlined by Table 7.25.
It will appear from this table that in all countries except India and
Pakistan this ratio was increasing during the earlier years of the period,
thus indicating that enrollment was rising faster than expenditure.
During the later years of the period this trend was reversed, with a
proportionately higher rate of increase in the expenditure on education
in all countries except India and Pakistan, which continued to experience a declining rate of increase in educational expenditure.

Some interesting characteristics of the production mechanisms of
the educational systems in the region seem to emerge from a study of
the unit of recurring expenditure on public education summarized in
Table 7.26. Using the retention ratio as a tentative indicator of output,

TABLE 7.26

Unit of Recurring Expenditure on Public Education by Level
in Selected Asian Countries, circa 1965

Country	First Level	Second Level	Third Level
China, Republic of			
(Taiwan)	12.0	43.0	197.0
Cambodia	26.0	111.0	212.0
India	6.5	13.0	181.0
Korea, Republic of			
(South)	6.6	17.0	143.0
Malaysia (West)	44.0	82.0	1,146.0
Pakistan	6.7	18.0	59.0
Singapore	60.0	78.0	766.0
Thailand	13.0	60.0	232.0

Source: UNESCO, Progress of Education in the Asian Region: A
Statistical Review (Bangkok: UNESCO, 1969).

and treating productivity as output-input ratio expressed in terms of the unit of expenditure, results for the first level appear as follows:

- South Korea and China are high in productivity (with large output and small input).
- Malaysia and Singapore are medium in productivity (with large output and large input).
- India and Pakistan are medium in productivity (with small output and small input).
- Cambodia and Thailand are low in productivity (with small output and large input).

A warning about the application of the economic concept of productivity in terms of the output-input ratio, input being the money cost, to educational systems should, however, be noted here. For one thing, as observed in Chapter 1, education is essentially a process of qualitative development of the individual, and its productivity cannot truly be measured in terms of economic cost and benefit. For another, any comparison of the productivity of the educational systems of different countries by their output-input ratio expressed in terms of cost only, can be highly misleading since it would place high-output-to-high-input countries at par with low-output-to-low-input countries. As a matter of fact a highly wasteful system with a very low unit cost of education may even look better in terms of productivity in the narrow economic sense. However, an interesting country profile seems to emerge from the data on the growth of education versus educational expenditure.

- The countries with the lowest unit cost are also the countries with the lowest retention rates, although the reverse is not true.
- The countries that have achieved the highest growth rates in the three levels of education are among those with the highest unit costs. Thus, contrary to popular notion, low cost and faster growth of education do not necessarily go together.
- The countries with the lowest unit cost are also the countries with the lowest per capita national incomes.

Thus an issue that is central to the development of education in the region, in both quantity and quality, seems to hinge on the ability of the countries in the last group, such as Bangladesh, India, Indonesia, and Pakistan, with the largest population in the Asian region except for Mainland China, to generate more resources for investment in education. The problem is thus bound up with the economic development of those countries. Some of the directions along which a plan-strategy may be designed in order to step up both economic and educational growth in mutually supporting roles have already been

TABLE 7.27

Public Expenditure on Education as a Ratio of National Budget
and National Income in Selected Asian Countries

Country	Public Expenditure on Education as a Percentage of National Budget	Total Public Expenditure on Education as a Percentage of National Income
Bangladesh	11.9 (1972/73)[a]	1.43 (1968/69)
Burma	16.8 (1967)	3.4 (1965)
Cambodia	21.6 (1967)	5.1 (1966)
Ceylon	12.9 (1965)	4.9 (1966)
China, Republic of (Taiwan)	19.3 (1966)	3.9 (1967)
India	–	2.1 (1965)
Indonesia	–	0.7 (1960)
Japan	20.1 (1967)	5.7 (1966)
Malaysia (West)[b]	19.0 (1969)	5.1 (1961)
Pakistan[a]	16.2 (1968/69)	1.4 (1968/69)
Philippines	–	3.5 (1966)
Singapore	19.3 (1967)	4.6 (1966)
Thailand	14.9 (1966)	3.4 (1966)

[a]Based on the budget estimates of Bangladesh Government 1972/73.

[b]Education in Malaysia (Ministry of Education, Malaysia, 1970), p. 52.

[c]Education in Pakistan (Paris: UNESCO, 1970), p. vi.

Sources: UNESCO, Statistical Yearbook, 1969; UNESCO, Progress of Education in the Asian Region: A Statistical Review (Bangkok: UNESCO, 1969).

indicated in the earlier chapters and will be elaborated in the next chapter.

It appears from a study of the national budgets that, compared to other countries in the region, these countries now allocate a proportionately smaller amount of their resources for education, as a ratio of their national budgets as well as of their national incomes, as shown in Table 7.27. It should be evident from this table that in the case of Bangladesh, India, Indonesia, and Pakistan there is scope for raising the allocation of resources for the education sector by intersectoral readjustments and a proportionately larger allocation to the educational sector out of the additional resources that may be generated.

TABLE 7.28

Public Expenditure by Level and Type of Education in Selected Countries (in percentage)

Country	Year	Central Administration	Preschool and First Level	Second Level General	Vocational	Teacher Training	Third Level	Others
Burma	1967	5.1	37.0	38.9	1.2	0.4	10.4	4.0[a]
China (Taiwan)	1967	1.1	43.4	26.0	7.8	0.2	12.8	8.7
India	1965	2.6	23.9	40.6	1.5	–	32.1	8.9[b]
Korea (South)	1967	5.1	72.6	21.0	0.1	–	0.9	0.1
Malaysia (West)	1967	16.7	45.4	27.6	0.4	4.9	4.3	0.7
Pakistan	1967	c	44.1	17.9	4.6	2.1	20.4	10.9[a]
Philippines	1964	c	93.4	–	–	–	6.5	0.1
Singapore	1967	2.5	50.6	27.9	2.8	–	13.7	2.5[b]
Thailand[d]	1967	2.5	51.4	12.5	9.6	4.2	16.7	3.1
France[e]	1967	2.9	33.2	28.8	12.9	1.2	19.6	1.4
United Kingdom	1967	3.8	23.7	28.7	8.5	–	23.6	11.7
United States	1967	c	71.8[f]	–	–	–	28.2	–
USSR	1967	c	14.7	45.8[g]	15.5[h]	–	12.3	11.7
Yugoslavia	1967	c	52.2	5.3	19.6	2.3	14.8	5.8
Japan	1967	7.4	38.0	38.4	i	–	12.7	3.5

[a]Including various subsidies; [b]including scholarships and grants to pupils; [c]expenditure on administration is distributed among various levels and types of education; [d]expenditure of the central government only; [e]expenditure of the Ministry of Education only; [f]including second level; [g]including first level; [h]including teacher training; [i]second level general includes vocational education.

Sources: UNESCO Statistical Yearbook, 1969; UNESCO, Progress of Education in the Asian Region: A Statistical Review (Bangkok: UNESCO, 1969).

An analysis of the budget of the education sector reveals an imbalance in the allocation of resources to the various levels within the sector of education, as shown in Table 7.28. This imbalance reduces the productivity of investment in the sector as a whole. It will appear from the table that what many countries in the region, particularly those with the lowest retention rate in the first level, now spend on the first level is hardly commensurate with the size of enrollment and the task involved. Its inadequacy stands out in sharp contrast with the disproportionately larger expenditure on higher education. It may be noted in this connection that in Japan the expenditure on elementary education was 84.3 percent of the total educational expenditure in 1885 and continued to be as high as 61.9 percent in 1935.

An analysis of the structure of the unit cost also shows considerable imbalance in the application of funds to the various components of education. What is most disconcerting is that the recurrent component of the cost, of which teachers' salaries now constitute the bulk, about 70 to 90 percent, has not been increasing with the increase in capital outlay. As a result, recruitment of additional teachers had to be altogether halted in Indonesia, and in several states of India and in one province of Pakistan trained teachers could not be provided with jobs. The inevitable consequence of such a state of finances is inadequately staffed schools, with its adverse effect on the quality and output of education.

Considering the educational tasks ahead of the countries in the Asian region and the present level of public expenditure on education, most countries in the region will have to brace themselves for rapidly rising expenditures on education. So far few countries have subjected themselves to the discipline of serious long-term planning to formulate realistic targets for meeting future educational needs, estimating the resources required, and indicating the ways and means of mobilizing such resources. The exercise undertaken by the Indian Education Commission in this direction is a commendable effort and needs to be followed up by more detailed and comprehensive planning to meet the occupational requirements, going down to the regional and local levels.

NOTES

1. UNESCO, Development of Education in Asia: Third Asian Ministers' Conference (Singapore: UNESCO, 1971), p. 12.

2. UNESCO, op. cit., p. 20.

3. Report of the Indian Education Commission (1964-66), p. 718.

4. Conference on the Application of Science and Technology to the Development of Asia (1968).

5. UNESCO, An Asian Model of Educational Development: Perspectives for 1965-80 (Paris: the United Nations, 1966), p. 108.

6. Ibid., p. 109.

7. Ibid., pp. 61-64.

8. Report of the President's Commission on Education in the Philippines (1970), p. 86.

9. UNESCO, Education in Pakistan (Paris: UNESCO, 1970), p. 53.

10. Report of the President's Commission, op. cit., p. 75.

11. Five-Year Plan of Ceylon (1972-76), p. 17.

12. I.I. Kaplan, Economics of Education in the USSR, cited by V.A. Zhamin in Noah, op. cit., p. 12.

13. U.S. Department of Health, Education, and Welfare, The Report on Higher Education (Washington: U.S. Government Printing Office, March 1971), p. vii.

8

SOME PLAN-STRATEGIES FOR EDUCATIONAL DEVELOPMENT: A CONCEPTUAL FRAMEWORK

The most telling lesson of the past decades of development is that the first imperative for each of the developing nations in South and Southeast Asia is to chart out a new path of growth strategy reflecting its own concepts of values and life styles, and suited to its own needs and conditions. The experiences of the past, the aspirations for the future, and the social, political, and economic realities in the Asian region indicate that the focal point of the new strategy should be the fullest development and utilization of the human capital in which the countries in the region are rich. This central strategy will determine the time path, the factor mix, and the parameters of growth.

This approach to plan-strategy has several implications. First, the targets, programs, and investments in different sectors, including education, will be oriented to this strategy. They will be woven into the overall plan as its integral and interacting parts, to enable all of these sectors to advance in harmony and in mutually supporting roles to the realization of the plan objectives. The emerging national plan will thus be the resultant of the sector plans integrated with a unified purpose and not of a mere aggregation of separate sector plans, as has been the practice in the past.

The preparation of such an integrated plan presupposes inter-disciplinary cooperation of systems analysts, educators, economists, sociologists, demographers, engineers, and specialists in all the various sectors, all working as a team. The sector specialists should be adequately oriented to the purposes and functions of the related sectors, and their perspective should be widened so that they can see and understand the roles of their respective sectors in the larger and more complex context of the interdependent and interacting roles of all the sectors in attaining the plan objectives.

Effective coordination at every level of planning is vital to the preparation of a well-integrated plan. Coordination should begin with communication among all those concerned with the formulation of the plan, long before the plans reach even the embryonic stage. It is also important that those who are responsible for policy-making decisions be actively involved in coordination, in order to avoid conflicts at later stages of plan-development. The planning authorities at the national, provincial, regional, and local levels provide the aegis for coordination. They can also serve as useful organs for collection and distribution of planning data and evaluation of progress in plan-implementation. The composition of planning authorities at each of the levels should, of course, be representative of the needed expertise and adequate in strength.

Second, since the core of the plan-strategy is the development and utilization of the human potential, the plan will have a much wider human base in terms of the involvement of the people, both as a means and as an end of development. An important criterion in the choice of technique will therefore be the extent to which it can contribute to the widening of this base during a given plan-period.

Third, in the economic sector the major thrust of this strategy will be in the direction of development of agriculture and more extensive use of labor-intensive technologies in industrial development, to achieve self-sufficiency in food and also generate more opportunities for productive work for more people. As indicated in Chapter 6, the vast possibilities in this direction are demonstrated by the performance of Mainland China and also that of Taiwan, in two ideologically different social settings. As already observed in Chapters 3 and 6, the goal remains progressive modernization of technology through a series of adjustments to the changing needs, in order to maximize the utilization of human capital during the period of transition.

It is, of course, recognized that the choice of technique is ultimately a matter of political decision. The strategy proposed in this chapter, however, rests on the postulate that hopefully the model of economic growth will gravitate around the central strategy, as mentioned above. In order to avoid increasing future unemployment (educated and uneducated) with its concomitant ills, it is indeed essential that the economic sector accept employment creation as an explicit variable in the construction of its growth model and provide a sufficiently wide and economically viable base for education. Such a marriage of the economic and education sectors would make a major departure from the past strategy by shifting emphasis to the complementarity of the roles of these sectors in developing and utilizing human capital as the prime factor of development.

PLAN REINFORCEMENTS

There are also other important preconditions that the society as a whole must create through its political, legislative and administrative organs to provide the needed underpinnings to reinforce the plan-strategy. As observed in Chapters 2 and 6, a number of social, demographical, political, and psychological factors have seriously slowed the pace of progress in the past, and they will continue to do so in the future if corrective measures are not adopted. Principal among them are (1) the rapid growth of population; (2) the disincentives to productive work that are caused by an irrational structure of wages and employment, a growing disparity in income, and the erosion of social and moral values; (3) overcentralization in administration and planning.

POPULATION CONTROL

The national plans in the Asian region clearly reflect the concern of the countries about the baneful effects of rapid growth of population, but the measures envisaged in these plans for population control do not appear to match the magnitude of the need. Considering the seriousness of the threat that the problem poses to all sectors of national development, population control needs to be viewed as a matter of prime national importance and therefore of direct concern to the national government. This is clearly an area in which time is of the very essence. While regional and local governments and voluntary agencies can with advantage continue to be associated actively with planning and implementation, it is evidently necessary to mount an adequate program of population control with utmost speed on a national and high priority basis, and suitable plans should be evolved to use both formal and nonformal education as instruments for the dissemination of population education.

INCENTIVES AND MOTIVATION

It was observed in Chapters 3 and 6 that psychological variables like habits, attitudes, and incentives play a crucial role, both as components of human capital and as factors of change. Resistance to change has proved to be the major impediment to progress in education as well as in other sectors. The very social structures, which are recognized as archaic and in need of change, stand as barriers against reform efforts and in many cases have stymied them successfully.

Even where the educational and social reforms came in the wake of a political movement, it appeared that the enthusiasm for reforms did not long survive the realization of the political objective. It is, of course, beyond question that an enlightened political leadership can be a powerful catalyst of change and progress. National goals and ideals explicitly and vigorously presented to the people can act as a fountainhead of inspiration. If they can be linked meaningfully the cultural heritage of the nation on the one hand, and with the universal structures of knowledge and values needed for progress on the other, they can be highly inspiring. The more inspiring they are, the further they penetrate the depth of the emotional life and the greater is the probability of their success in stirring the people out of their inertia and rigid adherence to traditions.

It is not, however, enough to rouse enthusiasm for the desired reform; the enthusiasm must be sustained long enough to produce results. The use of mass media, newspaper, films, radio, television, and public forums of discussion can be valuable aids, but what appears to be crucial is that an adequate action program be evolved to carry forward the reforms. It is also imperative that those who operate the program and also those to whom it is directed are sufficiently motivated to work the new program.

This is a task that has evidently proved to be most difficult and stubborn. Elimination of the obstacles in the way of accomplishing it is therefore an important prerequisite for the success of the future plans. It calls for a whole range of reforms through legislative and administrative action, as observed in Chapter 6, to ensure that (1) ability and achievement will be adopted as the criteria for recruitment and promotion in all occupations; (2) the traditional and occupational stratifications will be removed, to allow a fair allocation of high-level manpower to all sectors and to facilitate vertical and horizontal mobility among the various occupations; (3) the salary and wage structure will be rationalized to eliminate the grotesque disparities now existing between salary scales of different grades and to reflect the national needs and resources more realistically; and (4) production and distribution systems will be reformed to ensure an equitable participation of the people in the benefits of development.

Such a restructured system of incentives needs to be reinforced by additional reforms applicable to rural occupations, however. For example, the countries in the region still have extensive areas with a feudal agrarian system, where the farmers neither own the land they till nor get a just share of the produce, and are socially, economically, and politically in the grip of a small landed aristocracy. In such areas appropriate land reforms are obviously an essential precondition for motivating rural workers to take advantage of the "new seeds" and "new technology" and to make a greater effort to raise agricultural productivity. The experiences of the "Green Revolution" and the Comilla Rural Development Project indicate that people will be willing to abandon centuries-old traditions and change if the change is demonstrated to be beneficial to them and if they have the opportunity to change. In a different ideological framework and on a much larger scale, the nationwide changes in Mainland China also provide corroborative evidence in this regard. The conclusion thus emerges that people are best motivated towards a change when they are themselves meaningfully and beneficially involved in the process.

It should, however, be borne in mind that while some of the
archaic traditional structures have operated as disincentives to change,
a major disincentive to productive effort came in the wake of change.
The ill-conceived and ill-designed growth technique, the uncritical and
unintelligent application of the concept of market economy, and the pro-
pensity for gaining quick returns on investments, all combined to unleash
the forces of graft, corruption, and profiteering on a scale never known
before. Not only was the incentive for honest productive effort thus
weakened, but the whole value system stood eroded, endangering the
very foundation and objectives of national development. The reestablish-
ment of the values of honesty, fair play, and justice as the sheet anchor
of the reward system is therefore an imperative for the success of future
reform efforts.

What has been said above about an equitable sharing of benefits
and rewards as necessary to motivation is equally true of sacrifices.
Constraint of resources in the developing countries will compel them
to forego present consumption of many goods and services in order to
increase investment in future production. These sacrifices will be
better tolerated if they are equitably distributed. Thus an important
principle on which the incentive system is to be based is an equitable
sharing of benefits and sacrifices alike during the process of development. In other words, social justice is to be treated as a keystone of
the developmental process, motivated by an unequivocal commitment
to the goal of "growth with justice" and of life styles sustainable for
the nation as a whole.

INSTITUTIONAL CHANGES: DECENTRALIZATION OF ADMINISTRATION AND PLANNING

It was observed in Chapters 2 and 6 that the existing centralized
administration and planning were hardly conducive to generating and
sustaining community efforts at regional and local levels. A precondition for the success of the plan-strategy is, therefore, to evolve suitable and adequate institutional arrangements to enable the communities
of people at different levels to participate in both planning and performing the tasks that can most fruitfully be undertaken at regional and
local levels. This purpose cannot be served merely by creating or
expanding units of local government or establishing extension services.
Though such institutions and services are necessary inputs, they need
to be designed in such a way that the members of the community have
a sense of free, active, and effective participation and can gradually
move towards a state of self-reliance. The representatives of the
government will have to shed the robes of authority and don those of
friends and advisers, to make it clear that the relationship of the local
community with the representatives of the government is not one of
subserviency but of partnership in a common task.

As already observed in Chapter 6, the Comilla Cooperative model has immense possibilities as an institutional framework for planning and development at the local level. There can, of course, be many variants of this model to suit varying needs and conditions. What is of vital importance, however, is that (1) tasks at the local level that can be undertaken with local resources, supplemented by resources from other sources, if any, should be planned and executed by the people in the local community, assisted by various sector advisers; (2) the development programs of all sectors at the local level should be geared to these tasks; and (3) a pool of expertise and an interdisciplinary cadre of field workers should be created at the local level to advise and assist the local communities. Some key points in the plan-strategy follow.

NATIONAL OBJECTIVES IN EDUCATION

Given the plan reinforcements in the form of changes in social factors impinging on the education system, as indicated above, the planner's task is to induce changes within the system itself to meet the objectives set for the education sector in the overall plan for national development. These objectives are a crucial input in the design and structure of the education system. They determine the curricula, knowledge, skills, values, and attitudes that education in a given situation is expected to produce, and they serve as the motive force for educational changes. The plan-targets and programs all must naturally revolve around them in the time path until their realization. In translating these objectives into an educational plan, for the reasons discussed in Chapter 5 the planners will be prudent not to depend excessively on any single model. They should draw on the various models that are available, with suitable adaptations in light of social realities and the results of empirical studies developed and carried out within each country.

Most nations stress educational objectives, falling under the following broad categories: (1) personal: the development of the individual's innate powers and abilities; (2) economic: the development of the knowledge and skills of the individual for a productive role as a worker; (3) social and moral: the development of values and attitudes conducive to honest and responsible participation in social life; and (4) political: the development of a sense of national identity and public duty.

These categories are by no means exhaustive or mutually exclusive. The degree of emphasis laid on different categories by different nations will be found to vary according to their social situations. It is, however, of paramount importance to fruitful planning that the major objectives and their implications be properly identified, comprehended, and

spelled out. The planner's task is made easier in this regard if there
is a recognized public policy setting forth the national objectives in
education. In the past the lack of consensus on educational objectives
has wrecked reform efforts in more than one country in the region.
Where such a national policy does not exist, however, an essential
first step is to have one adopted by the accredited representatives of
the nation, with adequate public participation in its formulation.

ENDS VERSUS TECHNIQUES IN MODEL BUILDING

It is far more difficult to build a plan-model for effective implementation of the objectives. Some of them are clearly too abstract to
lend themselves to quantification, as required in a theoretical-
mathematical model. Here the planner is confronted with the admittedly
difficult technical problem of deciding how the abstract components of
the national objectives in education are to be treated in the plan-model.
As observed in Chapters 4 and 5, the increasing application of analytical methods in measuring the educational input and output has opened
up new possibilities in model building for education; however, the
results of the models so far developed have in many cases been vitiated
in varying degrees by their inherent limitations because of the difficulty
in coping with the numerous human and social variables involved. The
search for improved techniques must therefore continue. What is disturbing is that the rapidly spreading use of the analytical technique in
the social sciences seems to have shifted the focus to the technique
instead of to the ends it is intended to serve. As a result, those who
have the expertise often tend to shy away from the vital areas of human
and social concern for fear of committing a technical "incest."
The utter futility of any plan-model that is not responsive to the
national objectives, whatever its merit as a technical instrument, has
been amply demonstrated by the past experiences. It is therefore of
paramount importance that the educational plan be so designed that it
adequately reflects the national objectives. This is not an impossible
task, though ways may have to be found to accomplish it. Some of the
more recent models, two of which are discussed in Chapter 5, indicate
efforts to press further afield and probe deeper into education and psychology through empirical studies and to introduce into a model a number
of variables relating to the quality of education and also some value
biases. Continuing efforts in this direction are clearly necessary. In
the meantime, theoretical reasoning will have to be tempered by prag-
matism, where necessary, in evolving a plan-model, to avoid allowing
any of the major national objectives to be blurred or altogether ignored.
Even where the objectives may appear to be abstract, their implications for the operational programs may be capable of reduction to
concrete terms. For example, if education is intended to develop

values and attitudes conducive to honest and responsible participation in social life, as implied in the social objective, and to inculate a sense of national identity and public duty, as implied in the political objective, both the structure and contents of education must of course be so designed as to further these objectives. Two of the important and inescapable implications of these objectives are that (1) education, to be able to perform such a role, must have a nationwide base that enables it to reach all citizens, present and future, and (2) curricula, textbooks, and teacher education must be oriented to these ends. Schools acting alone cannot achieve these objectives. Suitable changes in public policy and social environment, as indicated in the previous section, must support the reform efforts within the education system. It must be made visible to the people that the society and education alike are structured on the values that the people are asked to cultivate. For example, an education system that does not provide for equal and fair access to education for any reason, whether social, economic, ethnic, or religious, is a negation of these values. It is conceivable that the present constraint of resources may continue to compel some countries to limit access to education at the second level and beyond for quite some time. In such a case, universal basic education assumes an added importance, both on grounds of equity and of national interest. All children should have at least enough basic education to compete for opportunities of further education. Talents are randomly distributed; they can be discovered only when every child has an opportunity for education. In either case, both equity and national interest also warrant an adequate scheme of financial support, so that inability to pay does not prevent a talented child from proceeding to further education. Universal basic education thus emerges as an area deserving of the highest priority in the new design of the structure of education. The public policy on the duration of basic education, the resources available, and the social and economic factors bearing on enrollment and attendance will naturally determine the time path in realizing this goal. The plan-strategy should be directed to shortening this path.

The countries in the Asian region are all committed to the goal of universal primary education of varying duration for children of the prescribed school age. Many of them have already achieved or are about to achieve universal enrollment. As already observed in Chapter 7, this apparently impressive performance hides appalling wastage at the first level and also the vast illiterate population of school age and above. Every year the number of children who drop out adds more to the children outside the school system than does the growth in population. The total number of illiterates also tends to grow progressively. Thus universal education in the larger sense of basic education for all citizens present and future remains a distant goal shimmering on the horizon, and the time path in reaching it within the frame of the present design of the national plans is very dim and hazy. If the development and utilization of human capital is to be the central strategy in planning future development, a radical change in the concept and structural design of the education system is clearly of great strategic importance.

FUTURE STRUCTURE OF EDUCATION

As indicated in Chapter 7, in concept the redesigned educational system should include all education within and beyond the school age, and education should be viewed as a lifelong process of renewal and regeneration of knowledge and skill. In structure it should be broad, flexible, and multidimensional. It should be broad enough to be able to treat and process the human "waste products" of the formal system of education (the dropouts), in a manner analogous to the use of "by-products" in industrial plants, and also to bring the adult illiterates under its ambit. It should be multidimensional, with a wide variety of courses, including full-time and part-time courses. It should be flexible enough to allow easy movement between full-time and part-time courses and between study and work, thus opening the door for work-oriented education and education-oriented work and setting into motion a dynamic process for the continuous renewal of education. The design of an educational pyramid having these salient features should provide for the dropouts to enter the nonformal education system and also for a two-way flow between the formal and nonformal systems. As noted earlier, the formal system should also provide some part-time courses, and both its full-time and part-time courses should be so designed that the active members of the labor force are not barred from them.

In the restructuring of education an important plan-strategy seems to lie in a rational and equitable distribution of resources between formal and nonformal and full-time and part-time education, both of which should be viewed as integral parts of the same national system. This will imply changes in the plan concepts and programs of many of the countries in the region.

Redesigning the Structure

The design of the educational structure will have to be radically different from that of the time-honored "lock-step" system. Educators will have to realize that there are other and more fruitful ways than the traditional formal system in which education can be produced. The new design should, within the limit of available resources, offer opportunities to link work with study and to change from full-time to part-time education and vice versa according to interest, ability, and needs,

without being hindered by age, break of studies, or a public examination
such as is now held at the end of each stage of education in many countries of the region. Such opportunities for further education, supported
by suitable reforms in the structure of salary and wages and an employment policy linking jobs to specific skills rather than to academic
degrees, are also likely to ease the pressure on formal full-time higher
education and to make technical-vocational education at the second
level more attractive. An important reason why high school graduates
flock to the colleges and universities is that, apart from the social
prestige attached to college education, an early option for specialized
training is regarded as an economic handicap. In the present scheme
of things the best-paid occupations require a higher level of general
education, and those who elect a vocational career early find the door
of higher education and higher occupations practically barred to them.
Not infrequently, students joining the technical-vocational courses at
the second level do so without any commitment to the vocation itself
but to use it as a springboard for moving into more remunerative occupations. This vicious circle seems to call for a strategy of simultaneous changes in social and economic structures conducive to occupational
mobility, both vertical and horizontal, and a redesigning of the educational structure to offer lifelong opportunities of further education
through part-time and full-time study. It may be noted in this connection that the barriers between formal and nonformal education have
largely disappeared in the socialist countries and that they have
established a close link between work and education. For example,
in the USSR[1] approximately half the students in engineering courses
at the universities are enrolled as part-time students with regular jobs.
Evening classes, correspondence courses, and instruction by television
make it possible for the workers to study without abandoning their jobs,
and leave of absence is freely granted to enable them to carry out laboratory work and appear at the examinations.[2] Ambitious workers wishing
to advance themselves educationally are allowed the opportunity of
returning to school without any great personal sacrifice. Periodical
renewal and updating of education for those engaged in research,
teaching, and technical and other professions is also an integral part
of the Soviet education system.

     The University of the Air, subsequently renamed the Open Uni-
versity, recently established in Britain, is an interesting alternative
system of higher education designed to meet the needs and aspirations
of those unable to secure admission at the British universities, who
number about a million a year. It accepts students "twenty-one or over,
requiring no formal entry qualifications, has no full-time students and
no students at all on its small campus."[3] The university offers foundation courses in science, the humanities, social science, mathematics, and technology, each of which comprises 34 weeks' work (34
units). Each week's study involves 10 hours of work "6 hours of self-
instruction, a half-hour of TV, a half-hour of radio, a half-hour of

self-assessment tests, a half-hour of 'subjective' assignments to be
graded later by tutors, about an hour of 'objective' assignments to be
graded later by computer and in science about an hour for home experiments."[4] The program is based on a nationwide tutorial system and
summer school and the production of vast academic materials. It has
250 local study centers, usually in universities, technical colleges,
or schools, at which the students may receive face-to-face instruction
or counselling from more than 3, 000 part-time academics. The Open
University has developed a teaching system capable of producing a
graduate at about 20 percent of the cost of a conventional university
education, with the added advantage that students can work for the
degree without any interruption in their employment.

Reordering Priorities

The priorities will have to be substantially reordered to make the
allocation of resources to nonformal education commensurate with the
tasks it is intended to perform within the framework of the overall
national plan. On the assumption that all education will be related to
the social and economic needs of the nation, a strategy that suggests
itself is to plan the creation of educational facilities at the local level
in the form of a "cluster" to serve the community as a whole. This
cluster will include a complement of schools with facilities for general,
technical, and vocational education at the first and second levels and
common centers of training to help both students and workers within a
community. Such a center might be a school laboratory, a rural or urban
workshop, a health center, an ordinary farm, or a demonstration farm.
    Since the major part of the nonformal education program will be
developed around specific tasks in agriculture, industry, and related
activities to meet the economic and social needs of the community,
teacher education will also have to be oriented to the new framework
within which the school and community are to work together.
    The concept of flexibility in the design of the educational struc-
ture further implies that if formal and nonformal parts of the system are
to interact to maximize the development of the nation's human capital,
a dynamic rather than a static view should be taken of the length in
years or the various levels and courses of education. As observed in
Chapter 3, development is essentially a process of progressive differentiation of tasks, with more people concentrating on more specific
tasks with increasingly specialized knowledge so that the tasks are
done better. If education is to play its crucial role in feeding this
dynamic process of change, the contents and length of courses will
have to be related to the requirements of the tasks involved at a particular stage of development.

In like manner, the divisions and levels in the educational structure also have to be related to the national needs and resources. For example, I have stressed that universal basic education is a critical factor in development; in the wider sense in which universal basic education has been used here, the task involved will be far from easy to accomplish even if given high priority, particularly in countries where first-level enrollment is still below 70 percent and the literacy rate under 50 percent. If the choice is between a slower pace of progress towards this goal with a greater length of individual education, or a faster pace with a shorter education, the latter seems to have a greater advantage in terms of the central strategy as enunciated in this study.

Historically the principal factors determining the period of basic general education appear to be a country's educational concepts, economic and social needs, and available resources. The observable trend has been one of extending the duration of general education as the country becomes more affluent, in view of the obvious benefits to the individual and the society flowing from a longer basic education. The organization of general education into two levels follows the traditional division of life cycles into those of childhood and early adolescence (which is now being increasingly questioned); but there is no worldwide uniformity in the length of these two levels. Nor is there any evidence of special merit in fixing the length of first-level education at five, six, or seven years, which appears to be the range in the Asian region. As a matter of fact, primary education lasts four years in some of the more developed countries, from ages seven to eleven in the USSR and from six to ten in West Germany, within the framework of a longer general education. An alternative strategy is to shorten "teacher-time per pupil per day" to enable a teacher to teach more students during a given school day and increase the nonteacher inputs that are conducive to self-study. Such a technique would include suitably designed textbooks and written materials programmed for self-instruction, with instruments of self-evaluation or of mutual evaluation by the students themselves. It would also include better library facilities and the use of media such as radio, films, and television. Under this strategy the total length of education in years might remain unchanged or even be increased, while the time saved by teachers is devoted to teaching a correspondingly larger number of students. There is a critical amount of educational exposure needed to provide the minimum of educational grounding as a safeguard against relapse into illiteracy; a longer length of educational exposure in years, even with shorter school days, seems to commend itself as the better choice at the first level of education.

VERTICAL AND HORIZONTAL BALANCE

Theoretically, a higher ratio of second- and third-level enrollment to total enrollment should mean a better balanced education system

in terms of human resource development, as is actually the case in the
more developed countries. However, the question of vertical balance
is inextricably bound up with that of horizontal balance, and unplanned
growth in either direction might aggravate the structural imbalance instead of correcting it. Besides, what is often overlooked is that balance
has significance only in terms of national needs and resources and
therefore warrants a strategy of horizontal and vertical growth that is
meaningfully related to the economic and social needs of a country.
Such a strategy is all the more necessary in the flexible and multidimensional design of educational structure, described above, which
would link education with work. In other words, priority assigned to
the second and third levels of education would not necessarily be based
on the assumption that they are vital to the supply of critical high-level
manpower, as was done in the past, but included in an objective assessment of national needs for other types of education, including nonformal
education. However, this does not mean that these levels of education
and their natural growth should be underemphasized, but that they
should not be overemphasized either. The countries in the Asian region
have already reached a stage at which the enrollment at these levels
will probably continue to grow at an increasing rate; however, second-
and third-level enrollment should not grow as rapidly as in the older
design, which was unrelated to the national needs and which left the
vast mass of people out of its ambit. The considerably higher unit cost
of education at the second and third levels makes any wastage correspondingly costlier. For this reason and also for the fact that the
second and third levels of education are directly involved in preparing
the future teachers and the core of professional leaders, the strategy
of development of these levels should stress the quality of the educational product. However, as a country advances the constraint of
resources eases, the job qualifications are upgraded, and the educational pyramid tends to grow wider at the middle and the top. During
the period of transition, nonformal education can be used to widen the
benefits of education as a complement to the facilities of formal
education.

THE "FITNESS" OF THE EDUCATIONAL SYSTEM

The most crucial implication of the central strategy of requiring
the economy and education to advance in mutually supporting roles in
the development and utilization of human capital is that the structure
and production function of education will be designed so as to fit economic and social needs. It is therefore imperative that long-range
studies be undertaken with a view to formulating enrollment policies
based on estimates of the manpower needs for economic and social
development. As observed in Chapter 5, the theoretical-mathematical

models that have so far been developed for forecasting manpower requirements and growth in enrollment are based on different approaches and
are subject to many limitations. However, they can serve as path-
finders: used as complementary methods and fed by empirical studies
undertaken within each country, they can be of great value to educational planning and will become progressively refined. The theoretical
character of these models also makes it necessary to adapt them to the
conditions peculiar to a region with a large rural sector and an abundant
supply of human capital. This will naturally imply changes in the basic
concepts and assumptions of the planning models to bring the entire
available stock of manpower within the ambit of the economic and education sectors of development.

"Fitness," that is, matching the educational output with the
demand for it, is admittedly a task with many difficulties in the present
stage of technical knowledge. The difficulties are compounded by the
debatable nature of the criteria for determining manpower requirements
for various occupations and for translating them into educational
qualifications.

As an economy grows in its absorptive capacity, job qualifications
tend to be adjusted upward, with relative salaries moving downward.
This has happened in most industrial countries. Thus fitness is a two-
way dynamic process determined by the changing educational status of
a country and its employment policy. Considering the lead time in
education and also the fact that the upgrading of qualifications is a
major source of increasing productivity, it will be a good development
strategy to plan a larger supply of trained manpower than indicated by
manpower surveys. For instance, educational growth was observed to
have led economic growth in Japan. The wisdom of such an approach
is also indicated by the fact that education, including nonformal education, is intended to be instrumental in providing skills for self-
employment, with the needed support from the economic sector,
including facilities of credit, marketing, supplies of raw materials
and equipment, and managerial advice.

While the need for all possible efforts to fit educational output
to occupational requirements is necessary in educational planning in
a developing country, the technical limitations in this regard make it
unlikely that a perfect fit can be achieved. This is a reality that has
an important bearing on the planning of educational strategy in meeting
the problem of "mismatch." As observed already, a study in the USSR,
which has the longest experience in manpower planning, has indicated
that the extent of mismatch was considerable in certain areas of highly
specialized skill. In the rapidly changing scene in the developing
countries of the Asian region, the chances of such mismatch are admittedly far greater.

In the event of a mismatch, one strategy would be to initiate
corrective measures by retraining the surplus manpower in a particular
field for employment in another in which there is a shortage, and also,

within the limits of balance, by re-engineering, to vary the occupational "mixes" used in meeting the production requirements of an industry.

An important planning strategy for reducing the incidence of the mismatch relates to the design of educational courses. In view of the long lead time in education and the comparatively higher cost of specialization, wisdom seems to warrant that not only at the second level but up to the first-degree stage of the third level the curriculum should be diversified as well as broad based, leading to intensive but relatively shorter programs of specialized training according to needs. Even in the professional courses the stress should be on preparing generalists with basic professional grounding, to be followed by specialized training for a year or two according to the developing needs. Such a design of general and professional education should make it easier for the planner to influence the supply over shorter periods, to meet unforeseen changes in the growth pattern. In such a design, high-level specialization would commence late at the third level, its size and direction depending on the changing technological needs.

It will also be necessary to build into the plan incentives and controls in the form of scholarships and subsidies to attract students to the critical areas of education, as indicated by the estimated requirements of trained manpower. In like manner, it may be necessary to discourage enrollment growth in areas of surplus, through deterrents such as more rigorous admission requirements and higher fees. While there can be no question about the need for assigning high priority to the critical areas of manpower supply, such priority cannot be assigned only to the finishing levels of education to the exclusion of all other levels. An important characteristic of the production function of education is that if production at one level is to be increased, production at the other related levels also has to be increased commensurately.

In terms of lead-time and fitness, short-term programs appear to have a two-fold advantage. First, the various types of nonformal education, including adult education and part-time courses, can be directly related to the observable tasks within a community. Second, since most of these tasks require comparatively simple technical skills, such as in agriculture, weaving, smithy, carpentry, storage of seeds, and use of fertilizer and pesticides, the required skills can be produced and most of the tasks performed within a short period of time, thus practically eliminating or greatly reducing the chances of a mismatch.

TECHNICAL-VOCATIONAL EDUCATION

What has been stated above on the strategy of avoiding over-specialized courses in liberal and professional education in coping with the problem of mismatch is equally applicable to technical-

vocational education. If the full potential of the available human capital
is to be utilized to make up for the present deficiency in physical capital, production will have to draw on capital-saving technologies on a
fairly large scale. During the period of transition, technologies will
not be identical even in the same field of production, and the skills
required for the bulk of the labor force will be in a wide range of intermediate technologies falling between the traditional and the modern.

This reality, as well as the requirements of the tasks to be performed in meeting the immediate economic and social needs of a country,
indicates some additional strategies in planning technical-vocational
education.

1. Technical-vocational education should aim at turning out, as
quickly as possible, more technically trained people at the intermediate
level and below than at the higher level. The bulk of the trained manpower will of course be in agricultural and related technologies, as
long as the rural sector remains the largest contributor to national
product and employment. The strategy should therefore be to plan short
"sandwich" courses alternating between formal training and on-the-job
training on farms, in industry, or in whatever the elected field of work.

The same strategy should also apply to subprofessional training
in education, engineering, medicine, and business administration. In
areas where subprofessional courses do not currently exist, such as
in medicine in Bangladesh, India, and Pakistan, the need for developing
them is clearly indicated. If the given resources are invested in a relatively large number of health technicians with basic training in medicine
and a relatively small number of qualified specialists, the national
needs in medicine and public health are likely to be much better met
than has been the case with investment concentrated on the training of
qualified specialists only.

2. Technical-vocational education should be designed as a part
of both formal and nonformal education within the overall multidimensional pattern of the educational system, as outlined in a foregoing
section. This strategy is warranted on the one hand by the limitations
of resources and on the other by the necessity of making the educational
system more responsive to developmental needs. The central strategy
of developing and utilizing human capital implies a symbiotic relationship in which education and economy motivate and sustain their mutual
growth, contrary to the assumption in the conventional approach to
growth that education is totally dependent on economic growth as the
source of its motivation. The studies discussed in Chapter 4 indicate
that education can also be an active agent of economic growth, since
a significant part of growth in several countries that could not be
accounted for by increases in the inputs of labor and capital as conventionally measured was ascribable to the quality of labor input, or
the productivity of investment in education and the training of the
labor force.

Past experience in the Asian region has shown that education as now designed, with a limited program of technical education developed through a few institutions of technical education outside the mainstream of education, is utterly inadequate as an active agent of growth. If education is to perform its instrumental role, it seems necessary to refashion technical education to enable it to permeate the entire educational system, with a curriculum suited to the needs of each age group. Nonformal technical education can be directly related to vocational needs within the framework of local community development plans. Technical education within the formal system will have to be meaningfully related to the mainstream of education, on a footing of equality with other courses. This will involve far-reaching changes in the traditional concept of both general and technical education. General and technical education should be viewed as complementary, and each should have elements of the other, depending on the level of education and the degree of specialization needed.

What is envisaged here, however, is something more than the manual training now provided at the first level, which has not proven very effectual, or a greater diversification of education at the second level with emphasis on the technical and commercial courses, although this is desirable. The essential strategy is to make technical education work-oriented and thereby reach more people. Whether the program is called vocational or prevocational is not so important as whether the skills acquired, even if very simple in some cases (as at the first level), have a meaning in the economic and social context. The program must extend beyond the classroom and in-school situations to its related fields of life-situation within the community. It thus implies much more than the acquisition of a skill, although of course this has its own value as a useful and satisfying source of neuromotor development. Exposure to life-situations in using and improving skills places these skills into perspective. The young people are thus enabled to see their relevance and better understand their social and economic environment. Not only skill, but skill relevant to a given social reality and an understanding of that reality appear to be essential conditions if technical education is to become an effective instrument of growth. Technical education as developed during the 1950s and 1960s lacked this social linkage and understanding.

However, the strategy does not imply that all forms of technical-vocational education are to be provided in every primary or secondary school. Separate schools, centers, or workshops may have to be set up for some forms of technical education, in which the skills involved are so specialized that training in these skills can most economically and efficiently be provided in separate institutions, especially equipped and staffed by specialist teachers. However, it would be a good strategy, as mentioned in Chapter 7, to plan such special centers or workshops as far as possible as part of a cluster of educational facilities available to the community as a whole.

SOME TRADITIONAL NOTIONS AND DEFINITIONS THAT ARE UNTENABLE IN CONTEMPORARY SOCIETY

The design of technical education as envisaged in this study will appear to run counter to some of the traditional notions about the contents and functions of education up to the second level; these notions strongly favor a liberal general education without any taint of technical-vocational education. The first notion reflects the dichotomy between the "cultural" and "utilitarian" aims of education, which, as observed in Chapter 7, can be traced to the influence of a bygone era when education was limited to an elite group and the process of economic growth was dehumanized in many ways. The second is the belief that education (in the sense of traditional liberal education) up to the second level should aim at general intellectual development and that an early exposure to the narrow specialization implied in technical education is detrimental to such development.

Both of these notions, historical byproducts of the social and educational evolution of Western society, have been unwittingly transferred to an entirely different social scene in the developing countries, in which neither underlying assumption seems to fit the realities of life. The value of general education, articulated by an adequate element of science, to development has been stressed more than once in this study, but the limited resources in the Asian region do not at present permit more than a fifth of the second-level age group to be enrolled in school and, under the traditional system, the bulk of the active labor force has no access to any education whatsoever. In such a context the debate over general versus technical education becomes totally academic, with hardly any relevance to the needs and realities of the situation in the region. Besides, as earlier noted, the present need for highly specialized training in technical education is very limited, though it will gradually increase with progressive modernization. Therefore the level, spread, and contents of general as well as technical education will have to be designed to fit the central strategy of maximizing the development of human capital to meet the changing technological needs.

GENERAL VERSUS TECHNICAL-VOCATIONAL EDUCATION

The dichotomic notion that the aims of general education are "cultural and humanistic" and those of technical-vocational education are "utilitarian and productivist" does not also seem to be consistent with contemporary life, even in the industrial societies. If by "culture" is meant a way of life, then culture has been profoundly changed by science and technology. With the development of democratic institu-

tions and the extension of education, and as both production and consumption have become increasingly governed by human values, the life
styles of the people and the norms and values of the whole society in
these countries have been transformed. The narrow traditional notion
of culture and cultural education has in this context become anachronistic, and there is clearly a need for a reexamination and redefinition
of some of the concepts and values that have hitherto determined the
structure of education.

Life in the contemporary world has become predominantly work-
oriented. Where work is no longer considered ignoble, and the human
values of dignity, honesty, and industry characterize individual work
habits, and where work that is well done yields a satisfaction over and
above the monetary reward, it becomes a part of the worker's cultural
life in a very real sense. To a perceptive mind, the work that a man
does, even though it is largely with his hands and for his living, can
also be highly creative and a source of joy and beauty as profound and
moving as a fine piece of art. The personal, cultural, social and economic aims of education thus converge as complementary and indivis-
ible components and merge into a single, unified, uplifting purpose.

Some of the classical concepts of education thus clearly need to
be reevaluated in the changing social context, especially in the developing countries, where the craze for book learning and the aversion
for manual work have stymied the effectiveness of education as an
instrument of development. The strategy lies not merely in assigning
a high priority to scientific and technological education, but also in
making such education integral to the mainstream of education, related
meaningfully to community needs. The "craft-centered education"
advocated for India by Gandhi contained the essence of such a strategy.
The immense possibilities of this "revolutionary experiment," to use
the words of the Indian Education Commission,[5] were apparently vitiated
by the narrow and rigid frame of "basic education" within which the
experiment was carried out.

QUALITY IN EDUCATION

Perhaps no aspect of educational planning has presented a greater
challenge to the planner than that of determining the mix of quantitative
and qualitative growth. As observed in Chapters 1 and 7, neither the
physical targets of growth as indicated in the national plans nor the
input-output or cost-benefit ratios were adequate and proper measures
of educational growth, since these indicators were not sensitive to the
quality factor. Quality is integral to the very concept of education,
since education is essentially a process of qualitative change through
the development of the innate capacity of an individual. Attendance at
school and the learning-teaching processes are means to this end, and

the desired social and educational changes that are the objective of
planned educational development are a function of quality in education.
Thus in any goal-oriented educational planning, as stressed in the
overall strategy, quality in education emerges as the central factor.

The term "quality" is semantically a slippery one and has often
been used to mean different things in different conceptual contexts.
For instance, as observed in Chapter 1, it may mean the "quality of
the product" or the "quality of the system." When it is used in terms
of the product, quality is measured by the level of development attained
by an individual regardless of the number of individuals within the
system; here the pursuit of individual excellence is the main concern
even though the number participating in the education system may be
very small, in the case of highly selective schools or school systems.
When "quality" is used in terms of the system it is measured by the
educational growth achieved by a number of students starting from a
given base in a given social and economic setting. In this sense the
"quantity of quality," or the number participating in the educational
system, is also an important factor in measuring quality, as in the
case of public education.

In either instance it should, perhaps, be stressed that quality
of education is not an absolute,[6] but has to be related to some explicitly stated standard that an institution has in view. For example, the
same level of excellence may be high in terms of modest aims and
medium in terms of higher aims. Thus an institution aiming to produce
technicians may turn out first-class technicians and be rated better
than a similar one that is aiming to train engineers and turns out
second-class engineers.

However, the concept of quality is capable of being carried to
a point of abstraction in pursuit of what is imagined to be perfect
quality, resembling a mathematical asymptote. The level of quality
to be sought must instead be objectively determined by social and
economic realities. It would be highly unrealistic for the planners of
an Asian country to pursue norms of quality that are either too abstract
for translation into operative programs or unsuited to the needs of a
developing country. "It would be patently absurd, for example, to
hold that identical school-building standards and specifications and
identical staffing standards should apply alike in an underdeveloped
tropical country and in a highly industrialized temperate country."[7]

The concept of quality has many dimensions from the standpoint
of practical planning. In the first place, the concept of quality at a
given time must be related to the stage of development of a country,
its need for further development, and the available human and material
resources. Thus, the quality requirements in technical education primarily depend on the technologies relevant to the country's stage of
development and needs. For example, the standard of training in agricultural technology that is relevant to a developed wheat-producing
country such as Canada or the United States has no meaning for the

rice-producing countries in South and Southeast Asia. In like manner, the standards of Eton, Harrow, Oxford, and Cambridge, whatever their value to English society, are totally incompatible with the social needs and conditions of the Indian subcontinent, as actually demonstrated by the unhappy results of the efforts made during the late 19th and early 20th centuries to transplant them there.[8] Thus quality has different meanings in different social contexts.

In the second place, even within a country quality is not a static concept, but changes with the country's changing needs, resources, and aspirations. As the level of attainment rises, the concept of quality also moves up in the scale. It is also relative to the boundaries of knowledge, and advances as the frontiers of knowledge are advanced by research. Thus the level of excellence attainable today in the sciences or social sciences is considerably different from that even a few decades back. Viewed in this context, the much-talked-about international standards become unreal except in certain sharply defined and highly specialized fields of higher education and technology such as the training of research mathematicians and physicists, airplane pilots, or the top-level managerial and engineering personnel of such modern industrial plants as those producing steel and hydroelectric or nuclear power.

In the third place, as observed in Chapter 1, the products of the educational system are human, and each one is unique. Even if the available human and material resources were enough to achieve the highest attainable level of excellence in a given stage and field of education, product quality would not be the same in all cases because of individual differences in innate capacities. Assuming what is improbable, that it were possible to control the social and economic environment affecting capacity and motivation to learn, the concept of quality control in the sense of uniformity of quality is thus ruled out as inapplicable to educational products. There are also certain desirable values and attitudes developed through education that are not quantifiable, though with the development and refinement of testing instruments the range of measurable qualities and abilities is progressively being widened.

In the fourth place, contrary to the notion held by some, quality and quantity in education are not mutually exclusive or incompatible; there is a "quality of quantity" and a "quantity of quality." Quantity and quality interact with each other within the complex web of social, economic, and psychological factors that impinge on educational growth. As observed in Chapter 7, neither a relatively small enrollment nor a higher unit cost necessarily results in better educational results. The notion that qualitative improvement can be accelerated in a nationwide public education system by restricting quantitative growth is not borne out by any historical evidence. On the other hand it is in the highest degree improbable that an educational system can experience quantitative growth without undergoing some qualitative changes in the process. At the same time it is beyond question that if the quantity and quality of the resource inputs do not match the student inputs into the educational system, its quality will be adversely affected.

"VALUE ADDED": A MEASURE OF QUALITY

In meeting the demands of such a multidimensional and dynamic concept of quality in education, there is clearly a need for a dynamic and imaginative plan-strategy — a strategy that can insightfully and realistically translate the implications of the desired qualitative changes into the needed changes in the educational system, in its aims, curricula, courses, systems of learning, teaching, evaluation, and motivation, and ultimately resulting in changes in the quality of the educational output. Keeping in view the interacting relationship between quality and quantity, the strategy should aim at maximizing the total value added through quantitative and qualitative growth in measurable qualities and abilities resulting from a given course or type of education at a given level, within the available resources. The efficacy of a given course of education can be measured in terms of value added as illustrated below:

Assuming that P = ability at the commencement of the course, and

Q = ability at the end of the course,

$Q - P = V$, the educational growth resulting from the course, or value added.

N = total number of students

V_k = value of the kth student

Therefore

$$\text{Total value,} \quad N\bar{V} = \sum_1^N (Q - P)_k$$

The total value added in a public education system is thus influenced by both the quantitative and qualitative aspects of growth.

There does not appear to be any golden rule that determines the mix of quantity and quality necessary to maximize educational growth. The weight to be assigned to either factor will have to be objectively determined by the functions that education of a particular level or type is intended to perform in a given social and economic situation. For example, in the Asian situation emphasis on quantitative growth at the level of basic education (that is, first-level formal education and nonformal education) is indicated as a good strategy for several reasons: (1) The command of the basic tools of knowledge and skill is likely to increase labor productivity. (2) The equalization of opportunities of education is likely to promote social and occupational mobility and hence is an incentive to better efforts. (3) Since differences in native ability are reflected in the product quality, to the extent that universal basic education helps in discovering the talented and enabling them to proceed to further education, it also contributes to the qualitative growth of the education system.

HIGHER EDUCATION

On the other hand, the strategy seems to lie in the direction of stressing the qualitative aspect of growth in higher education. This is warranted not only by the limitations of resources and the high unit cost at this level, but more importantly by the functions that education at this level is intended to perform. For example, higher education has to supply the teachers needed for other levels of education and it has to spearhead reforms in the contents and methods of education through advanced study and research. At the advanced level one of its major functions is to apply the fruits of knowledge in solving social and economic problems and accelerate the process of technological change. It is also the crucible of creative, inventive, and innovative ideas. It thus serves as the source of motive-force for change. In all of these functions quality is of the first importance. Besides, there are certain areas of highly specialized training, such as training in advanced study and research in the sciences and in engineering and technology, where training does not become critical unless it reaches a certain quality level determined by the rising level of knowledge and technology in the global context. It was observed in Chapter 1 that scientific knowledge is growing at a breathtaking speed, practically doubling itself in 10 to 15 years. Viewed in the context of the Asian situation, a realistic strategy would be to aim at reaching and maintaining the international standards in selected fields according to a country's needs and resources. As observed in Chapter 4, it is in the knowledge sector that the fastest and most fruitful return may be expected from investment in human capital.

THE SOCIAL MILIEU: "TRADE-OFFS"

The planner is not a completely free agent in devising his strategies. The social milieu in which he works imposes many limitations. His choice of weight and of trade-offs is greatly fettered by the limitations of resources, the pressures exerted by the social, political, and economic aspirations of the people, the quality of the existing teachers, the rate at which better teachers can be inducted, and not least the home and neighborhood environment of the students. Within these and other limitations the planner will have to map out his strategy to influence the quality of output by influencing the input. As earlier mentioned, empirical studies are needed to determine the relationship between input variations and qualitative increments. Theoretically it should be possible to influence the input through judicious resource allocation to foster qualitative growth in the desired way. There is also rationality in the generally recommended strategy of stressing modernization of the curriculum and textbooks, improvement and expansion of teacher education, development of technical-vocational education, including agricultural education, improvement of teaching methods, and use of such aids as films, radio, and television.

However, efforts in these directions were thwarted in the past by the irrational forces of resistance to change. Some of these forces are located within the educational system, in the principles and practices developed over the years and encrusting a subculture unresponsive to the needs of a changing society. If this crust is to be broken and the forces of resistance overcome, past experiences indicate the need for unifying the forces of change in a "critical mass," not at one single point, but at several vital points, including the heart of the system, which is the concepts, values, and motivation underlying it.

The new design of the educational system, with its broad, flexible, multidimensional structure, linking formal and nonformal education, work, and study, and with access to "recurrent" education through part-time courses and even an "open university," as well as facilities for returning workers to full-time courses of formal education for professional development, appears to be the most important first step in the direction of the needed change.

EXAMINATIONS

Examinations not only measure but also motivate educational growth. As observed in Chapter 7, in many countries of the Asian region the examinations used measure mechanical memory and not intellectual development, and instead of motivating the growth of the creative and analytical powers of the mind they stifle them. Many a reform effort has been wrecked by the prevailing examination system. The success of any new design of education thus presupposes a radical reform in the concept and method of examination. Examinations should become an integral part of the very educational process, measuring and motivating educational growth daily, weekly, monthly, and continuously throughout the courses.

Examinations are to be designed as instruments for testing the power to reason, to analyze, and use knowledge in solving problems, allowing both teachers and students to participate in using them

within the normal learning-teaching process. The reform of the examinations is thus a prerequisite for the success of other educational
reforms and also for ending the baneful effects of an examination system that has proved to be a source of fear, friction, and frustration.

Three other strategic points through which a "critical mass" of
qualitative change can be introduced into the educational system are
higher education, teacher education, and educational administration
and supervision.

"CRITICAL MASS" IN HIGHER EDUCATION AND TEACHER EDUCATION

Institutions of higher education and teacher education are directly
concerned with the education and training of teachers. Educational administration is concerned with their recruitment and the supervision of
their work. Changes at these levels have a multiplier effect felt down
to the first level. It is also at these levels that the search for new
teaching methods and innovations has to be undertaken. Because the
numbers involved are relatively small, it should be easier to allocate
the resources necessary to substitute input of better quality for that of
inferior quality and produce a "critical mass" faster. However, if
these areas are to act as catalysts of change within the whole system,
past experience in the region indicates that (1) the resources employed
in these fields, both human and material, should be of the very best
quality available; (2) their programs of education should be directly
geared to the changing needs of the society; (3) their performance
should be evaluated in terms of their creative, inventive, and innovative contributions to the educational curriculum and technology and
to the solution of other educational problems; and (4) research in education should not remain confined to professional institutions of teacher
education, which have traditionally suffered from an isolation from the
mainstream of higher education and research. Advanced study and
research in the sciences, the social sciences, and the applied sciences, including agriculture, at the universities can be fruitfully
linked to contemporary problems in general, technical, and professional
education, and thus make a positive contribution to educational concepts and technology.

NONFORMAL EDUCATION, MOTIVATION FOR CHANGE: EDUCATION CORPS

Nonformal education is another strategic and highly promising
base for launching the reform efforts. If an effective program of
nonformal education directly related to the development goals and

tasks within a community can be planned, the entire community can be involved in a meaningful process of change, extending to the school, the home, and the society. The experience of the USSR indicates that a nationwide program to replace mass illiteracy by mass education and productive employment of the members of the labor force can be mounted successfully if the political leadership is willing and prepared to undertake the task.

Keeping in view the vast numbers involved in the Asian region, the ineffectiveness of the traditional methods of education, and the inadequacy of the supply of qualified teachers for meeting even the needs of formal education, the success of the program of nonformal education seems to depend on several factors. Major among them are (1) the ability of the planners to design a sound program of education relevant to the development tasks to be performed; (2) the ability to produce educational materials suited to the interests and needs of the nonschool population; (3) the ability to develop an appropriate educational technology, including the use of the mass media such as radio and television; and (4) the availability of teaching and administrative personnel. The first three factors primarily hinge on technical expertise and resources. Many of the countries in the region have already built up cores of technical expertise that can be expanded rapidly according to need. Given the national commitment to the program, the need for resources can be met by mobilizing local resources within a community according to a phased plan.

The problems of the teaching and administrative staff are also not beyond solution. Besides using the part-time services of the full-time staff of existing schools and participants from other sectors in implementing the program of nonformal education, educated youths may also be drafted annually into this program in the required number for a specified period of time. As already observed, the latter technique has been tried out in several Asian countries, on a voluntary basis in some and on a compulsory basis in others. The experiences of these countries seem to indicate that if a nationwide program of nonformal education is to be mounted as a part of the overall development of the community, the task must be approached as a national duty and shared by all. In that case, the service rendered under this program will have to form a part of the compulsory national service, or else an integral part of the educational process and a requirement for the successful completion of a prescribed course of education. As indicated earlier, it is being increasingly recognized that an exposure to the realities of life through participation in solving the economic and social problems confronting a society is a valuable education experience. In many of the more developed countries, work experience in the field is a requirement of the educational program. This is indeed a social necessity in the developing countries in view of the shortage of educated manpower and also the catalytic influence that a highly motivated corps of educated young people can have on the process of change.

PRIORITIES IN EDUCATION

One of the most difficult problems in planning is the establishment of priorities among the competing claims of the various goals of
development in the allocation of the limited resources likely to be
available during a given time. Grotesque distortions in the growth
pattern have indicated the lack of success of past efforts in this direction and the need for more judicious selection of the criteria for establishing future priorities.

The governments of all developing countries are admittedly under
great social and political pressures to move rapidly in all sectors of
development, which however desirable is far from practicable, not only
because of the lack of resources but also because of the lack of time
and the technique needed for their use. Resources, technique, and a
period of gestation are interrelated factors of growth. If our analysis
in this study is correct, the problems of distortion facing the countries
in South and Southeast Asia are not the outcome so much of their effort
to move in all directions at the same pace as of their choice of wrong
priorities. It is evident from the investment pattern that during the
1950s and 1960s the social sectors, including education, and also
agriculture, the major segment of the economic sector, were placed
much lower in the scale of priorities than was warranted by the goals
and needs of development. In like manner, in the choice of technology
proper weight was not given to those technologies that were likely to
produce better and quicker results in terms of productive employment
of the labor force. As observed in Chapter 4, the core of development
dynamics is the technological change accompanying increasing application of specialized knowledge and a greater division of labor with
more individuals concentrating on more specific tasks so that the
tasks are done better. The aim of the developing countries is to move
in the direction of progressive modernization of technology through a
series of adjustments to the changing needs in order to maximize the
utilization of human capital during the period of transition. The concept of priority must therefore be related to both the time and technique
of growth within the dynamic frame of the central strategy of development and utilization of human capital.

Theoretically speaking, the order of priorities should follow the
order of the estimated marginal return on investment in the various
subsectors of education. The level of investment in the different subsectors will increase or diminish according to the demand so that the
marginal rates of return for all subsectors will ultimately be equal.
Such a perfect equilibrium is hardly attainable in the sector of education, in which the human and social variables are preponderant,
many of which do not lend themselves to measurement by the available
instruments.

The problem of developing the criteria for establishing priorities within the education sector is further complicated by the following factors: (1) The national objectives in education are not all capable of being translated into quantifiable schedules of educational supply and demand. (2) These objectives are so interrelated that it is not possible to arrange them according to their relative importance in the form of a ladder of priorities. (3) In like manner, the different levels and types of education are also interdependent, and a weight to one subsector involves a corresponding weight to a related subsector. (4) The lead time in education renders it highly difficult to forecast the appropriate level of investment in a subsector in terms of the national needs in a rapidly changing society. (5) Neither the unit cost nor the cost-benefit ratio is a dependable guide in view of the difficulty demonstrated in Chapter 4 of capturing and measuring all the benefits accruing to the individual and the society from investment in a particular educational program.

"CHAIN" OF PRIORITIES—NOT A "LADDER"

It will appear from the foregoing discussion that the interdependence of the various levels and types of education rules out the practicability of arranging the priorities in the form of a ladder and renders it necessary to arrange them in the form of a chain, reflecting the complementary relationship of the various subsectors. However, the role that each subsector of education is required to perform in supporting the central strategy of the development and utilization of human capital will determine the units of weight to be assigned to it in the scale of priorities.

Establishment of priorities is a matter of policy prescription, and each country will naturally have to develop its own criteria for determining the priorities in education according to its own national objectives, needs, resources, social realities, and values. However, to the extent that the countries in the Asian region have a common identity in their development goals, social conditions, and educational needs and problems, a basis for the development of some common criteria appears to exist. The following common criteria seem to emerge from the foregoing analysis of the national objectives of development and of the educational needs and problems in the countries in the region:

1. To what extent does an educational program contribute to the national objective of equalizing educational, economic, and social opportunities? From this point of view, special weight would be due to formal and nonformal basic education, part-time courses for further education, and financial assistance schemes.

2. To what extent is an educational program likely to contribute to the skills needed for increasing productive employment, including self-employment? Technical-vocational education within the formal as well as the nonformal system, higher professional education, and scientific and technological research should rate highly according to this criterion.

3. To what extent does a program have a "multiplier effect"? That is, to what extent do improvements resulting from the program have a direct effect on a number of other areas of education in the form of a chain reaction? For example, higher education and teacher education are responsible for the supply of teachers for various levels and types of education, and advanced study and research lead to innovations in educational curricula and technology. These are likely to produce a multiplier effect throughout the educational system, formal and nonformal.

4. How much is a program likely to cost? Both unit cost and total cost are important factors from the standpoint of resources. Even though the money-cost may not be a reliable measure of the benefits flowing from an educational program, the competing claims of various programs for the limited resources lend a special importance to the cost criterion in determining priorities. In the Asian region nonformal education and primary education have an advantage over other areas of education in terms of unit cost. This criterion is also applicable to specific projects within a level or type of education in determining the relative value of alternative choices.

5. How long is the lead time involved in the implementation of a program? Though a long lead time is inescapable in the case of some programs, as in producing medical and engineering graduates and masters and Ph. D.'s of higher education, the countries in the region are under social and political pressure to spread the benefits of development as widely and as quickly as possible. Shorter programs, such as subprofessional courses, extension courses, and part-time courses, with a higher rate of turnover, have distinct advantages over longer programs in some areas. This implies that the longer courses should also continue but on a limited scale.

6. What is the estimated value of the indirect benefits that accrue to the individual and the society from an educational program, other than those that are measurable? As observed, some of the results of an educational program cannot be captured by analytical instruments employed to compute the return on investment in the program, though these benefits may be of great value to the individual, family, and neighborhood. For example, a basic general education through primary and adult education bestows immense benefits on the individual and the neighborhood by enriching the cultural life and fostering habits and attitudes conducive to the national purpose, with their good effects on home, school, and society. Even though the

assessment of these benefits can only be subjective, it is important that they are not overlooked and that they are assigned due weight in view of the importance attached to them by the countries in the region.

7. To what extent does a program serve as a foundation for other educational programs? An important characteristic of the production function of education is that the output of one level, type, or course becomes the input of a related level, type, or course. Thus first-level education has a foundational value for second-level education, and second-level education has a similar value for higher general, technological, and professional education. In like manner some courses, such as those in mathematics and the basic sciences, provide the foundation for specialized technological-professional education.

8. What is the value of the program as a source of motivation for creative, inventive, and innovative work? Such motivation is basic to qualitative improvement in education and a prerequisite for breaking down the barriers of resistance to change within the educational system and also outside it in the economic and social sectors of development. Advanced study and mission-oriented research with a critical role to play in accelerating the process of change should rate high in this criterion. Suitable reforms in examination and administration also appear to deserve special weight.

9. To what extent does a program contribute to a reduction in the unit cost through modified techniques? Development of materials programmed for self-instruction and assignment of lessons through suitably designed radio and television programs can substantially cut down teacher cost, which is now the major component of the recurrent cost in the Asian region. Through suitable changes in educational technology and through part-time courses designed on a graduated scale, it is also possible to shorten the time of formal education, thus reducing overall cost, easing pressure on the formal system, and increasing the rate of turnover. Recent studies indicate that there is no evidence supporting the traditional belief that the longer a course lasts and the larger its curriculum content, the better will be the educational result.[9] The will to learn, the teaching technique, and the aids to self-instruction appear to be more important factors in influencing the results of an educational program.

10. How far does a program contribute to the national pool of knowledge and skill, to enable the nation to stay within the mainstream of world knowledge in those areas? As already observed, though the present educational needs of the developing countries vary considerably from those of the industrial countries, in certain areas of education and training, such as higher scientific and technological research, aviation, and management of modern industries, the investment will be fully fruitful only by attaining the current world level of technical competence.

It is evident that the above criteria are not mutually exclusive. This reflects the interrelationship of the different areas of education.

They also do not exhaust the range of needs and interests shared by the countries in the region. These criteria are intended to bring into focus the major areas of critical need in educational development within the central theme of the present study.

The weight that should be assigned to each of these criteria in their present or a modified form is naturally a matter of social decision in light of a country's needs and conditions. However, whatever may be the scale of weight emerging from the values assigned by a developing country to each of the criteria, it is likely that some of the areas of education will gain a multiple weight by this scale.

FINANCING OF EDUCATION

The strategy in financing educational development has to be thought of in the international as well as the national context, inasmuch as the sources of finance have both a national and international dimension.

As observed in Chapter 2, internationally the two most important elements affecting the resource position of a developing country are international aid and international trade. There is clearly scope for improving the contribution of both in financing development. Progress in this direction seems to depend on a more enlightened appreciation of the interdependence of the nations and on the realization that the cause of global peace and security is served better by increasing investment in development than by increasing the stock of armaments.

It was noted that the flow of international aid has shown a trend of faltering growth, and in terms of the GNP even a decline. In the Asian region the part of aid applied to education was as low as 3 percent. If aid even on the present scale is to be more productive than has been the case in the past, a two-fold strategy seems to be indicated: (1) all aid should be applied to genuine development, and (2) the military component of the aid should be converted into a human component, representing ideas, knowledge, and skill in a two-way flow. This would have a catalytic effect on development and also on the international exchange of knowledge in the true tradition of scholarship.

Nationally, some of the directions along which efforts can be made to generate more resources for investment in development have been indicated in Chapters 2 and 6. So far as the pressing need for larger investment in the education sector is concerned, several strategies for mobilizing additional resources seem to follow from the analysis of the data for the Asian region that are presented in Chapter 7.

1. In countries where the level of investment in education falls in the lower half of the range as a percentage of the GNP or of the national budget within the region, there is evidently scope for raising

the level immediately by intersectoral readjustments in the allocation of the available resources.

2. Several countries in the region spend 20 percent of their national budgets and 4 to 5.7 percent of their GNP on education. These levels should be attainable by other countries in the region and can therefore be adopted as targets to stimulate planned growth in educational investment within a reasonable period of time. The plan for a gradual increase in the expenditure on education that was recommended for India by the Indian Education Commission, to reach a level of 6 percent in 1985/86, appears to be reasonably graduated.

3. The strategy of setting targets of educational expenditure as a percentage of the GNP, which is very often stressed in literature on educational planning, may serve as a stimulus to larger investments in education. It does not, however, seem to have a rational basis as a guide to the financial input necessary to produce the output desired from an educational system. The current level of expenditure as a ratio of the GNP in the more developed countries can be quite misleading. For one thing a given ratio of the GNP in these countries means much more money than the corresponding ratio in the developing countries. For another, the developed countries have reached their present levels of educational expenditure not because they had set such targets in advance but because rising levels of investment in education were found necessary to meet their educational needs. Thus in their case the educational expenditure bears a meaningful relationship to the changing educational needs of the society. The strategy of setting targets of educational expenditure in the developing countries has not related educational expenditure to educational needs in the same way. It seems to reflect the traditional notion that education can grow only when economy grows and not vice versa, contrary to the central thesis of this study that the relationship between education and economy is symbiotic, that each feeds the other's growth. A rational approach seems to be to treat educational expenditure as an investment in the human component of capital, and to cost it as other factors of production are costed, keeping in view the goal of maximizing employment and adjusting technology to the changing needs of development. Technically this is no longer considered as impracticable. Some of the analytical methods already available for computing educational supply and demand were discussed in Chapter 5.

4. In the case of the areas of education that are costly or have long lead time, the most commonly employed strategy is to phase their development in such a way as to distribute the financial burden over a sufficiently long period of time and spanning several plan periods, if the plans are of short or medium range, as they usually are. The resources released through this strategy can then be applied to low-cost and quickly gestating programs of education that accelerate the growth of productive employment in areas that do not require long and specialized training. An important caveat in phasing the plans of

development of costly areas of education is that if the size of the program is smaller than what is needed to reach a "critical mass," the entire investment may be wasted. This is particularly true in the case of higher education and research, where the input of teachers and equipment must reach a minimum level for effective work and therefore cannot be determined as a ratio of the number of trainees.

5. As observed in Chapter 7, the goal of universal education is yet to be achieved in a number of countries in the region. The impediments in the way of realization of the goal include limited resources, rapid growth in population, and a high rate of attrition. This is an area of education, along with basic nonformal education for the nonschool population, that is central to the objectives of economic and social development. It is therefore also at the center of the social and political pressure on the governments in these countries. It is necessary to consider the impracticability of halting expansion altogether, the trend in enrollment growth, the present resource constraint, and the time needed to evolve remedies for wastage. The simple mathematical model in Appendix B shows how the growth in enrollment and the growth in expenditure can be spread over a period (the span of ten years used in this model is illustrative) in easy stages, with a proportionately smaller burden in the initial years.

6. There is a need for intrasectoral readjustments in resource allocation within the education sector to correct the inter-level and inter-type imbalance noted in Chapter 7. This imbalance is apparently caused by a distorted notion of priorities and a disharmony between national objectives and plan-strategies. This distortion was most conspicuous in technical-vocational education throughout the region compared to other levels and at the first level in India and Pakistan compared to the third level.

7. In many countries capital outlay was not matched by the current outlay required for educational development. This inevitably had an adverse effect on the fruitfulness of the investment as a whole. The strategy should be to economize on capital expenditure and invest more in such other input as teachers, books, and laboratory and other equipment. Construction of ostentatious buildings has many disadvantages: (1) It uses up resources that could be applied to qualitative improvement of education. (2) The cost of maintenance of such buildings is also higher and accordingly increases the ultimate burden of current outlay. (3) Being discordant with the other buildings in the neighborhood, they also become a source of social and ecological disharmony. If the technique of planned development through the participation of the local communities and of education at the local level is related to the development tasks to be performed within a community, a large part of the capital outlay can be passed on to the local communities. Such a strategy of burden sharing is also quite in line with what has been a time-honored tradition in the countries in the Asian region. As earlier mentioned, another important measure of economy

would be to establish the educational institutions in a cluster to serve a community as a whole and thus allow the use of the available accommodation, equipment, and staff for multiple educational purposes.

ADMINISTRATION

As observed in Chapters 1, 6, and 7, the archaic structure of educational administration in the region has been a major impediment to change and also an important cause of the alienation of the youth. One of the principal reasons for the failure of the various reform efforts has been that the structure of administration entrusted with implementation of these reforms was itself in need of reform. It has remained a relic of the bygone colonial era, so wrapped up in its institutional memory that even the able and talented become atrophied parts of an ineffective structure.

Certain general strategies, such as decentralization of administration, active participation of the community in plan formulation and implementation, development of an effective system of communication and feedback, and rationalization of the system of recruitment, promotion, and salary structure to provide incentives for creative and productive effort are essential structural reforms to break the hard shell that has grown around administration. If administration is to perform its critical role as the nerve center of the educational system, other measures are also necessary: (1) The administrative personnel must have the knowledge of and skill in the use of the modern techniques of management, since education has in recent years grown into a vast "industry," and traditional methods of management are no longer adequate for the complex task of educational development. (2) The concept of renewal of education through "recurrent" education should be equally applicable to the administrative personnel. (3) The performance of the educational administration at various levels should be under continuous evaluation through the application of modern methods of research to the various educational activities. (4) A team of diverse talents representing various skills and interests, rather than only "administrators" in the traditional sense, should be made responsible for developing and implementing educational plans and policies at the top level. (5) There should be an inflow into this team of talented persons from the field who have demonstrated creative and innovative ability.

Educational administrators have in the past played an integrative and conservative role in preserving the existing structures and values. If they are now to be cast into the role of agents of change and innovation, some special strategies seem to be necessary:

1. Individuals with creative minds will have to be attracted in sufficient number to careers in the management of education. The

success of the multidimensional education system proposed in this study to move the nation progressively towards the goal of the most productive development of its human capital will depend largely on the professional competence, insight, leadership, and creativity of the administrative organ, not only at the top level but at all levels. It should perhaps be stressed that the leadership role is not an authoritarian one. Its function is preeminently to stimulate, sustain, and coordinate the creative efforts that spring from within and from below. It therefore implies a cooperative partnership within which the various component parts of the education system have the freedom as well as the opportunity to search and experiment.

2. Those involved in administration must have sufficient exposure to field experience outside formal education for a proper perception of the needs and problems of the society and of the kind of education relevant in that context. This is especially true in the case of higher education, which, as observed in Chapter 7, tends to isolate itself from the life of society and become a major cause of the alienation of youth. If the institutions of higher education are to be made responsive to social and economic needs, the rigid traditional classroom, lecture-reading format will have to be changed to a flexible and dynamic work-study format. If the universities and colleges are to serve as the wellspring of innovation for progress and produce the "multiplier" effect in changing education as well as society, both faculty and students must be exposed to meaningful life experiences outside the campus. This will call for several changes in the well-established pattern of higher education:

1. The admission policy should favor students with "field experience"; such experience for a specified period could be a requirement for admission to the graduate program—this would be especially relevant in countries where educated youths are required to serve compulsorily for a given period in the implementation of the development program. Such a change in the admission policy is also likely to reduce the number of those who now hang on and "mark time" in institutions of higher education.

2. Provision should be made for financial aid to students with work experience. It may be noted that the costs of higher education are likely to be reduced because the students are better motivated.

3. The change should be supported by a comprehensive scheme for educational internships of students in government departments, industry, business, community development, and other forms of social service. Higher education will thus become mission oriented and recognize work and experience as an integral part of education. A trend in this direction is visible even in capitalist industrial countries. The "work-study approach for technical training at Northeastern University in Massachusetts and the small-group-centered, community-problem-oriented format at Staten Island Community College"[10] are some of the notable examples of work-study programs of education in the United States.

THE STRATEGY OF STRATEGIES

Finally, a word on the strategy of strategies. As already observed, development is a dynamic process of change, and both education and technology have an adaptive role to play within the complex web of numerous interrelated and interacting forces. It cannot be overstressed that the crisis in development throughout the Third World also involves a crisis in values underscoring the vital role of both education and society in the reorientation of the value moorings to provide a socially stable and politically viable base for national development and to motivate national efforts in this direction. If the high social cost of violent explosion, which has already been paid by some of them, is to be avoided, the strategy of strategies seems to lie in aiming at growth with justice, with the thrust of the development effort towards maximizing employment and productivity at the community and human level and enriching the quality of life.

This strategy implies five important steps: (1) a firm and unequivocal commitment of the political leadership to the goal of social justice and an equitable distribution of the benefits of development; (2) consciously opting for a style of life consistent with social realities and values, which may mean for many countries an austere level of consumption, but which may yet be rich in its intellectual and cultural content; (3) the creation of a trained and highly motivated cadre of workers, preferably drawn from among the educated youths, to fill the present educational gap and provide the much-needed educational input in the rural areas where the majority of the population has no access to education; (4) the building of appropriate institutions to stimulate and sustain development efforts at various levels; and (5) an adequate machinery for continuous evaluation of the planning performance, with the decision-making authority sufficiently decentralized to encourage local initiative and innovativeness.

It is, above all, of paramount importance that the plan-strategies keep the human dimension in the symbiotic growth of education and economy in constant focus and do not allow means to overshadow the ends at any stage.

NOTES

1. K. Nozkho et al., Educational Planning in the U.S.S.R., including a report by an IIEP Mission to the USSR headed by R. Poignant (Paris: UNESCO/IIEP, 1968).

2. C.E. Beeby, ed., Qualitative Aspects of Educational Planning (Paris: UNESCO, 1969), p. 267.

3. Peter J. Smith, "Britain's Open University," in Saturday Review (April 29, 1972), p. 40.

4. Ibid., p. 49.

5. Government of India, Report of the Education Commission (1964-66), p. 14.

6. Beeby, op. cit., p. 116.

7. Ibid., p. 30.

8. Eric Ashby, Universities: British, Indian, African (Cambridge, Mass.: Harvard University Press, 1966), pp. 47-72.

9. Tosten Husen, "Does More Time in School Make a Difference?" in Saturday Review (April 29, 1972), pp. 32-34.

10. U.S. Department of Health, Education, and Welfare, Report on Higher Education (Washington, D.C.: U.S. Government Printing Office, 1971), p. 64.

Growth Profiles, Selected Countries in South and Southeast Asia, 1969-70

(I) Country	Population (in millions)	Growth Rate (in percent)	Growth Rate of GNP (in percent)	Growth Rate of per Capita Income (in percent)	Percent of GNP Spent on Education
Bangladesh	74[a]	3.3[b]	4.0	0.7	1.43
India	546.9[c]	2.5[d]	4.9	2.4	2.6
Indonesia	116[d]	2.5[d]	5.0[e]	2.5	1.1[d]
Malaysia	10.9[b]	2.7[b]	6.0	3.3	5.0[h]
Pakistan	60[b]	2.5[b]	6.0	3.5	1.4
Philippines	38[b]	3.5[b]	5.0[f]	1.5[g]	6.7

[a]1972/73; [b]1970; [c]1971; [d]1969; [e]estimated for 1969/70 to 1973/74; [f]estimate for 1971-74 is 5.5; [g]estimate for 1971-74 is 2.0; [h]1967.

(II) Country	Public Expenditure on Education (in percent)	Enrollment First Level (in millions)	(in percent)	Second Level (in thousands)	(in percent)	Third Level (in thousands)	(in percent)
Bangladesh							
1954/55	-	2.7	40.0	333	4.0	27	
1972/73	11.9	6.3	58.0	1,930	14.0	121.7	1.4
India							
1965	6.1[a]						
1950/51	-	19.5	42.6	3,120	12.7	360	0.9
1968/69	-	55.5	77.3	12,270	13.3	1,690	2.9
Indonesia							
1967	-	13.0	72.0	1,500	11.0	119	
Malaysia							
1970	19.0[c]	-	92.0 (age 6-11)[d] 54.0 (age 12-14)[d]	-	18.0[d] (age 15-16) 4.0 (age 17-18)[d]	-	1.0[d]
Pakistan	16.2[e]						
1954/55		1.5	30.0	500	6.0	40	
1969/70		4.2	47.0	1,400	12.0	75	1.6
Philippines	22.3	-	108.6[e]	-	35.4	-	17.5[e]

[a]As a percentage of plan allocation in Fourth Five-Year Plan; Rs. 6.1 billion; [b]Rs. 912.5 million in 1952; Rs. 2.6 billion in 1960; [c]1969; [d]1968; [e]1964/65.

(III) Country	Distribution of Graduates (in percent) Humanities and Social Sciences	Sciences, Engineering, and Agriculture	(IV) Vocational-Technical Enrollment
Bangladesh	81	19	1954/55 Diploma 483; Degree 184; 1969/70 Diploma 9,000; Degree 2,500
India	73[b]	27[b]	1968/69 Diploma 48,000; Degree 25,000
Indonesia	90	10	
Malaysia	91	9	(1967) Diploma 1,827; Degree 49
Pakistan	67[a]	33	1954-55 Diploma 1,371; Degree 1,348; 1969-70 Diploma 15,000; Degree 8,300
Philippines	80[c]	20	1969-70 102,070 (under Bureau of Vocational Education Programs)

[a]Second level only; [b]1964; [c]1966; 52 percent in education.

Sources: First Five-Year Plan of Bangladesh (1973-78); Five-Year Plan of Ceylon (1972-76); Fourth Five-Year Plan of India (1969-74); First Five-Year Plan of Indonesia (1969-74); Second Five-Year Plan of Malaysia (1971-75); Fourth Five-Year Plan of Pakistan (1970-75); Four-Year Development Plan of the Philippines (1971-74); The Phillipines Education Survey Report, 1970; IBRD World Tables, 1971; Education in Malaysia 1970 (Kuala Lumpur, 1970); UNESCO, Education in Pakistan, 1970; Pakistan Education Index, 1970; UNESCO Statistical Yearbook 1969.

A MATHEMATICAL MODEL SHOWING THE DISTRIBUTION OF
GROWTH IN ENROLLMENT AND EXPENDITURE OVER A
PERIOD OF TEN YEARS

In this model the total number of children of 6 to 11 years of age
to be enrolled by the tenth year is assumed to be n_t and the number of
the same age group already enrolled in the base year (year preceding
the plan-period) as n. The balance of children remaining to be enrolled
in ten years is n_t - n represented in the model as 100. It is also
assumed that this number is evenly distributed within the age range.
This model can have many variants by varying the ratio of initial entry
into Grade 1 and the rate of progression.

Grades	Years									
	1	2	3	4	5	6	7	8	9	10
1	10	12	14	16	18	20	20	20	20	20
2	—	10	12	14	16	18	20	20	20	20
3	—	—	10	12	14	16	18	20	20	20
4	—	—	—	10	12	14	16	18	20	20
5	—	—	—	—	10	12	14	16	18	20
Total	10	22	36	52	70	80	88	94	98	100
Ratio of expenditure (in percent)	10	22	36	52	70	80	88	94	98	100

MUHAMMAD SHAMSUL HUQ, currently Executive President of the Foundation for Research on Educational Planning and Development, Bangladesh, was a Fellow at the Woodrow Wilson International Center for Scholars, Washington, D. C., from 1971 to 1973. His professional experience ranges from teaching economics and education to planning and administering education in various positions including those of Director of Public Instruction in former East Pakistan and Vice-Chancellor of Rajshahi University. He was Chairman of the Inter-University Board in 1965, and Minister for Education and Scientific Research in the last cabinet of former Pakistan.

Mr. Huq's participation in educational planning at an international level began with a UNESCO educational survey of fifteen Asian countries undertaken with three other Asian educators in 1959. He was Chairman of the Committee on International Cooperation for Financial Assistance at the Commonwealth Education Conference held in New Delhi in 1962 and a member of the Paris 1971 UNESCO International Committee of Experts on the formulation of a policy for training abroad.

His publications include: Changing Education in England (Dacca: Talim Publications, 1948), Compulsory Education in Pakistan (Paris: UNESCO, 1954), and Education and Development Strategy in South and Southeast Asia (Honolulu: East-West Center Press, 1965). He is a contributor to the new edition of the Encylopedia Britannica ("Patterns of Education in South and Southeast Asia") and Lexikon der Padagogik (Verlag Herder, Freiburg im Breisgau).

THE MAOIST EDUCATIONAL REVOLUTION
                    Theodore Hsi-en Chen

THE PROVINCIAL UNIVERSITIES OF MEXICO: An Analysis
of Growth and Development
                    Richard G. King, with Alfonso Rangel
                    Guerra, David Kline, and Noel F. McGinn;
                    foreword by Philip H. Coombs

EDUCATIONAL PROBLEMS OF DEVELOPING SOCIETIES: With
Case Studies of Ghana, Pakistan, and Nigeria
                    Adam Curle

TEACHERS AS AGENTS OF NATIONAL DEVELOPMENT: A Case Study
of Uganda
                    David R. Evans

PLANNING OCCUPATIONAL EDUCATION AND TRAINING
FOR DEVELOPMENT
                    Eugene Staley

NON-FORMAL EDUCATION: An Annotated International Bibliography
                    edited by Rolland G. Paulston

EDUCATION AND DEVELOPMENT IN RURAL KENYA: A Study of
Primary School Graduates
                    Lewis Brownstein